Linguistic Philosophy

RP: 153 (attn to subj. mattr, not lang. used to describe it)

RP: 160 Wittg. quote: unable to notice what's always before dr eyes. Cf. enclosv interp.

RP: 172: young Wittg demanded "that meanings be sharp, regardls of what socl life or efctv intercourse may require."

RP: 2 Dummett quotes re importnc of gettg clear abt meanings of words

RP: 179 at "RP?"

181 RP: 'most existg usage strikes many as intolerably messy in comparison to the precisn + coherenc of abstract formal systems'

SUNY series in Philosophy

George R. Lucas Jr., editor

Linguistic Philosophy

The Central Story

Garth L. Hallett

STATE UNIVERSITY OF NEW YORK PRESS

Published by
State University of New York Press, Albany

For information, contact State University of New York Press, Albany, NY
www.sunypress.edu

Production by Diane Ganeles
Marketing by Anne M. Valentine

Library of Congress Cataloging-in-Publication Data

Hallett, Garth.
    Linguistic philosophy : the central story / Garth L. Hallett.
        p. cm. — (SUNY series in philosophy)
    Includes bibliographical references and index.
    ISBN 978-0-7914-7361-0 (hardcover : alk. paper) —
    ISBN 978-0-7914-7362-7 (pbk. : alk. paper)
    1. Language and languages—Philosophy.   I. Title.
P107.H347 2008
401—dc22
                                                            2007024535

10 9 8 7 6 5 4 3 2 1

Contents

PREFACE

"The aspects of things that are most important for us," Ludwig Wittgenstein observed, "are hidden because of their simplicity and familiarity." We fail to be struck "by what, once seen, is most striking and most powerful."[1] The story here recounted illustrates Wittgenstein's point. For the central, most significant issue of linguistic philosophy is one its devotees did not explicitly state or address, in so many words, even at the peak of linguistic interest in the last century. Yet it is an issue that has divided linguistic and nonlinguistic philosophers, and it has lost none of its interest in our day. Simply put, the question is this: to what extent should *language, as medium* of communication, determine what we say? Clearly, the linguistic medium employed (whether standard or stipulated, natural or artificial) does and should play some role, for the realities we describe, report, explain, or otherwise characterize do not by themselves tell us what words to use. For example, the flakes falling from the sky do not tell us to call them snow rather than rain, sleet, or butterflies; the English language does. The flakes and the language, together, dictate the right term to use. Or so it might seem. However, in the history of thought and especially in recent times, there has been profound disagreement on how much authority to grant language as a determinant of truth or assertability, and on how its authority, whether slight or great, should be understood and exercised.

Talk about language's "authority" to determine what we say may sound strange, partly because it is unfamiliar, partly because it seems inappropriate. Speech, after all, is determined by thought and thought is determined by the objects of thought. There, it seems, is where authority resides—in thought and its objects. Speech is doubly derivative. However, the dependence also runs the other way. As chapter 1 will note, language largely determines not only how we speak but also how we think and how we conceive the things we think and speak about. The question is, just how deep and decisive should its influence be?

vii

Evidently linguistic, this question is also clearly philosophical. For, though it extends far beyond philosophy, it implicates the whole of philosophy: it concerns "Body and mind are identical," "Meaning is use," or "God created the universe" as much as it does "It's snowing," "Napoleon invaded Russia," or "Molecules consist of atoms." Further, the question arises more frequently and acutely in philosophy than it does, say, in chemistry, geometry, or coffee-break gossip. For in philosophy, language has faced more numerous, powerful rivals than it has in most other disciplines or areas of discourse. Furthermore, as even the present introductory study will attest, the issue of language's authority is so complex and difficult that only philosophy can adequately address it. And philosophers have, in fact, come closest to confronting the issue. They may not have asked squarely "How much authority should language exercise in determining what we say?" but they have repeatedly beaten around this bush.

The general question can be put in sharper focus: Should the language employed be recognized as the principal factor bridging the gap between reality and its proper description? From Plato to the present, most philosophers, favoring one or the other of language's competitors, have implicitly denied language such a role. Somewhat more explicitly, numerous linguistic philosophers, accepting language's authority, have answered in the affirmative. (It is this, primarily, that makes them linguistic philosophers, as I here use the term, and not merely philosophers who study language.) They have differed notably, however, in their understanding of language's guidance. My hope and expectation is that mapping this multiplicity of views, both negative and positive, will help readers reach greater clarity on this crucial issue of linguistic philosophy—indeed of philosophy in general.

Whereas the claims of "ordinary language" were briefly debated in the last century, the authority of *language* to determine what we say, though profoundly challenged for millennia, has never been explicitly debated. Herein lies the answer, or at least a principal answer, to a possible puzzle. How strange it may seem, on reflection, that there should be such a thing as "linguistic philosophy." After all, there are no linguistic physicists, anthropologists, historians, or zoologists. The very notion that there might be sounds bizarre. But if specialists in other fields feel no need to obsess about language, why should philosophers? To this query the present work furnishes a reply, perhaps the most important. Outside philosophy and other areas of speculative inquiry, there is little need to say much about language, because there is relatively little disagreement about how to employ it. Inside philosophy, where, for reasons that will appear, basic disagreement prevails about the authority of language, there is consequently much disagreement about how to use it. As long as this disagreement persists and pervasively affects philosophical practice in

fundamental ways, language will demand constant attention. When and
if philosophers reach consensus with regard to language's authority, there
will be no such need.

A linguistic philosopher, too, can long for that day. In response,
therefore, to the common complaint that linguistic philosophers are interested only in words, I proffer a parable. Two men are confined in a
prison cell. One, lounging against the wall, is observing the other sawing
away at the cell window's bars with a nail file. "Strange man!" comments
the first. "He has no soul, no vision. He is interested only in bars." No,
he is interested in freedom. So, too, is the linguistic philosopher who saws
on the bars of language. He desires to be free simply to use language, as
those beyond the bars do, without the constant, distracting need to talk
about language. But he and his cellmates will not enjoy that freedom so
long as there persists such deep and widespread disagreement, among
both linguistic and nonlinguistic philosophers, about the authority and
proper use of language. The bars are still as solid today as they were fifty
or a hundred years ago—or two thousand.

It may appear that in answering one puzzle I have introduced another. What subtle insanity or perverse ingenuity am I attributing, by in-
sinuation, to philosophers, that they should have constructed and
inhabited a linguistic prison while the rest of humanity enjoyed greater
freedom from linguistic obstacles and distractions? None—I intend no
such imputation. Philosophers' linguistic problems have arisen, I suggest,
not from thinking more confusedly than other people but from thinking
more about confusing problems—problems that, to borrow a phrase,
"have the character of depth": "their roots are as deep in us and the forms
of our language and their significance is as great as the importance of our
language."[2] What presently appears greatly needed is not a return to relative unreflective unanimity in verbal practice, but, rather, an advance to
relative *reflective* unanimity—or at least to greater consensus than currently exists.

Previously, I addressed this issue systematically. Here, I review it historically, with a broader audience in view. This explains the book's style.
In any reader likely to read such a work, I can presume a certain amount
of philosophical background, but I cannot assume that all readers will be
well acquainted with every one of the thinkers, from Plato to Jürgen
Habermas, here considered. Accordingly, though individual discussions
may interest specialists as well as nonspecialists, I shall typically say more
by way of introduction and explanation than I would if I were writing
solely for the former.

I am grateful for the assistance of generous readers: Suzanne Cun-
ningham, Gerard Hughes, and Nicholas Rescher, who read the whole
work in various drafts; and Robert Audi, Michael Barber, Scott Berman,

William Charron, William Rehg, and Joseph Salerno, who offered helpful comments on one or more chapters. May their tribe increase! My thanks also to Victoria Carlson-Casaregola for her careful stylistic editing.

I dedicate this work to the memory of Frederick Copleston, admired teacher, friend, and confrere and the author of a highly regarded nine-volume history of philosophy. I would be gratified beyond my expectations if in the present chronicle I could emulate the accuracy, fairness, clarity, and order that have made Copleston's history of such service to so many for so long.

1

The Issue of Language's Authority

INTRODUCING ERNEST GELLNER'S *Words and Things*, Bertrand Russell wrote disparagingly of "linguistic philosophy, which cares only about language, and not about the world."[1] Though this blanket characterization is a travesty, as is Gellner's equally caustic account, the travesty contains some truth. The philosophy that Russell and Gellner targeted—the kind centered in Oxford and Cambridge during the middle decades of the last century—represented an antithetical moment in the dialectical development of Western thought. For millennia, language had not received its due. In reaction, during those several Oxbridge decades it often received more than its due. Now, as subsequent thought swings uncertainly between these prior extremes, we can ask, aided by reflection on discussion to this point in time: where should the pendulum come to rest? What claims can validly be made on language's behalf? Clearly, language serves as a means of communication in philosophy and elsewhere, and as a crucially important instrument of personal reflection. Clearly, too, language can be an object of philosophical or scientific scrutiny, as can history, law, life, evolution, or the galaxies. What more, though, might be claimed specifically for language? One common response is the following.

Foundation

René Descartes made the question of knowledge foundational. More recently, there has been a widespread tendency to place the question of meaning before the question of knowledge and to focus on language as basic. In partial explanation of this shift, Michael Dummett has written that

> once we have achieved a successful analysis of the meanings of the expressions with which we are concerned, then questions of justification may arise, which it may be more or less difficult to

1

settle. But, until we have first achieved a satisfactory analysis of the meanings of the relevant expressions, we cannot so much as raise questions of justification and of truth, since we remain unclear about what we are attempting to justify or what it is about whose truth we are enquiring.[2]

Here, one might wish to distinguish between "satisfactory analysis" of expressions and adequate unreflective understanding of their meanings. However, from at least the time of Plato, philosophers have seen the need to scrutinize the meanings of the expressions they employed. Thus, as Dummett observes, "Someone who accepted Descartes's perspective according to which epistemology is the starting-point of all philosophy might impatiently concede that it was advisable, before undertaking any discussion, first to agree about the meanings of any possible ambiguous terms, but regard this as a mere preliminary to a philosophical enquiry rather than as part of one."[3] Yet it is more than that, Dummett argues; for this initial task is difficult as well as fundamental. "Only when it is clearly grasped how hard it can be to attain an adequate analysis of the meaning of an expression having the kind of generality or depth that makes it of interest to philosophers, can the analysis of meaning be seen as a primary task of philosophy."

With this much many would agree. For reasons like Dummett's, they would see the analysis of meaning as *a* primary task of philosophy, but not necessarily as *the* primary task. Though preliminary to some important matters, clarification of meaning might be subsequent to others. For elucidation of individual meanings would require clarity about the nature of meanings and their proper analysis, and light on these underlying issues might be sought from epistemology, ontology, anthropology, psychology, logic, or elsewhere. Dummett, however, suggests a stronger sense in which the analysis of meanings is "the starting-point, something that must be settled before anything else can be said."[4] He writes that

the theory of meaning is the fundamental part of philosophy which underlies all others. Because philosophy has, as its first if not its only task, the analysis of meanings, and because, the deeper such analysis goes, the more it is dependent upon a correct general account of meaning, a model for what the understanding of an expression consists in, the theory of meaning, which is the search for such a model, is the foundation of all philosophy, and not epistemology as Descartes misled us into believing.[5]

Examples suggest why even linguistic philosophers might hesitate to go as far with Dummett as these words suggest.[6] To take a single instance, con-

sider a famed saying of the later Wittgenstein, which was itself an analysis of meaning and laid the basis for other analyses: "For a *large* class of
cases—though not for all—in which we employ the word 'meaning' it can
be defined thus: the meaning of a word is its use in the language."[7] Most
philosophers of the past would have contested such an identification, and
Wittgenstein might have agreed with them had he shared their metaphysical, epistemological, or psychological views. However, he did not believe, for example, in Plato's eternal, unchanging "Forms," independent
of human thought or the flux and flow of temporal, sensible realities. He
did not believe in Aristotelian essences or in the corresponding "concepts"—the mental likenesses abstracted from sensible realities and expressed by general terms—with which Thomas Aquinas and others
populated the mind. He did not believe in the flow of images, word for
word, through the minds of speakers; or in the "felt meanings" that
William James correlated with even such expressions as "not," "never,"
and "not yet." He did not believe in the projective "thinking out" of
words that Wittgenstein himself had once postulated, or in the "logical
atoms" thus allegedly picked out. He did not believe in any of these can-
didate meanings for words. This multiple disbelief explains why he could
make the suggestion he did, equating words' meanings (in most contexts
of their discussion) with the words' established uses. So in this instance as
in others, a problem arises for the idea that with the "analysis of meanings" one reaches rock bottom and one's spade is turned. Primacy may
often lie elsewhere, in one's views, not of language or word meanings, but
of Forms, universals, essences, thought, and the like. The linguistic views
may be derivative, and pre-Cartesian philosophers may have been right in
recognizing no one part of philosophy as foundational for the rest.[8] However, the foundational perspective is not the only one that assigns a special place to language.

Worldview

In the eighteenth century, Johann Herder pioneered a theme that has since
been variously orchestrated by Wilhelm von Humboldt, Edward Sapir,
Benjamin Lee Whorf, and others. According to Herder, language "determines the boundary and the outline of all human cognition."[9] According
to Whorf, "We dissect nature along lines laid down by our native languages."[10] For Sapir, the forms of language "predetermine for us certain
modes of observation and interpretation"—indeed, "no matter how so-
phisticated our modes of interpretation become, we never really get beyond
the projection and continuous transfer of relations suggested by the forms
of our speech."[11] A people's language, it is suggested, shapes their *Weltanschauung*, their worldview.[12]

Such claims, like Dummett's, might have a stronger or a weaker sense. The idea might be, for example, that different languages just package the same reality differently, much as different metric systems measure the same weights, speeds, or distances differently, without disagreement. Or the contention might be, more significantly, that different languages engender conflicting views of reality: some right, some wrong, or perhaps none of them perfectly accurate. In the Herderian tradition just indicated, the authors' examples and modes of expression may sometimes suggest something more than packaging but they seldom impose a stronger sense.[13] I think this emphasis is right. Yet a case can be made for language's ability to beget reality and not merely to organize it. Thinkers have adduced many individual instances of this ability. At the extreme, it has been suggested that the substantive "God" begot belief in God. More plausibly, the terms "true" and "good" have been held responsible for belief in properties denoted by these allegedly nondenoting expressions. At least as plausibly, Wittgenstein held that single terms for a whole class of things may evoke belief in essences shared by all members of the class, that verbal parallels with verbs that denote mental acts may suggest similar referents for verbs that function differently, and so forth: repeatedly and variously, surface features of language may conjure up nonexistent entities (see chapter 8). However, even if extensive,[14] such influences as these would still be piecemeal, whereas for thinkers in the Herderian tradition the influence of language is systematic and all-embracing: language's influence is comprehensive because thought's coverage is comprehensive and language pervades thought. The connection appears, for example, when Whorf writes: "The categories and types that we isolate from the world of phenomena we do not find there because they stare every observer in the face; on the contrary, the world is presented in a kaleidoscopic flux of impressions which has to be organized by our minds—and this means largely by the linguistic systems in our minds."[15] Language shapes our views of the world because it shapes our *thinking*.

Thought

"Concepts and ideas," notes Hilary Putnam, "were always thought important; language was thought unimportant, because it was considered to be merely a system of conventional signs for concepts and ideas (considered as mental entities of some kind, and quite independent of the signs used to express them)."[16] Now the pendulum has swung far in the opposite direction, thanks largely in recent times to the later Wittgenstein.[17] "When I think in language," he observed, "there aren't 'meanings' going through my mind in addition to the verbal expressions: the language is itself the vehicle of

C~M

thought."[18] This does not signify that all thought is linguistic—that, as he had once tentatively put it, "thinking is operating with language."[19] The concept "thinking" is more varied than that.[20] However, Wittgenstein's remarks do raise a question of great interest and importance: can linguistic thoughts—the ones expressed by utterances—be had nonlinguistically?

To spotlight the significance of this query, I suggest the following test. Pick out any sentence so far in this chapter. Let the sentence be short (e.g., "We dissect nature along lines laid down by our native languages"), or let it be as lengthy as you please. Now do this: have the same thought, non-linguistically. Do it without words. If, as I expect, you have no idea how even to begin, or if, having made the attempt, you at least have doubts whether what you did, nonlinguistically, really had the same meaning as the words, you may appreciate the importance of language for thought. For, instead of citing the sentences in the preceding pages, I could have substituted those in this chapter, this book, or any other work of philosophy—indeed in any other work on any other topic. Try random statements in the morning paper; try "Thompson was acquitted" or "Stocks climbed higher today."

Though some of Wittgenstein's examples may suggest the possibility of meaning-equivalence between a nonverbal thought and a verbal utterance,[21] in general he, like numerous other linguistic philosophers, reacted critically to the idea that thoughts expressed in a conventional language are simply verbal renderings of thoughts entertained or entertainable nonlinguistically or in a natural, transnational language of the mind. To clarify verbalized thoughts, they would agree, one should look to language—to linguistic practice—and not to any ghostly, nonlinguistic equivalents in the mind. For Wittgenstein and like-minded thinkers, "Words have meaning only in the stream of life."[22]

Dummett becomes more specific. Speaking of what he would prefer to label "linguistic philosophy" rather than "analytical philosophy" (were the former expression not tied, in his view, "to that quite special version of analytical philosophy that flourished at Oxford in the 1950s and 60s"), he writes:

> The basic tenet of analytical philosophy, common to such disparate philosophers as Schlick, early and late Wittgenstein, Carnap, Ryle, Ayer, Austin, Quine and Davidson, may be expressed as being that the philosophy of thought is to be equated with the philosophy of language: more exactly, (i) an account of language does not presuppose an account of thought, (ii) an account of language yields an account of thought, and (iii) there is no other adequate means by which an account of thought may be given.[23]

The accuracy of this sketch might be questioned for one or the other of
the thinkers Dummett lists. Nonetheless, the claims he cites further illustrate the perspective here being suggested. Many linguistic philosophers
would agree that to a much greater extent than has often been recognized, an analysis of language is required for an analysis of thought rather
than the other way around.

Since language and thought encompass all discourse, on whatever
topic, it might seem that no stronger claim than this might be made for language. However, to study language or thought is not to study morality, in-
flation, continental drift, subatomic particles, or the cosmos. Language or
thought is just one reality among many. And to analyze thought or its expression is not to judge or validate it. Analysis of how people do speak or
think does not automatically indicate how they should speak or think. So a
still more significant claim on language's behalf remains to be considered.

Authority

A passage in G. E. Moore's *Principia Ethica* (1903) can aptly intimate the
claim and its significance. For Moore, the question how "good" is to be
defined is the most fundamental question in all ethics. This question is
not merely verbal, he notes, nor is the desired definition of the sort that
interests lexicographers. "If I wanted that kind of definition," he explains, "I should have to consider in the first place how people generally
used the word 'good'; but my business is not with its proper usage, as established by custom."[24] How, then, does Moore conceive his task?
Though perplexing, his answer is also revealing. "I should, indeed, be
foolish," he explains,

> if I tried to use [the word "good"] for something which it did not
> usually denote: if, for instance, I were to announce that, when-
> ever I used the word "good," I must be understood to be think-
> ing of that object which is usually denoted by the word "table."
> I shall, therefore, use the word in the sense in which I think it is
> ordinarily used; but at the same time I am not anxious to discuss
> whether I am right in thinking that it is so used. My business is
> solely with that object or idea, which I hold, rightly or wrongly,
> that the word is generally used to stand for. What I want to dis-
> cover is the nature of that object or idea, and about this I am ex-
> tremely anxious to arrive at an agreement.[25]

As I say, this explanation is puzzling. Moore would like his use of the
word "good" to agree with its familiar sense, yet he sees no need to determine whether it does, in fact, do so. Though his concern is with the

object that he believes the word is generally used to stand for, he feels free to ignore whether the object he describes is indeed the one which that word denotes. Who knows? Perhaps it is the object usually designated by the word "value" or "fruitfulness" or "satisfaction"; it does not matter. His account will still be an account of good, regardless of how anyone else uses the word "good." Thus Putnam comments:

> Moore writes as if there were an *object*, "the concept Good," that one could pass about, inspect under a microscope, perhaps take to pieces (be careful not to break it!). The word, on this view, is only a convenient if accidental label for this object. Once we have had our attention called to the object, we can simply forget about the word and concentrate on the object. But what is this object?[26]

If Moore has used the wrong word, how will our attention be called to the intended object? If our attention is directed to some other object, or to no object at all (such, perhaps, not being the customary employment of the word "good"), how can he expect us to accept his account as accurate?

Later, Moore himself characterized the pages from which I have quoted as a "mass of confusions."[27] My present purpose, however, is not critical. I quote Moore because his account is so typical—not in its explicitness, which is relatively rare, but in what it makes explicit. The general stance revealed vis-à-vis language is that of countless thinkers. It would be nice, they might concede, if their use of words agreed with other people's, but that does not really concern them. Words, they hold, can for the most part take care of themselves. If expressions are ambiguous, indicate the intended sense. If they are not sufficiently precise for one's purpose, sharpen them. Where necessary, fashion new ones. Otherwise, get on with the business at hand. Describe or define the good, give an account of causes, explain right action, investigate identity, freedom, time, truth, happiness, or what have you. Only if language is the object of inquiry will language dictate any answers. Otherwise it will not. Such is the overall attitude.

How, though, can any nonlinguistic reality, by itself, dictate any *answer*, in German, French, Hopi, or Swahili? How can Moore's object, for example, tell him what English term to use in naming it? How can it inform him what English words, if any, to employ in describing or defining it? How can it instruct him about defining or describing? How can it teach him the syntax, lexicon, or semantics of any language, actual or ideal? Ever since Plato's failed attempt in the *Cratylus*, philosophers have recognized that words cannot be read straight off from reality. To know what words to use in order correctly, accurately to report, describe, or explain any reality, you need something more than just the reality. The question is: will that something more be language, the medium employed in the reporting, describing, or explaining, or will it be something else? Doubtless language has some title to determine what we should say, but how much? If little, where does authority principally reside? What, if not the language employed, can determine, together with the realities described, what words to use in describing them, when making statements in that language?

To clarify the issue, let me highlight the sense, already indicated by the preface's first paragraph, in which the word "language" is here being used. Noting the diversity of conceptions of language, Mario Bunge comments: "As in the case of other important concepts, one may hope that of language to be eventually defined (implicitly) by a comprehensive theory or system of theories."[28] For reasons that will emerge, I do not share this hope or the methodological assumptions that underlie it. In any case, no such definition has garnered consensus, nor is any such needed for present purposes. For the moment, let one basic distinction suffice. Dictionaries, reflecting usage, define language both as communication (e.g., "the use by human beings of voice sounds, and often written symbols representing these sounds, in combinations and patterns to express and communicate thoughts and feelings"[29]) and, more typically, as instrument or medium of communication (e.g., "a system of words formed from such combinations and patterns, used by the people of a particular country or by a group of people with a shared history or set of traditions"[30]). Discussion about the authority of language to determine what we should say implicitly picks out the latter sense: language, in this context, is the instrument or medium, not the communication effected by its means. It is, for example, the natural language I am here employing as I write, not my use of it to say the things I am saying.

A quotation from Gilbert Ryle may help lodge this distinction, so crucial for all that follows, firmly in the reader's memory:

> A Language, such as the French language, is a stock, fund or deposit of words, constructions, intonations, *cliché* phrases and so on. "Speech," on the other hand, or "discourse" can be conscripted to denote the activity or rather the clan of activities of saying things, saying them in French, it may be, or English or some other language. A stock of language-pieces is not a lot of activities, but the fairly lasting wherewithal to conduct them; somewhat as a stock of coins is not a momentary transaction or set of momentary transactions of buying, lending, investing, etc., but is the lasting wherewithal to conduct such transactions. Roughly, as Capital stands to Trade, so Language stands to Speech.[31]

This is how I shall use the word "language": for the "stock of language-pieces" and not for the "clan of activities." For this is the sense needed in a discussion of language's authority. A natural language may derive its grammar, pragmatics, semantics, and lexicon from the linguistic practice in which it figures; its expressions may derive their meaning from the various "language-games" in which they occur. Still, a language is not a language-game: it is not any mode or style of discourse (narration, argumentation, explanation, prediction, evaluation, exhortation, etc.) in which the language is employed, much less is it identical with the individual utterances that make use of it. The medium is not the message. Hence, to question the message is not to question the medium, or vice versa. To accord authority to the medium is not to accord authority to the message, or vice versa. Despite their intimate connection, the two are distinct.

This first clarification permits a second: using a language must be distinguished from choosing a language. Though obvious, this distinction merits mention since, as a later chapter will bring out, very different considerations apply to the reasonable selection of a language or terminology than to the reasonable employment of the language or terminology selected. Typically, on most occasions, there is little reason to consider what language to speak: one speaks one's mother tongue with those who share it, and their language, if possible, with those who do not understand one's own. Typically, too, there is little reason to make up new meanings for the words of the language spoken. But whatever the idiom adopted, there is always reason to consider how to use it—often much more reason than is recognized. (Witness Moore.) So the question to be considered here (what we should say) has far greater real-life relevance than the other (what language we should say it in), especially since it is a question about which there has been much greater disagreement. Nobody questioned whether Moore should write in English, but critics did seriously question whether he should use that language the way he did, with slight regard for its customary employment.

The notion of language as a determinant of truth or assertability also merits a word of explanation. Many, perhaps most, philosophers have supposed that language alone can furnish answers to some questions (e.g., concerning the marital status of bachelors). Most, however, including linguistic philosophers, have recognized that language cannot by itself furnish answers to most questions. Typically, neither language alone nor reality alone suffices to indicate what we should say, nontautologically, about any reality; but language and the reality to be described may do so, together. If drops of water are falling from clouds, then, given the meaning of "rain" in the English language and a desire to inform English-speaking hearers of the state of the weather, we should say, "It's raining" and not "It's snowing," "It's sleeting," or "The weather is fine."

The notion of language as a principal determinant of truth and assertability has evoked a common reaction. "This," writes John Mackie, "is the basic problem for linguistic philosophy, to decide whether it is concerned with grammar or metaphysics, with language or the world. And if it is to tell us something about the world, on what evidence or on what arguments will its conclusions rest? If we want to learn about the world, no strictly linguistic evidence will be at all conclusive."[32] True, but the linguistic evidence may be conclusive when joined with the nonlinguistic. The issue that Mackie slights is this: to what extent should language be recognized, in philosophy and elsewhere, as the arbiter of what we should say? Here, I suggest, is the central question for linguistic philosophy in its confrontation with nonlinguistic philosophy; and "the basic problem for linguistic philosophy" is, not to decide whether to talk about language or the world, but to decide what role, in either area of discourse, language should be accorded.

What more, I asked earlier, might be claimed for language, besides its utility for interpersonal communication and personal reflection and its status as a worthwhile object of philosophical and scientific study? The chief response I can now suggest is this: "Authority." It is authority that a long tradition has largely denied to language; that many linguistic philosophers have claimed for it (though not in so many words[33]); and that critics have contested. This three-part story—first negative with regard to language's authority, then positive, then critical—is the one I shall here recount. Though the latter parts of this dialectical tale will be more helpful in reaching a balanced assessment of language's due, the story would not be complete, nor would linguistic philosophers' claims be fully intelligible, without some account at the start of the views against which they have reacted. If, in the famed "linguistic turn," linguistic philosophers turned *to* language, what did they turn *from*, and why?

For an initial sample reply, we can glance again at Moore and at the tradition he represents. In defense of this tradition, Gellner commented: "that usage cannot settle normative issues about how we *should* think, is something so obvious that it has never in the past been doubted. On the contrary, it was taken for granted, and just this was the reason why pre-linguistic philosophers did not appeal to usage."[34] Young Moore was just such a pre-linguistic philosopher. Typically and reasonably, he had stipulated no alternative sense for the word "good" and had introduced no alternative idiom to replace standard English; so if language was to exercise any authority on this occasion, it would have to be through common English usage. Moore, however, saw no point in examining usage. Where, then, did authority reside? What dictated what he should say? According to Peter Hacker, "Moore conceived of himself as engaged in the analysis of mind-independent concepts, which, when held before the mind, could be seen to be either composite or simple. . . . According to his official doctrine, it is possible to analyze a concept (or the meaning of a term) without attending to its linguistic expression."[35] Thus Moore could, for example, declare: "'right' does and can mean nothing but 'cause of a good result,' and is thus identical with 'useful.'"[36] Regardless of how people actually employ the term, this is what it must mean. The concept, in concert with other concepts, so decrees.

Disconnected from usage, Moore's "concepts" were disconnected from language as ordinarily defined (a "system of words" or its communicative use).[37] In this they resembled, for example, Plato's Forms (examined in chapter 3), and they therefore raise similar problems. If no answer can be read off from the reality to be described, by itself, how can an answer be read off from these concepts or Forms? How can they tell us what we should *say*? Indeed, what need have we of any such nonlinguistic intermediaries between reality and its expression? Why not pass directly from the reality to the expression via the meanings of the terms employed? Why not turn to language for guidance?

Perhaps we do and should, but how? The answer may look easy: just talk as other people do; speak the language—Spanish, Greek, Russian, or Hindi—as it is spoken. However, speakers frequently make incompatible assertions. Even when they agree verbally, their words are often loaded with conflicting theories and beliefs. They commonly employ forms of speech that, as suggested earlier, may be seriously misleading. They speak vaguely, confusedly, mistakenly. All or most of them may agree in saying things that just aren't so. Their linguistic behavior, as Richard Rorty has piquantly observed, mixes "mumbles, stumbles, malapropisms, metaphors, tics, seizures, psychotic symptoms, egregious stupidity, strokes of genius, and the like."[38] So one wonders: should philosophers and other careful speakers follow suit? Perhaps some wisdom or valid normativity lies concealed within actual verbal practice, but, if so, it is well concealed. It seems at first glance that one might as well consult astrologers as consult everyday speakers as oracles on what to say. But if everyday language cannot guide us, what language can? Linguistic philosophers have no ready response. They may agree (or many may) in stressing the authority of language, but they are far from agreeing on how its authority should be described or exercised. Here is another reason for dwelling on the longer, positive part of the coming account. Not only is it likely to prove more profitable: it will also prove more difficult. It is easy to criticize Moore, but what positive guidance can be offered him? How should he have conducted his inquiry? The answer to such a query is as difficult as it is fundamental.

Such, then, is the direction this study will take. It will focus, historically and critically, on the question of the proper role of language in determining what we say when we make assertions, whether in philosophy or elsewhere. (For easy reference, let us label this question, concerning language's authority to govern language's assertoric use, the "Issue of Language's Authority.") In this formulation, notice the verb "say." The utterance "Wor thup banalitous" says nothing. Neither, despite its English words, does "I brain my see." Neither, in the sense of making an intelligible assertion, does "I fly my identity." However, such linguistic aberrations hold slight practical significance for philosophers, or for others. For the most part, philosophers have taken for granted the authority of language to determine grammaticality and intelligibility, but not to determine *what* to say grammatically and intelligibly. Concerning the authority of language to determine truth or assertability, they have been very far from agreement.

So understood, the Issue of Language's Authority is a major theme of linguistic philosophy, but in what sense is it as central to linguistic philosophy as this work's title suggests? This question, opening large historical and theoretical perspectives, the next chapter will address.

2

The Question's Centrality

THE SUGGESTION THAT the Issue of Language's Authority is central to linguistic philosophy could create an unfortunate impression. If the chief question of linguistic philosophy concerns the use of words, then, it might seem, linguistic philosophy is interested primarily in words and not in nonlinguistic reality. It cares, as Russell put it, "only about language, and not about the world." How, then, is the suggestion to be understood if not in this reductive, off-putting sense?

The metaphor of "centrality" can be unpacked in terms of frequency, influence, and importance. If, one way or another, linguistic philosophers have frequently addressed the Issue of Language's Authority, and their answers to it have influenced their treatment of many other issues and have influenced it importantly, then the issue is central to linguistic philosophy. So might other issues be—for instance the one cited in the last chapter concerning the relation between language and thought. However, if, in addition, the answers given or not given to this issue have weightier implications, not only within linguistic philosophy or within philosophy generally but beyond, than does the stance adopted on any other issue in linguistic philosophy, then the Issue of Language's Authority can, in that sense, be termed *the* central issue of linguistic philosophy. It is central, and it is more important than any other central issue. Let us focus first on the issue's centrality (its frequency and influence) within linguistic philosophy, then on its importance.

Centrality

A verdict on the issue's centrality to linguistic philosophy depends on how one defines "linguistic philosophy." In Rom Harré's characterization, "Linguistic philosophy is not a set of doctrines, but a critical technique."[1] Similarly, for Bernard Williams, "linguistic philosophy, or linguistic analysis, is not a branch of philosophy but a method of philosophy, a method which could be applied to philosophical questions raised in all branches."[2] This seems like equating empirical science with its experimental procedures or impressionistic painting with its impressionistic technique. There is more to any type of philosophy—for example, dialectical, phenomenological, pragmatic, existential, or linguistic—than its distinctive approach. However, verbal infelicities aside, what is the "critical technique" here in question, the "method of philosophy" on which emphasis is thus placed?

"Linguistic philosophy," writes Maurice Cornforth, "is concerned with words. And its philosophical techniques consist of posing every problem with which it is concerned in the form, 'How, in this instance, are words being used?' For linguistic philosophy, every philosophical problem concerns the use of words, and is therefore to be solved by the method of inquiring into the uses of words."[3] In this sort of account, linguistic philosophy takes its name not only from its linguistic approach but also from its linguistic domain. Linguistics is the empirical study of natural languages, philosophy of language is concerned with the underlying nature of the phenomena that linguistics studies, and linguistic philosophy studies the language of philosophical problems.[4]

Even within these narrow limits, the Issue of Language's Authority could still be central; attention would just shift from correct statements about nonlinguistic reality (e.g., good) to correct statements about the corresponding words (e.g., "good"). However, as Antony Flew observed in the 1950s, "to concede that it is sometimes illuminating to think of philosophy as some special sort of study of language, or to allow that there is value in methods derivable from this way of thinking, is not to commit anyone to conducting all discussions and presenting all papers exclusively in the formal mode of speech, with display of talk about words, expressions, and sentences; specimens neatly deployed between inverted commas."[5] In talk about matter, rights, identity, time, or causality, the guidance of language might be tacit, as it is in talk about stocks, crops, politics, or the weather. In this account, which does more justice to the full historical reality,[6] "'linguistic philosophy' is not one branch or field of philosophy; like the philosophy of science, or history, or religion, or ethics; or like the study of Kant or Hegel."[7] It is coextensive with the whole of philosophy; but, whatever the area, it is philosophy conducted in a new, linguistic key. What this means, above all, is that language acquires new authority.[8]

Recognition of its authority is discernible, for example, in the view Cornforth cited above. "Clearly," it has been said, "'language-analytical philosophy' refers to a way of doing philosophy which involves the belief that the problems of philosophy can be solved, or must be solved, by means of an analysis of language."[9] I imagine many linguistic philosophers would bridle at this comprehensive claim, especially in its restrictive form, as I do. However, the generality of the claim suggests the prevalence of the belief in question, and that in turn suggests widespread acceptance of language's authority. If philosophers have turned to language for solutions, it is because they have accepted the authority of language to dictate the solutions.

Consider examples already seen. Moore's great question concerned the nature of the good. The good, he concluded, was a single, simple reality, as indefinable as yellow. Later he recognized that we use and understand the word "good" "in a considerable number of different senses."[10] Without acknowledgment of language's authority, this recognition would have had no significance for his quest. Linguistic analysis would have appeared as irrelevant as it did in *Principia Ethica*. Again, we have seen Wittgenstein remark, in answer to previous problems concerning the meanings of words, that for a large class of cases in which we employ the word "meaning," the meaning of a word can be characterized as the word's use in the language. Earlier, he was not interested in how we employ the word "meaning" (or *Bedeutung*); later, he was, because he accepted the authority of language. Philosophers may not disregard the senses of the terms they employ. Examples to come suggest how characteristic is the connection here illustrated: recourse to language for answers to philosophical problems typically reflects recognition of language's authority to determine the answers.

Without necessarily subscribing to the thesis that language can solve all philosophical problems, in the last century many came to accept language's guidance still more widely than just in philosophy or in solving philosophy's problems. Whether writing, speaking, or assessing others' assertions, on whatever question, they took into account the claims of the idiom employed. This above all—this authority accorded to language—accounted for the quantity of dust the "linguistic turn" kicked up.

Importance

The metaphor of "centrality," I suggested, can be unpacked in terms of frequency, influence, and importance. If "linguistic philosophy" is broadly, realistically conceived, then numerous thinkers classifiable as linguistic philosophers have, with varying degrees of explicitness, addressed the Issue of Language's Authority. What is more, their answers to it have notably affected their treatment of many other questions. In this sense, the issue is central to linguistic philosophy. It is *a* central issue. I now suggest, moreover, that the Issue of Language's Authority may be termed *the* central issue of linguistic philosophy, in the sense that it is more important than any other central issue: it exerts greater influence and has more weighty implications, not only within linguistic philosophy but also beyond.

Of the rivals the last chapter cited, the first, foundational question appears largely a nonissue. All would agree that discussion cannot profitably proceed without our first understanding the meaning of our words, whereas not even Wittgenstein, the paradigmatic linguistic philosopher, would claim that the study of language, abstracted from all else, can be singled out as foundational, as "first philosophy." Only in the total stream of thought and life can meanings be clarified. Whether the stream of thought is largely linguistic, as Herder and others have held, and whether, indeed, linguistic thoughts can only be had linguistically are important questions. However, these questions we seldom need to consider, whereas the Issue of Language's Authority confronts us at every turn. Every time we proffer an utterance or assess another's utterance, we accept or reject the authority of language to determine what we should say. And on this question, disagreement has been and still is both pervasive and profound.

The full case for the primacy of the Issue of Language's Authority will emerge only gradually in the course of the present study. Chapter by chapter, case by consequential case, in one major thinker after another, the suggestion will appear ever more plausible that the question of language's authority is indeed the most important issue raised by linguistic philosophy. However, here in advance this promissory note may be received with some skepticism. So let me add a more modest claim by way of motivation: whether or not, in the end, the Issue of Language's Authority is accorded primacy, the issue merits fuller, more systematic scrutiny than it has so far received.

Ian Hacking's *Why Does Language Matter to Philosophy?* is revealing in this regard. He writes, "Aside from what, in the opening chapter of strategy, I called the minor reasons why language has persistently mattered to philosophers, there need not be any true and interesting general answer to my question. Indeed, I am sure that no such answer is valid over the whole domain of Western philosophizing from Plato to the present."[11] The basis for Hacking's sureness does not include attention to the question here addressed. That question—the Issue of Language's Authority—does concern the whole of Western philosophy from Plato to the present, fundamentally; and if a true and interesting response can be given to it, favoring language's authority, then a true and interesting general answer can be given to Hacking's question, "Why does language matter to philosophy?" But nothing in the literature alerted him to this possible reply. Relatively few philosophers have focused on Hacking's question, and far fewer have focused, clearly and explicitly, on the issue of language's authority, inside and outside philosophy (as distinct, say, from the authority of "ordinary" language, within philosophy).[12] In this respect, most philosophers have resembled Moore. And many, like Moore, have had reasons that seemed to exempt them from seriously attending to language.

Recall Gellner's comment "that usage cannot settle normative issues about how we should think." Thinking, it is felt, should regulate speaking, not vice versa. And the thinking that does the regulating is not itself linguistic—at least not in the sense of employing inwardly the same signs as occur outwardly in linguistic intercourse. Such mental surrogates would be no help. Duplicating outer speech, they would raise the same question: why use these words, inwardly or outwardly, rather than others in the language? Thought, then, should not be confused with language, and primacy, it is held, belongs clearly with the former. To any readers harboring such notions as these, claims of language's authority may appear suspect and a book-length study of language's prerogatives may appear a misguided enterprise.

I had such possible readers in mind when I proposed trying to entertain nonverbally any of the thoughts expressed verbally here or in any other work. I know I can't pull it off, but suppose I could. Where would authority lie? Would the nonlinguistic version of the thought validate the linguistic one? Would it tell us what we should say? Certainly the realities we speak of don't—not by themselves. An automobile accident, for example, does not come with labels attached, informing us what words to describe it with, in English, Russian, or Cantonese. And the most perfect mental representation of the accident would do no better. How, then, can the mental intermediary get us from the reality to the words? This question deserves more attention than it has typically received. The more closely we study it here, the more plausible it will appear that language is, and should be acknowledged as, a more important determinant of utterances' truth and assertability than is private, nonlinguistic thought.

Even so, surely *reality* is the chief determinant? Surely, then, that is where emphasis should fall? Granted, but in defense of a focus that may otherwise appear misplaced (confer statements such as Mackie's and Gellner's), let me note, first, that the determination of truth by both language and reality does not resemble the independent pulling by two horses, one weak and one strong, hitched to a single wagon: neither the role of language nor the role of reality can be understood independently of the other. To understand a descriptive expression (e.g., "red"), we must know what reality it is used to describe; to know what reality that is (e.g., red), we must understand the language used to indicate it. Immanuel Kant said something similar. However, the "categories of the understanding" that subtly, powerfully shape our conceptions of reality are not, for instance, Kant's twelve, transcending times, cultures, and languages, but those of our mother tongues, assimilated before we undertake the study of philosophy or anything else. These familiar concepts, which we acquire with minimal linguistic reflection, we also employ with minimal linguistic reflection. They resemble spectacles that we look through but seldom at. Thus, with our mental gaze fixed on the topics of reflection and discussion, the concepts we employ tend to fuse with the realities considered and discussed. ("We predicate of the thing," wrote Wittgenstein, "what lies in the method of representing it."[13]) When and if the fusion is detected, the reality may look very different. The next chapter, on Plato, will offer a first example of such fusion and its momentous implications.

There and in subsequent chapters, I shall adopt the same procedure as in the last, using specific thinkers and their specific doctrines to introduce themes of general interest, as I did with Moore, and addressing the themes critically as well as historically. The chosen thoughts and figures will give sharper focus to the discussion, while opening large perspectives.

3

Plato's Recourse
to Nonlinguistic Forms

THE THESIS IS plausible and intriguing: at the dawn of Western philosophy, Plato already took a "linguistic turn," not merely in the sense that
he scrutinized language, but in a stronger sense more pertinent to this
study. In the *Cratylus* he may have questioned the linguistic guidance that
the *Phaedo* attributed to the Forms and, consequently, may have recognized more fully the role of language in determining what we should say.
Whatever the truth of this surmise, the story deserves telling, for it illustrates the following facts of great importance for the issue that here concerns us: (1) thinkers are more likely to ignore the authority of language
than explicitly to contest it; (2) this neglect may radically affect their conceptions of reality; and (3) repeatedly, realities thus conjured up pose as
major rivals to language as arbiters of truth or assertability. So it was in
Plato's case and so it was in others we shall consider; but few examples
demonstrate more clearly than Plato's *Phaedo* that the Issue of Language's Authority is no mere "matter of words."

The *Phaedo*

Perhaps more fully than any other of Plato's writings, the *Phaedo* encapsulates the distinctive philosophical outlook known as Platonism. The best
known and most discussed of the dialogue's arguments, tentatively proposed, makes a case for the existence of nonsensible Forms, our recollection of them in this life, the preexistence of the soul, and, by implication,
the immortality of the soul (the question raised by Socrates's imminent
death). The starting point of this progression is linguistic: "'When people
are asked something, if the question is well put, they themselves explain
everything—and yet if they hadn't got knowledge and a right account of

19

C—M

the matter <u>stored away inside them</u>, they couldn't do that.'"[1] We have knowledge, for example, of equality, and on the strength of this knowledge, we may declare two sticks equal or unequal in length. Since sensible objects such as sticks cannot impart such knowledge (the debate about the reason given for this denial need not here detain us), '"we must have acquired knowledge of the Equal Itself before we began to see and to hear and to use our other senses.'"[2] Similarly, before we entered this sensible world, we acquired knowledge '"not only of the Equal and the Greater and the Smaller, but of all such things.'"[3] "For our discussion now," Socrates concludes,

> is concerned with the Beautiful Itself and the Good Itself and the Just and the Holy, no less than with the Equal; in fact, as I say, it is concerned with all those things to which, in our questions and answers, we attach as a sort of hall-mark of identification the words "that which *is*, all by itself." We must, then, have acquired our knowledge of all these things before being born.[4]

Note that the argument ends, as it began, with "our questions and answers." These linguistic performances are to be explained through knowledge of the Forms. Yet the Forms, be it noted, are not themselves linguistic. They are neither Greek nor Latin nor Hebrew, and they have no labels attached (e.g., "in ancient Rome call me 'aequalitas,' in modern London call me 'equality'"). So we wonder how they can help in choosing the right expression, for instance for the sticks. Will recollection of the nonlinguistic paradigm inform would-be English-speakers that "equal" is the right word to use, and will it indicate whether that word is verb, noun, or adjective, or all three, or something else? How, for example, will we know to apply the word to a particular relation between objects, lengths, numbers, and the rest, and not, for instance, to a color or a bridge?

To all such queries the answer is the same. The Form is deaf and dumb. It is as uncommunicative as the color or the bridge. Though I should gaze all day at the blue of the sky, I would not thereby learn the meaning of "blue" or "sky"; though I stared holes in the Golden Gate Bridge, it would not teach me the meaning of "bridge" (or "pont" or "ponte" or "Brücke"). And Plato's Forms—Equality Itself, Beauty Itself, Virtue Itself—can do no better. No nonlinguistic entity can convey, on its own, the grammar, semantics, or pragmatics of a language—that is, the rules relating words with words, words with things, or words with actions—let alone those of all languages.

We might therefore suggest that in order to ask and answer questions about any reality, we need to know not three things (the reality, the language, and the pertinent Form), but just two: the reality spoken of and the

language used to speak of it. If, for example, we see two sticks and measure their length, the semantics of the English word "equal" will then tell
us whether to call the sticks equal in length. A nonlinguistic "Form" is superfluous. However, with regard to moral terms (Plato's chief interest) the
sufficiency of reality plus language looks more problematic. And even
with regard to nonmoral terms such as "equal," Plato may not have stum-
bled through sheer inadvertence. His attitude need not have been, "Language can take care of itself; there is no problem there." The *Phaedo*'s
allusions to what people "call" pleasure, courage, or temperance suggest a
different explanation[5]—what Nicholas White has termed "Plato's refusal
to trust hearsay." "Plato would not grant that the observation of the way
in which a term was customarily used, or the expressed views of ordinary
speakers on its meaning, could be taken as evidence carrying any particular value."[6] Word usage looked as fluctuating and uncertain as temporal,
sensible reality; sureness and stability would have to be found elsewhere—
in Equality itself, Beauty itself, Truth itself, and so forth.

The *Cratylus* calls this solution into question. The clarity with which
it indicates the linguistic gap left by the theory of recollection is one reason for surmising that the *Cratylus* may have been written later than the
Phaedo.[7] The *Cratylus* may have targeted the *Phaedo*'s theory of recollection, as the *Parmenides* targeted its theory of Forms.

The *Cratylus*

White has remarked that "because language is not the chief issue of any
other dialogue, people tend to think that it is as if Plato in the *Cratylus*
were taking time out from his usual interests. But the *Cratylus* is not an
isolated work."[8] Of particular interest here, the *Cratylus* recognizes and
addresses the very issue the *Phaedo* failed to confront: how can a Form—
how can any nonlinguistic reality, by itself—tell us what we should say?
According to one of the dialogue's disputants, Hermogenes, it cannot do
so; there is no correctness of names other than by convention and agreement.[9] According to Cratylus, on the contrary, the reality named may itself determine how it should be labeled. Indeed, ontology may override
convention: though all may call a man by a given name, that may not be
his real name.[10]

As initially stated by Hermogenes, Cratylus's view is still indefinite:
"Cratylus, whom you see here, Socrates, says that everything has a right
name of its own, which comes by nature, and that a name is not whatever
people call a thing by agreement, just a piece of their own voice applied to
the thing, but that there is a kind of inherent correctness in names, which
is the same for all men, both Greeks and barbarians."[11] In explication of
this "correctness," Socrates first traces names to other names from which

they are derived, then focuses on elementary names, not explained through other names. At this level, he suggests, perhaps a name "is a vocal imitation of that which is imitated, and he who imitates with his voice names that which he imitates."[12] For example, the Greek words for flowing, running, whirling, and the like all imitate these realities' rapidity of motion by means of the letter rho with which the words start; for "the tongue is least at rest and most agitated in pronouncing this letter."[13] This mimetic solution, to be sure, is a desperate nonstarter; and Socrates's efforts to make it work only succeed in making it look ridiculous.

Hermogenes's alternative view comes off no better; for, as formulated by Socrates, it presents an easy target. Socrates elicits Hermogenes's agreement that whatever name we decide to give each particular thing is its name, and that it makes no difference whether the giver be a whole population or a private individual. "Well, then," comments Socrates, "suppose I give a name to something or other, designating, for instance, that which we now call 'man' as 'horse' and that which we now call 'horse' as 'man,' will the real name of the same thing be 'man' for the public and 'horse' for me individually, and in the other case 'horse' for the public and 'man' for me individually?"[14] As Rudolph Weingartner notes, such a position, which Socrates proceeds to critique, hardly merits the name "conventionalism."[15] When, therefore, the extremes represented by Hermogenes and Cratylus have been rejected, all avenues of solution are not closed. In 434E–435D, Socrates can correct both the extreme individualism of the one and the extreme realism of the other, and suggest an alternative direction by arguing that "both convention and custom must contribute something towards the indication of our meaning when we speak."[16] Just what they contribute, and how, he does not spell out. The issue is left for future generations of philosophers to grapple with—or to ignore. Some, we might say, have written a footnote to the *Cratylus* by the ways in which they have grappled with the issue; others have written a footnote to the *Phaedo* by the comparable ways in which they have ignored it. Later chapters will track the former alternative; here, let us further illustrate the latter.

Historical Perspectives

Of special interest for its historical importance and its relevance for the next chapter, on Thomas Aquinas, is the tradition in which general concepts and their abstraction from particular realities play a role comparable to that of Forms and their intuition and recollection in Plato's *Phaedo*. Frederick Copleston illustrates this tradition through a standard example: "Thus the intellect as active abstracts the universal essence of man from a particular image, leaving out the particularizing notes which confine the image to being the image of this or that particular man, and impresses it on the intellect as passive. And so the universal concept is born."[17] Since, in this typical account,[18] no mention is made of language or of any particular language and its words, we may wonder what makes this universal concept the one expressed by the English word "man." How is that connection made? Right from the start, it would seem, before any abstracting occurs; for the particulars chosen for consideration are called men; and no things called by other names (e.g., chimpanzees) are considered. If, however, this is what qualifies candidates for inspection, *Cratylus*-style queries arise. Should we be guided by whatever people, reflectively or unreflectively, happen to call "men"? If yes, then why suppose a common essence? If no, then what class of things should we examine for the essence in question? And why, if we do spot an essence in another class of things, should we call it the essence of "man"? So long as such questions as these are not addressed and answered, the "concepts" abstracted without regard for language may operate with equally little regard for language. Like Moore's "concepts" and Plato's Forms, they may compete with language for hegemony. And indeed, as we shall see, they do and repeatedly have.

This sample, like the preceding, corrects the possible impression that debate about language's authority can have little substantive significance. What we say, it is thought, or what words we use, is of secondary importance. What should we think? What are the facts? The reality described is what matters, not the arbitrary signs used to describe it. Imbued with this attitude, Moore went about laying the foundations of ethics—and built them on sand. Ignoring the link with language, Plato made an equally shaky case for preexistence, Forms, recollection, and the immortality of the soul. Of comparable significance, the linguistic gap left by Copleston's Thomistic account calls into question widely held views concerning the fundamental relationship between speech, thought, and world: are there in fact such things as Aquinas's essences, and are they captured by mental concepts, and do these provide the basis for truth in mental judgments, and do linguistic utterances simply give external expression to these inner representations? From such examples, it is clear that language matters, and so does attention to language.

The last-cited example makes the point most powerfully; for in the history of Western thought it is difficult to discern any configuration more comprehensive and momentous than the one exemplified by Aquinas and evoked, more generally, by Wittgenstein when he wrote: "Thought, language, now appear to us as the unique correlate, picture, of the world. These concepts: proposition, language, thought, world, stand in line one behind the other, each equivalent to each."[19] Wittgenstein's own early theory, which he here had in mind, and other theories back through the centuries, have played innumerable variations on the same central theme: words, thoughts, and things are seen not just as being causally related to one another, but as running parallel. One way or another, words are paired with thoughts, and thoughts with things. On the basis of this isomorphic matching, truth may be achieved. If the thoughts are arranged as the things dictate, the thoughts are true. If the words are arranged as the thoughts dictate, the words are true. Such is the direction in which authority is exercised. The truth of judgments or beliefs is primary; the truth of utterances is derivative and subordinate; and language, as a mere means of communication, is accorded slight authority.

The next chapter, on Aquinas, will illustrate what has arguably been the most plausible and popular variant of this overall scheme—the one in which universal concepts, mirroring universal essences and expressed by universal terms, figure as the key components. From this variant we shall then turn to young Wittgenstein's refined, very different version—the one from which he eventually freed himself when, in his later thought, he left behind the whole three-tiered, isomorphic conception of language, thought, and world that, in varied forms, long dominated Western thought.

4

Aquinas and the Primacy of Mental Truth

"**I**T SEEMS," REMARKS Wittgenstein in his *Blue Book*, "that there are *certain definite* mental processes bound up with the working of language, processes through which alone language can function. I mean the processes of understanding and meaning. The signs of our language seem dead without these mental processes; and it might seem that the only function of the signs is to induce such processes, and that these are the things we ought really to be interested in."[1] Figuratively stated, many have viewed public language as though it were a mere code, instrumentally convenient but having no life of its own; all meaning and truth lay in the language translated by the code—that is, the language of the mind. In this conception, the transition from one language to the other, the mental to the spoken, has appeared to pose no more problem than, say, the transition from English to Morse Code: one just needed to know the pertinent conventions. Neither, it seemed, did any linguistic gap open between reality and its mental expression; for the signs of the mental language were natural, not conventional: they mirrored reality as no external, physical signs could. Thus, to cite the last chapter's example, whereas a nonlinguistic Form transcending all empirical realities might not indicate whether to call a pair of sticks equal, the mental concept of equality could. From the equality of the sticks to the corresponding concept to the code word "equal" the links, natural then conventional, looked unproblematic. Connected with reality by similarity and with speech by convention, *thought* could tell us what to say.

Aquinas as Paradigm

This general viewpoint, whose pertinence for our theme can readily be sensed, found paradigmatic expression in Thomas Aquinas's repeated assertion that truth resides primarily in the intellect.[2] More specifically, truth lies primarily not in things, nor in words, nor even in concepts or their formation, but in the act of judgment affirming or denying, combining or separating.[3] In simple illustration, "one who thinks that to be separated which is separated in reality, has a true opinion—for example, one who thinks that man is not an ass. And the same is true of one who thinks that to be combined which is combined in reality—for example, one who thinks that man is an animal. But, on the other hand, one who relates things in thought in a different way than they are in their own proper nature has an erroneous opinion—for example, one who thinks that man is an ass, or that he is not an animal."[4]

According to Aquinas, true judgments reveal two levels of correspondence with reality. First, the individual concepts that judgments employ are likenesses of the essences of things.[5] Whereas, for example, the senses form likenesses of the various shades or intensities of white, the intellect forms a likeness of the essence common to all whites. Whereas the senses form likenesses of the various colors, shapes, and sizes of human beings, the intellect forms a likeness of the essence common to all human beings. And so forth. These intellectual likenesses, serving as mental "words," furnish components of affirmation and negation in judgments. What distinguishes true judgments from false is a second level of correspondence: true judgments join what reality joins (e.g., man and rational) and disjoin what reality disjoins (e.g., man and ass). Without this further correspondence, there would be no truth in the primary sense of the term; and without the underlying correspondence at the level of the concepts, there would be neither truth nor falsehood in the primary sense of the terms.

For Aquinas, verbal truth ("vox vera"[6]) carries so little weight that he can state on one occasion "Truth is only in the mind."[7] Not resembling the realities they indicate, as mental representations can and do, words serve merely to communicate thoughts.[8] And their truth can be known only by reference to that of the thoughts they express. Thus, in Aquinas's view, mental truth enjoys a double primacy relative to verbal truth: primacy both in the order of value and in the order of knowledge. Verbal truth is for the sake of mental truth, and not vice versa. And verbal truth is known from the truth of the thoughts expressed, and not vice versa.

This is important, for it locates Aquinas on one side of a great divide in Western thought. In terms of mere verbal matching, we might either define true statements as those that express true judgments or define true judgments as those expressed by true statements. The equivalence works either way. But is there no exit from this charmed circle? On what side can understanding be found? For millennia, most philosophers—whether rationalist, empiricist, or other—agreed in replying, "On the mental side." Aquinas here stands as their representative. More specifically, he represents what is perhaps the most plausible and historically widespread version of mental primacy, matching universal terms with universal concepts and universal concepts with universal essences or natures, then combining the concepts in true judgments expressed by true statements.[9]

To many, only the mental exit from the definitional circle has seemed possible, for the linguistic exit has looked hopeless. Mental likenesses seem an evident fact of life, and so does their importance for speech. But the word "man," for example, does not resemble a man, nor does the word "rational" resemble rationality. In the *Cratylus* Plato was right to give up on the audible resemblance of words with reality as a key to truth. But if the key is not to be found in Platonic Forms, where else can it be found save in the mediating action of the mind? And how else can that mediation operate save through resemblance of some sort if, indeed, truth is correspondence? The fundamental correspondence must be that of thought with reality, not of speech with reality.

For most linguistic philosophers, it is the mental exit, not the linguistic, that looks hopeless. Here, taking Aquinas as exemplar of the mentalistic tradition, we can sample the reasons for the negative side of this judgment and leave the positive part, favoring language, for later. Why does the solution via inner similarity appear so doubtful?

Difficulties

Consider the simple statement, "This summer I vacationed in Switzerland." From a Thomistic viewpoint, mental representation for the verb and its tense looks least problematic: just abstract the essence of vacationing and the essence of pastness and combine them.[10] What, though, of the first-person subject "I"? My human nature, of which I might perhaps form an abstract mental likeness, is shared with other persons, so does not pick me out, as does this first-person pronoun. Rather, according to Aquinas what individuates any corporeal substance like myself is prime matter (roughly, the undifferentiated stuff of which physical bodies are formed) "signed by quantity." It can hardly be supposed that this "signing" appears in thought by my mentally representing, even sketchily, the volume, contours, posture, or location of my body throughout the vacation, let alone my bones, brains, tissues, organs, thoughts, habits, and the rest. But anything less—anything at all realistic, psychologically—would be both incomplete and inaccurate as a depiction of the reality expressed by the pronoun "I." It would be a mere sketch, no more required for the sense and accuracy of the words than is an illustration in a book.

The problems worsen for Switzerland. How deep in the earth and high in the sky does that country extend? How can I form an accurate representation of all its borders, through plains and mountains and the middle of lakes? How, in the narrow confines of my mind, can I represent the land's full dimensions, so many miles this way and so many that, and all that lies within them? If possible, the difficulties grow still worse for "this summer." Does a summer have prime matter to individuate it? Though confined to planet Earth, does it occupy a space? What mental likeness might be formed of any summer, let alone of this particular one? I need not insist. In chapter 1, I questioned the possibility of nonverbally thinking the sense of any sentence in that chapter. Now I can add the nonphilosophical, everyday statement, "This summer I vacationed in Switzerland."

Were it not for the number and explicitness of Aquinas's statements about concepts as likenesses and knowledge through resemblance,[11] one might be tempted to explain them away: Aquinas just went along with some traditional terminology,[12] without taking it very seriously.[13] Such a concession should not be lightly made. If the viewpoint that Aquinas's wording suggests is as hopeless as it appears on closer examination, that needs to be clearly recognized. For here is language's foremost historical rival for authority: essentialistic, nonlinguistic thoughts, related to reality not merely as arbitrary signs, as words are, but through resemblance with reality, as words are not and cannot conceivably be. The word "animal," say, does not look or sound like any animal, much less like animality, and neither could any other written or spoken expression. Where else, then, might we seek correspondence with reality than in the mind?

I would like, if possible, to make the present critique less one-sided and balance it with actual or conceivable lines of response. However, for this purpose I have found no helpful stimuli to my thinking. Even the fullest account of conceptual "likenesses" or "similitudes" in Aquinas's thought that I have come across does not address difficulties of the kind that I have just sketched.[14] And I have never encountered any representative of this tradition who has made a serious effort, in the manner I have illustrated here, to spell out the mental contents for any single statement. The details, it seems, could take care of themselves. The basic account had to be correct. And indeed if, despite the difficulties that appear for pronouns, proper names, definite descriptions, and other familiar expressions, the tradition which Aquinas represents got the universal terms right, that would be an important achievement. It might be difficult to understand how any complete judgment save the simplest and most conveniently chosen (e.g., "Man is rational") could be formed with just universal components, but these components might still exercise the sort of primacy supposed. So let us examine the heart of the system, and focus on a simple, universal concept of a kind Aquinas often cited—for instance, "blue."

I pick this particular color concept (not Aquinas's favorite, "white") because Moore gave such a revealing account of it, in agreement with

Aquinas's general viewpoint. Musing to himself in his *Commonplace Book*, Moore remarked:

> This character wh. we express by "is a shade of blue," is, of course, something which is common to all shades of blue—something which they have "in common." Some people seem loth to admit that they have anything "in common." And of course this character is not "in common" to both of 2 blue shades, in the sense that it is a part or constituent of both . . . Obviously this character also is not identical with any shade which possesses it, nor yet with any other shade of colour that we *see*. It is not similar in shade to any shade that we *see*. So that, if it is "seen" at all, it is only in a completely different sense.[15]

With similar emphasis, Moore affirmed: "*All* the shades we *see* occupy some position in the colour octahedron; but 'blue,' in the sense in which many of the shades in the octahedron are 'blue,' occupies *no* position in it: therefore it is not seen."[16]

What all shades of blue have in common is something that can be truly said of all of them. For example, they are all members of the disjunctive class (cobalt or aquamarine or turquoise or . . .) designated by the common term "blue." Or, they all belong to a continuum of shades labeled "blue" and bordered roundabout by colors that bear other labels. This disjunctive membership, or position within a linguistically defined continuum of colors, is not, to be sure, something that can be "seen." Neither, however, is it something of which one might form an abstract mental likeness. I can form no such likeness of disjunction as such, much less of this particular disjunction with its constituent shades. Talk of abstraction suggests leaving out the sensible particulars, but to leave out the shades of blue that form the continuum or disjunctive class would be to leave out the content of the concept "blue." In Wittgenstein's comparison, it would be like stripping an artichoke of its leaves in search of the real, essential artichoke and concluding that, since no single leaf belongs to the essence, the essence is invisible and intangible and can only be captured by an intellectual likeness. Thus, recourse to inner resemblance works no better for "blue," it seems, than it does for "I," "this summer," or "Switzerland."

The like holds, I suggest, for "vacation," "rational," "animal," and other general terms. This I can state with some assurance for several reasons. First, for no general term that I consider do I discover any abstract essence, of which I might form a mental likeness in the manner suggested by Moore's account of "blue" or Copleston's account (in the last chapter) of "man." Second, essentialists do not base their position, inductively, on a varied sampling of general terms ("chair," "nation," "percentage," "variety," "thought," etc.), but on a priori reasons. Third, these reasons appear weak, suggesting slight reflection of the requisite kind.[17] Fourth, I discern potent influences that, rather than any genuine intuition, can account for the conviction that to the general terms of language abstract essences do and must correspond. Let me start with the a priori reasons and their weakness.

"Well, then," asks Socrates in the *Republic*, "shall we proceed as usual and begin by assuming the existence of a single essential nature or Form for every set of things which we call by the same name?"[18] Shifting the focus from the things to the names, we might ask, "Shall we assume that names do and must function in this way—to pick out essences?" How might that be shown? "Signs," wrote Gottlob Frege, in pragmatic reply, "would hardly be useful if they did not serve the purpose of signifying the same thing repeatedly and in different contexts, while making evident that the same thing was meant."[19] So, is the word "healthy" useless if it describes now people, now climates, medicines, diets, or complexions? Does such contextual variation throw us into confusion? We might reply for Frege that at least the word means the same thing when, for example, it is predicated of persons.[20] But what does such talk of "sameness" signify? Does it simply contrast the single sense with the broader range of senses (for diet, complexion, etc.), or, more strongly, does it assert the inner homogeneity of that single sense? The former looks a safe reply, the latter does not. When people ask, as some still do in defense of essences, "Why would we use the same word if it didn't pick out the same thing?" they have not reviewed alternative conceptual structures—qualitative continua, family resemblances, overlapping fibers, causal connections, and so forth—and found them impractical, implausible, or nonexistent. They simply have not considered them. And we can sense why they have not.

For the most part, the essentialistic view of speech, thought, and reality is not based on argument but is taken for granted. Various prereflective influences powerfully suggest it. For example, the sameness of the appearance of single words on various occasions suggests a similar sameness in their referents or meanings. Or the singular form of abstract nouns suggests a single referent (knowledge is one thing, beauty is one thing, and so forth). Or the association of proper names with single, constant referents (Caesar, Denver, the Alamo) serves as an implicit model and suggests a similar function for general names: no doubt they, too, pick out some one entity—if not a single concrete referent—then a single essence or nature common to the various things called by the common name. After all, do not all houses, say, have at least this in common, that they are houses? And are not all books books, all people people, all laws laws? It is easy to get caught in this web and to stay trapped in it. Searching for essences (that for some reason prove elusive, despite their supposedly crucial role in our mental and linguistic lives), we may fail seriously to question whether there are such things.

The web's tentacles extend farther. We *think* what we say, the mentalist may insist, and if that amounted to no more than saying it, or saying it twice (first privately, then publicly), we would be doing no more than a computer might be programmed to execute. Surely human thinking is different. Resemblance, instantiated by mental images, suggests how it differs. And abstractive, intellectual resemblance does so most decisively. A computer cannot form *that* kind of likeness. The question is, can we? For example, can we form a likeness of what all and only blues—or all and only vacations, animals, human beings, and so on—have in common, if in fact they share no single, invariant, nondisjunctive essence? Or should we turn elsewhere for what makes human thought distinctive—for instance to our ability to examine shades of blue and determine whether, and in what sense, they do or do not have anything in common? (How could we program a computer to determine whether Moore was right about blues?)

Significance

I could continue this critique, but enough has been said to suggest the seriousness of the difficulties facing the tradition that Aquinas represents. As I remarked at the start, the importance of that tradition for the Issue of Language's Authority can readily be sensed. Anyone who places meaning and truth primarily in the mind and views public language as a mere code is likely to adopt an attitude like Moore's: "I am not anxious to discuss whether I am right in thinking that [the word "good"] is so used. My business is solely with that object or idea, which I hold, rightly or wrongly, that the word is generally used to stand for." Authority lies in the object or the idea (the essence or the concept that mirrors it), not in language.

In illustration of this tendency, consider Aquinas's claim that unjust laws are not laws.[21] People call them laws. It is handy to have an expression that covers both just and unjust laws. If we restricted the term in the way Aquinas enjoins, we might have to introduce a new term to fill the spot on the conceptual map that "law" presently occupies. However, such linguistic, pragmatic considerations did not concern Aquinas. The essence of law was stated in the definition: "an ordinance of reason for the common good, made by him who has care of the community, and promulgated."[22] Unjust laws, which did not further the common good, did not satisfy this definition; therefore they were not laws.

The essentialistic form of the mentalistic tradition begets more conflict with the authority of language than does any other version. As a sample alternative form, consider Russell's explication of truth in terms of image propositions (e.g., of a window to the left of a door) expressed by verbal propositions (e.g., "The window is to the left of the door").[23] In such examples, wrote Russell, the "general nature of the formal correspondence which makes truth or falsehood can be seen."[24] In this empiricist account, no essences appear that might challenge the customary or stipulated application of terms (e.g., "door" or "window"). The images are particular, not general, hence can dictate no expansion or restriction of terms. Through the ages, a major challenge to the authority of language has come, instead, from the generality of essences and corresponding mental concepts, from belief in the abundance of such essences and concepts, and from belief in their teleological and conceptual primacy relative to words. "There are some philosophers," wrote Moore,

> who say that there are no such things at all: that general ideas are pure fictions like chimaeras or griffins. . . . But a majority of philosophers would, I think, say that there are such things; and *if* there are, then, I think there is no doubt that they are one of the most important kinds of things in the Universe. *If* there are any at all, there are tremendous numbers of them, and we are all constantly thinking and talking of them.[25]

On this common assumption, mere words merit less attention. In the essentialistic tradition that Aquinas represents, the teleological and conceptual primacy of the mental relative to language translates into practical, normative primacy of the mental.

5

The *Tractatus*

Precise Thought versus Imprecise Language

THE MENTALISTIC TRADITION represented by Aquinas continued strong for many centuries and carried into the twentieth century. Many, like Moore, still believed in essences captured by universal concepts and expressed by universal terms. Many, like Russell, relied more on mental images. Some, like young Wittgenstein (as we shall now see), turned to atomic names for atomic objects, picked out in thought. Yet, whether essentialist, empiricist, or atomist, all, like Aquinas, paired words with thoughts and thoughts with things, isomorphically. All explained the truth of words through the truth of thoughts. And all explained the truth of thoughts through the arrangement of thoughts' components—concepts, images, atomic names—mirroring the arrangement of the things represented. Humanity and rationality are indeed joined in reality, as in the judgment "Man is rational." The window is indeed to the left of the door, as depicted by the mental images. The atomic objects are indeed arrayed as portrayed in the speaker's thinking-out of the words. In these variants of the same basic scheme, words and their truth pose no separate problem. To determine what to say, you must understand what is true; and to understand what is true, you must examine thought, not language.[1]

In the eighteenth century a groundswell of resistance set in against this tradition. However, many who turned from an isomorphic, mentalistic perspective did not straightway switch to a linguistic one. Kant, for example, did not. Though he occasionally stressed the linguistic nature of thought, the authority of language played a very limited role in defining the twelve basic categories of the understanding that, in Kant's account, govern thought about empirical reality, and in defining the key concepts that he employed in his account of human understanding. Kant's theoretical ambitions repeatedly determined what words to apply, regardless of the words' familiar meanings or any stipulated substitutes. Here, in these theoretical ambitions, lay language's new rival. Kant had a tower to build, and ordinary word meanings were not suited to his purposes, so could be ignored. I can leave this major competitor—philosophical theory construction—for later consideration, for it is still very much alive.

Gottlob Frege's favored challenger is not. With respect to the Issue of Language's Authority, Frege too, like Kant, was a transitional figure. Though Frege reacted sharply against the psychologism of his day and of previous centuries, he did not turn to language as the chief locus of meaning and truth, but to "thoughts" (e.g., "laws of nature, mathematical laws, historical facts"[2]) that, as he conceived them, were neither linguistic nor psychological. Like Plato's Forms, they constituted a realm of eternal, unchanging realities, distinct from the world of experience. For Frege, not only does truth not reside in language, but language, in its existing condition, is the enemy of truth. He may have transmitted something of this antilinguistic bias to later philosophers, for example to Russell and the early Wittgenstein. Overall, however, Dummett plausibly views Frege's influence as working in language's favor:

> For if one accepts the initial step—the extrusion of thoughts and their components from the mind—one may yet feel unhappy with the ontological mythology which, as we have seen, was already in some tension with Frege's more detailed accounts of particular senses. One in this position has therefore to look about him to find something non-mythological but objective and external to the individual mind to embody the thoughts which the individual subject grasps and may assent to or reject. Where better to find it than in the institution of a common language?[3]

This shift did not occur immediately, however. As Aristotelians abandoned Platonic Forms and Frege abandoned mental meanings without turning to language, so it was for Wittgenstein, in whose thinking the full conversion to acceptance of language's authority would eventually occur. Although the author of the *Tractatus Logico-Philosophicus* dropped Frege's "thoughts," he did not turn straightway to "the institution of a common language," but substituted a new mythology of his own.

That mythology and its components—the atomic names and atomic objects just mentioned—have enjoyed no greater vogue than did Frege's "thoughts." So, skipping the *Tractatus*, I might cite one or two further transitional thinkers, then pass to someone like Rudolf Carnap, who paid more heed to the authority of language. However, the progress of Wittgenstein's thinking cannot be understood without reference to the *Tractatus*; and Wittgenstein is the most important single figure for the story here being told. In a progression without close parallel, Wittgenstein strongly influenced three philosophical movements of the last century: the logical atomism classically formulated in his youthful *Tractatus*, the logical positivism of the Vienna Circle, and the linguistic philosophy represented by his posthumously published *Philosophical Investigations*. These influences, reflecting stages in Wittgenstein's philosophical development, relate importantly to the Issue of Language's Authority, so will receive successive attention here—the first in the present chapter, the second in the next chapter, and the third in chapters 8 and 9.

A supplemental reason for examining the *Tractatus* is the attention it permits and requires to one of the chief complaints blocking acceptance of language's authority: its fuzziness, its imprecision. In this regard, already near the start of his philosophical career, before he wrote the *Tractatus*, Wittgenstein made a decisive move. Could it be, he wondered in an early notebook, that the sentences in ordinary use have only a vague, indefinite sense? For example, "When I say, 'The book is lying on the table,' does this really have a completely clear sense?"[4] To this "EXTREMELY important question," he replied: "If the proposition 'The book is on the table' has a clear sense, then I must, whatever *is the case*, be able to say whether the proposition is true or false."[5] But how can this be, since there could very well occur cases in which, going by just the phrase "lying on the table," I should be unable to say whether the book is lying on the table? There appeared only one solution: "It seems clear that what we MEAN must always be '*sharp*.'"[6] The personal act of meaning goes beyond the language spoken and adds the requisite precision.

For the Issue of Language's Authority, this move was momentous. If truth was the prime desideratum of declarative utterances, and their truth depended on their sense, and their sense depended on thought and not on language, there was no clear way to decide between one expression and another. For speakers, it seemed, might project their words as they pleased. Thus, in young Wittgenstein's thought, no positive answer to the Issue of Language's Authority emerged, but merely a negative verdict against existing languages' authority. I shall first describe more fully how Wittgenstein reasoned himself into this linguistic cul-de-sac, then how, later on, he reasoned himself out of it.

The *Tractatus*'s Linguistic Dead End

The *Tractatus* echoes the notebook pages just quoted. Number 4.023 reiterates the two-value requirement: "A proposition must restrict reality to two alternatives: yes or no." Between yes and no, true and false, there can never be any third possibility; there is no place for "neither true nor false" or "undecided." Number 3.11 indicates the key role of thought in determining a statement's sense: "We use the perceptible sign of a proposition (spoken or written, etc.) as a projection of a possible situation. The method of projection is to think out the sense of the proposition."[7] From these two premises it follows that what we mean must be sharp,[8] leaving no gap between yes and no; but how is such sharpness achieved? Different lines of reasoning converge on the same solution. Whereas the physical analysis of physical objects leads to atoms that can in fact be split, the logical analysis of propositions leads beyond the reach of any microscope to objects so simple that they cannot be logically dissected any further.

A first line of thought, reflecting the notebook requirement that, whatever is the case, we must be able to say whether a proposition is true or false, proceeds as in the *Investigations'* retrospective account:

> [O]ne is tempted to make an objection against what is ordinarily called a name. It can be put like this: *a name ought really to signify a simple.* And for this one might perhaps give the following reasons: The word "Excalibur," say, is a proper name in the ordinary sense. The sword Excalibur consists of parts combined in a particular way. If they are combined differently Excalibur does not exist. But it is clear that the sentence "Excalibur has a sharp blade" makes *sense* whether Excalibur is still whole or is broken up. But if "Excalibur" is the name of an object, this object no longer exists when Excalibur is broken in pieces; and as no object would then correspond to the name it would have no meaning. But then the sentence "Excalibur has a sharp blade" would contain a word that had no meaning, and hence the sentence would be nonsense. But it does make sense; so there must always be something corresponding to the words of which it consists. So the word "Excalibur" must disappear when the sense is analysed and its place be taken by words which name simples. It will be reasonable to call these words the real names.[9]

Similar reasoning had led Russell to the conclusion that the referents picked out by genuine names would be "such things as little patches of colour or sounds, momentary things."[10] The existence of such items, being contingent, was not logically guaranteed, but it was assured by the speaker's direct acquaintance with them. A person could not name them without their existing to be named, any more than a person could attach a label to a nonexistent object.

For more than one reason, young Wittgenstein could not rest content with Russell's empirical referents. For one thing, doubtless they still retained too much complexity (a sound has volume, timbre, and pitch; a color patch has size, shape, shade, and saturation), and complexity was what differentiated propositions, which are true or false, from names, which are not. "A name," the *Tractatus* declared, "cannot be dissected any further by means of a definition. . . . Names *cannot* be anatomized by means of definitions."[11] What we call names can be, but that just shows they are not genuine names but veiled propositions. Consider the *Investigations'* sample utterance: "My broom is in the corner."[12] The word "broom" indicates a fact, statable in a proposition ("The broomstick is fitted into the brush"). So does the word "broomstick" and the word "brush." So, in turn, do the words (e.g., "bristle," "segment") that indicate the parts of the broomstick and the brush. Far along in this progression, we may reach such things as Russell's color patches, but not at the end of it. For just as the union of broomstick and brush is a fact, statable in a proposition, so too is the union of size, shape, shade, and saturation in a color patch. What, though, of these further constituents (e.g., this specific shade of brown)? They, too, were unacceptable as the ultimate atoms of logical analysis, for a reason that, in the present limited discussion, can be suggested as follows.

Echoing Frege, the *Tractatus* asserts: "Only in the nexus of a proposition does a name have meaning."[13] Only in an utterance such as "My broom is in the corner," as thought out by the speaker, do the words "broom" and "corner" pick out a specific broom and a specific corner. At the fully analytic level, where names link with names in elementary propositions, only in the nexus of the total utterance do the ultimate, genuine names pick out their specific referents. So doing, they connect the utterance with reality in a way that permits truth and falsehood. "One name stands for one thing, another for another thing, and they are combined with one another. In this way the whole group—like a *tableau vivant*—presents a state of affairs."[14] Not only does the proposition present a possible state of affairs; it states: "This is how things stand."[15] If they do so stand, the proposition is true; if they do not, it is false.

Now, suppose we had a name for a specific shade of brown, not further analyzable. By itself, the name might look logically simple. However, when used in a proposition, where alone it would have meaning, this name would reveal logical complexity. For from the assignment of that shade to some spot it would follow that no other shade of brown, and no shade of any other color, was in the same spot at the same instant. All competing hues would be logically excluded. Thus, though the shade named might be simple and not further analyzable, the name would be far from logically simple: closer analysis of its meaning in use would reveal, in addition to its positive content, enormous negative content: not a, not b, not c . . . not y, not z. In his search, then, for truly atomic names Wittgenstein was led to a realm as metaphysically remote as Plato's Forms or Frege's "thoughts." The utterly simple objects picked out by thought must be of a radically different kind than any we experience.

Enough has now been said to indicate more fully why no clear answer to the Issue of Language's Authority emerged from Wittgenstein's early thinking. A first reason is already evident. As the notebooks assert and the *Tractatus* amply confirms, "There is enormously much added in thought to each sentence and not said."[16] Thinking out the sense of their words, speakers connect them with myriad invisible objects, unknown to science or to introspection and joined in relations yet to be identified by logical analysis. Thus, with thought, not language, determining sense and sense determining truth, the link between truth and linguistic expression is cut, or at least greatly obscured. How freely, one wonders, can words be meant one way or another? ("Can I say 'bububu,'" inquires the later Wittgenstein, "and mean 'If it doesn't rain I shall go for a walk'?"[17]) The notebooks link this source of obscurity with another, which the *Tractatus* also repeats and fully confirms: "The tacit conventions on which the understanding of everyday language depends are enormously complicated."[18] Thus, even if the razor-sharp Tractarian truth-conditions derived from language, not thought, who could say what they are? What imperceptible logical atoms, how arranged, establish the truth of any utterance? Finally, the project that the *Tractatus* envisioned to lay bare these hidden truth-conditions proved chimerical. It was not possible to construct "a sign-language . . . governed by *logical* grammar," excluding all the errors and confusions occasioned by everyday language.[19] The difficulties that Wittgenstein encountered in his efforts to carry out this enterprise eventually led him to reject the whole Tractarian scheme of language, thought, and world. The fly, as he would put it, was finally freed from the fly-bottle.[20]

Wittgenstein's Later Critique

In a fly-bottle, the fly enters through a hole in the bottom, drawn by the fumes of beer in a trough surrounding the hole. Since it then flies only upward or sideways, never downward, in its efforts to escape, it is effectively trapped, for there is a stopper in the top. Thus, driven by the conviction that meaning had to be sharp, that names had to have existing referents, and that they had to occur in logically independent elementary propositions, young Wittgenstein kept flying upward in search of objects that might satisfy his requirements and never found any. The stopper was stuck firmly in the top. Though troubled by this failure ("Our difficulty was that we kept on speaking of simple objects and were unable to mention a single one"[21]), the youthful author of the *Tractatus* did not seriously reconsider the convictions that forced him in that futile direction.

Why must names have existing referents? What is wrong, for instance, with "Excalibur," even if someone, unbeknownst to the speaker, has reduced the sword to filings? In the *Investigations*, the buzzing fly is made to reply: "'What the names in language signify must be indestructible; for it must be possible to describe the state of affairs in which everything destructible is destroyed. And this description will contain words; and what corresponds to these cannot then be destroyed, for otherwise the words would have no meaning.'"[22] To weaken the hold of such thoughts, Wittgenstein comments: "In a sense, however, this man is surely what corresponds to his name. But he is destructible, and his name does not lose its meaning when the bearer is destroyed."[23] "Tom died last month," we say, and language functions perfectly well.

Again, why must the sense of our utterances be sharp? Must someone who says and means "Tom died last month" mentally specify the time zone for "last month" and the precise boundaries from pole to pole that define it? Hardly, yet the utterance serves its purpose, as does a lamp, and where precisely does the light of the lamp cease and the darkness begin? "'Inexact,'" observed Wittgenstein, "is really a reproach, and 'exact' is praise. And that is to say that what is inexact attains its goal less perfectly than what is more exact. Thus the point here is what we call 'the goal.' Am I inexact when I do not give our distance from the sun to the nearest foot, or tell a joiner the width of a table to the nearest thousandth of an inch?"[24] With numerous such therapeutic remarks as these, the later Wittgenstein addressed the obsession with precision that underlay the Tractarian requirement of atomic names in elementary propositions.

Dummett finds Wittgenstein's treatment of this issue inadequate. It is evident, he writes, "that we have an intuitive sympathy with Frege's view that a vague expression is one which is, to that extent, defective in sense: any account of vagueness which failed at least to explain this intuitive feeling would be inadequate."[25] The words just quoted from the *Investigations* contain an implicit response to this demand: the term "inexact" is a reproach, in relation to some purpose (as is "vague," on most occasions); hence, tautologically, inexactness is always a defect. It is a defect when giving the distance from the sun, instructing a cabinetmaker, reporting one's age, specifying the mass of an electron, citing a law in court, or predicting the weather. Whatever the context and whatever its requirements, vagueness (with respect to those requirements) is always a flaw. However, Dummett continues:

> At the same time, we have also a contrary intuition, that vagueness is an indispensable feature of our language, that we could not operate with language as we do unless many of its expressions displayed this feature: and it is equally a requirement on any satisfactory account of vagueness that it should at least explain our having this intuition also. Wittgenstein gave powerful expression

to this latter intuition in some passages in the *Investigations*, in
which he ridicules Frege for believing that vagueness is always a
defect our only response to which must be to seek to eliminate it:
but Wittgenstein can hardly be claimed to have offered any explanation or analysis of the indispensability of vagueness, let
alone a rebuttal of Frege's grounds for thinking that it has to
be eliminated.

From what Wittgenstein said and his reasons for saying it, it is clear what
direction his response would take. He would distinguish between relative,
context-sensitive exactness, which does not exclude a verdict of "undecided" in real or imaginary cases, and absolute, Tractarian exactness,
which permits only truth and falsehood, whatever the circumstances. He
had seen where the demand for this latter sort of precision led. He had
perceived, more deeply and acutely than any other thinker on record,
how impossible it was to satisfy that demand—and also how pointless.
No purpose of actual discourse, on any occasion, requires that utterances
cut reality with a precision greater than that of any laser. This realization,
born of Wittgenstein's long struggles, is reflected in *Investigations* §70:

> When I give the description: "The ground was quite covered with
> plants"—do you want to say I don't know what I am talking
> about until I can give a definition of a plant? My meaning would
> be explained by, say, a drawing and the words "The ground
> looked roughly like this." Perhaps I even say "it looked *exactly*
> like this."—Then were just *this* grass and *these* leaves there,
> arranged just like this? No, that is not what it means. And I
> should not accept any picture as exact in *this* sense.

Tractarian exactness is a chimera.
    Calling into question the need for greater exactness than the words of
any language can impart, Wittgenstein thereby cast doubt on the need for
thinking out the words' sense on one's own. For example, "Does someone who says that the broom is in the corner really mean: the broomstick
is there, and so is the brush, and the broomstick is fixed in the brush?—
If we were to ask anyone if he meant this he would probably say that he
had not thought specially of the broomstick or specially of the brush at
all."[26] But suppose he did think of the broomstick and the brush as he uttered the words: would that mental performance affect the words' sense?
If, in his private imagination, he put the broomstick in wrong or pictured
too many bristles, what difference would that make? Would the utterance
be false, or would anyone understand it differently? Wittgenstein's *Blue
Book* anticipates the *Investigations*' reply:

The sign (the sentence) gets its significance from the system of signs, from the language to which it belongs. Roughly: understanding a sentence means understanding a language. As a part of the system of language, one may say, the sentence has life. But one is tempted to imagine that which gives the sentence life as something in an occult sphere, accompanying the sentence.[27]

By the time Wittgenstein wrote these words, his linguistic turn was complete, affecting, as we shall see, not only what he said about language but how he used language. With the *Tractatus*'s "occult sphere" no longer competing for primacy, the "system of signs" acquired new authority.

6

Carnap's Limited Linguistic Turn

IT IS QUESTIONABLE whether the early Wittgenstein, who stressed the need to "think out" the sense of our statements, should be included in Dummett's list of those for whom "an account of language does not presuppose an account of thought." The inclusion of Rudolf Carnap occasions no similar doubts, for he abandoned the *Tractatus*'s logical atoms and the need to identify them in thought. Thus, in comparison with the early Wittgenstein, Carnap took a decisive linguistic turn. However, in comparison with the later Wittgenstein, he did not: for Carnap, language acquired more authority than in the *Tractatus* but less than in the *Investigations*. The same might be said, more generally and for similar reasons, of the Vienna Circle of which Carnap was the foremost member. However, I shall focus just on Carnap—on his linguistic turn, then on its limits.

The Turn

Wittgenstein strongly influenced the thinking of the Circle, which worked through much of the *Tractatus* sentence by sentence and several of whose members, including Carnap, had personal contact with the author. "For me personally," recounts Carnap, "Wittgenstein was perhaps the philosopher who, besides Russell and Frege, had the greatest influence on my thinking."[1] The influence shows, for example, in Carnap's early (1932) taxonomy of propositions:

> (Meaningful) statements are divided into the following kinds. First there are statements which are true solely by virtue of their form ("tautologies" according to Wittgenstein; they correspond approximately to Kant's "analytic judgments"). They say nothing about reality. The formulae of logic and mathematics are of this kind. They are not themselves factual statements, but serve

43

for the transformation of such statements. Secondly there are the negations of such statements ("*contradictions*"). They are self-contradictory, hence false by virtue of their form. With respect to all other statements the decision about truth or falsehood lies in the protocol sentences.[2]

These last, like Wittgenstein's "elementary propositions," were basic and determined the truth-conditions of more complex statements. However, unlike the *Tractatus*'s elementary propositions, Carnap's protocol sentences were clearly empirical, referring either to sense phenomena such as Russell's color patches (Carnap's first preference) or to physical objects such as sticks and stones (his later preference). For Carnap, and the Circle generally, eschewed the metaphysics of the *Tractatus*, with its never-spoken names for never-identified logical atoms. All meaningful statements of fact, declared Carnap, are "*empirical statements* and belong to the domain of empirical science."[3] Within this realm, "The analysis of the concepts of science has shown that all these concepts, no matter whether they belong, according to the usual classification, to the natural sciences, or to psychology or the social sciences, go back to a common basis. They can be reduced to root concepts which apply to the 'given,' to the content of immediate experience."[4]

As Wittgenstein had recognized, the "root concepts" of our language are imprecise, and so too are any concepts based on them. To achieve greater definiteness, Carnap suggested recourse, not to private, pinpoint thinking-out of utterances' sense, as in the *Tractatus*, but to public "explication." "By an explication," he wrote, "I understand the replacement of a pre-scientific inexact concept (which I call 'explicandum') by an exact concept ('explicatum'), which frequently belongs to the scientific language."[5] Here, "The only essential requirement is that the explicatum be more precise than the explicandum."[6] Accordingly, "the interpretation which we shall adopt . . . deviates deliberately from the meaning of descriptions in the ordinary language. Generally speaking, it is not required that an explicatum have, as nearly as possible, the same meaning as the explicandum."[7] Rather, it suffices that the explicatum satisfy the following four requirements, "to a sufficient degree":

1. The explicatum is to be *similar to the explicandum* in such a way that, in most cases in which the explicandum has so far been used, the explicatum can be used; however, close similarity is not required, and considerable differences are permitted.
2. The characterization of the explicatum, that is, the rules of its use (for instance, in the form of a definition), is to be given in an *exact* form, so as to introduce the explicatum into a well-connected system of scientific concepts.

3. The explicatum is to be a *fruitful* concept, that is, useful for the formulation of many universal statements (empirical laws in the case of a nonlogical concept, logical theorems in the case of a logical concept).

4. The explicatum should be as *simple* as possible; this means as simple as the more important requirements (1), (2), and (3) permit.[8]

"If there is one concept that might be said to provide a key to Carnap's philosophy," observes Peter Achinstein, "it is *explication*, a concept that has had considerable influence on many philosophers."[9] Certainly, with regard to the Issue of Language's Authority, it marks an important development. With public explication replacing private thinking-out, the *Tractatus*'s linguistic dead end ceases. If it's a whale and the word "fish" still has its prescientific meaning, call it a fish; if the word has been explicated to exclude marine mammals, don't call it a fish.[10] Language, whether explicated or unexplicated, will codetermine, along with any reality, what to say about that reality. Or so it would seem in theory. For Carnap stressed the *"relativity of all philosophical theses in regard to language* [his italics], that is, the need of reference to one or several particular language systems."[11] However, despite the need thus implied to heed the authority of language, in Carnap's practice it didn't always work out that way.

Limits

Wittgenstein was largely responsible for Carnap's most notorious disregard of language's authority. According to the *Tractatus*, supposedly factual utterances that do not picture reality in the way prescribed are *unsinnig*, nonsensical. Having abandoned the *Tractatus*'s metaphysics and replaced its logical atoms with empirical data, Carnap and the rest of the Circle concluded that, aside from logical and mathematical propositions, statements that are not empirically verifiable are meaningless. This "principle of verification" or "verifiability principle" became the group's most distinctive doctrine. It was their way of distinguishing decisively between the nebulous deliverances of a Hegel, Heidegger, or Bergson, on the one hand, and the relative clarity of scientific discourse, on the other.

One can sense why such a restrictive principle raised a storm of protest, especially in its earlier formulations. After the passage already quoted, dividing statements between tautological, contradictory, and empirical, Carnap trenchantly concluded: "Any statement one desires to construct which does not fall within these categories becomes automatically meaningless."[12] The metaphysician, whose utterances are not empirically verifiable, "has not asserted anything, but only expressed something, like an artist."[13] For in such statements, Carnap explained,

Concepts are introduced which are irreducible either to the given
or to the physical. They are therefore mere illusory concepts
which are to be rejected from the epistemological viewpoint as
well as from the scientific viewpoint. No matter how much they
are sanctified by tradition and charged with feeling, they are
meaningless words.[14]

"No information has been communicated to us," Carnap insisted, "but
mere verbal sounds devoid of meaning though possibly associated with
images."[15] The same holds for "all philosophy of value and normative
theory"; in this domain, too, all "the alleged statements" are *"entirely
meaningless."*[16] Thus, Carnap expressed agreement with David Hume
that (in Carnap's terms) "only the propositions of mathematics and empirical science have sense, and that all other propositions are without
sense."[17] They are mere "pseudo-statements."[18]

It is evident, I think, that in these early texts Carnap's restrictive use of
such terms as "meaning," "sense," "statement," and "assert" lacks linguistic backing, whether from usage or from any personal "explication"
or stipulation of a narrower meaning. Under "water," the dictionary spec-
ifies the chemical composition, H_2O. Under "sentence," "statement,"
"meaning," "sense," "assert," and the like, it cites nothing comparably
precise; it does not specify the logical composition, as it were, required for
meaning, sense, assertion, and the rest. And it is right not to do so. The
typical speaker would, for example, receive with puzzlement the claim
that metaphysicians and ethicians "say nothing," or "make no assertion."
Following his own instructions for "explication," Carnap might have introduced more exact concepts in place of the imprecise familiar ones,[19] but
that would have served no purpose. His impressive-sounding claims
would have been revealed as mere tautologies: nonempirical statements
are not empirical, statements that cannot be empirically verified cannot be
empirically verified. So advised, metaphysicians and ethicians might cheer-
fully agree and carry on as before.

Here, then, is a puzzle. Despite his linguistic turn, despite his attention to language, in practice Carnap accorded very limited authority to
language. Why? With old rivals and obstacles eliminated, what new ones
can perhaps be discerned in his thought, competing with language for
hegemony? I suggest that ideology or worldview played a role, and so did
scientific, theoretical ambitions.

First, worldview. A close friend of Wittgenstein thus contrasted young
Wittgenstein's *Weltanschauung* with that of Carnap and the Circle:

A whole generation of disciples was able to take Wittgenstein for
a positivist because he has something of enormous importance in

common with the positivists: he draws the line between what we can speak about and what we must be silent about just as they do. The difference is only that they have nothing to be silent about. Positivism holds—and this is its essence—that what we can speak about is all that matters in life. *Whereas Wittgenstein passionately believes that all that really matters in human life is precisely what, in his view, we must be silent about.*[20]

Wittgenstein drew the line for one reason, Carnap drew it for a very different reason, and the fuzziness of everyday terms stood in the way of any sharp, definitive delineation. Wittgenstein, however, wanted to "hit the nail on the head,"[21] as did Carnap. So they appropriated definitive-sounding expressions—"senseless," "meaningless," and the like—for their purposes.

A less apodictic approach would have noted the indefiniteness of such semantic expressions and the great variety of doctrines and utterances falling under an umbrella term such as "metaphysics." That is, it would have attended more to details. "What makes it difficult for us to take this line of investigation," the post-*Tractatus* Wittgenstein surmised, "is our craving for generality."[22] Among the main sources of this craving, he cited, appositely, "our preoccupation with the method of science."[23] By this, he explained,

I mean the method of reducing the explanation of natural phenomena to the smallest possible number of primitive natural laws; and, in mathematics, of unifying the treatment of different topics by using a generalization. Philosophers constantly see the method of science before their eyes, and are irresistibly tempted to ask and answer questions in the way science does. This tendency is the real source of metaphysics, and leads the philosopher into complete darkness.[24]

The Vienna Circle, with its strong scientific and mathematical bent,[25] notably exemplified the thrust toward reductive generalization. Carnap voiced the common viewpoint and spirit of the Circle when he asserted, as we have seen, that all concepts, in whatever field, "go back to a common basis. They can be reduced to root concepts which apply to the 'given,' to the content of immediate experience."[26] The verifiability principle traces negatively the same border that this account traces positively. All concepts and statements that are not thus reducible are meaningless. Such a principle, lacking linguistic backing, may qualify as the sort of "metaphysics" Wittgenstein had in mind. Certainly it led to complete darkness. Endlessly refined and revised, the verifiability principle led nowhere, for the familiar expressions employed in its formulation could not bear the theoretical weight imposed on them. They could not serve to mark off, once for all, the distinction between sense and nonsense in such a way that science lay on one side of the divide and nonscientific discourse lay on the other. But so long as the dream persisted, it fostered the sort of linguistic disregard evident in Carnap's formulations. Looking back in the 1960s, Carnap reflected:

> Unfortunately, following Wittgenstein, we formulated our view in the Vienna Circle in the oversimplified version of saying that certain metaphysical theses are "meaningless." This formulation caused much unnecessary opposition, even among some of those philosophers who basically agreed with us. Only later did we see that it is important to distinguish the various meaning components, and therefore said in a more precise way that such theses lack cognitive or theoretical meaning. They often have other meaning components, e.g., emotive or normative ones.[27]

Here, Carnap's claim has become more circumspect. It concerns only "certain metaphysical theses," not "all metaphysics,"[28] "metaphysics in its entirety,"[29] or "all philosophy in the old sense,"[30] as previously. And the modifiers "cognitive" and "theoretical" add some precision. However, not enough. In what special sense of the term did Hegel, say, advance no "theories"? And what special relation to knowledge or cognition does the term "cognitive," unaided by any Carnapian explication, here signal?[31]

Carnap's personal use of the terms "know" and "knowledge" is revealing. He remarks, for example: "It is true that a person will, as a rule, attribute the predicate 'hard' to a thing *b* only if he knows it to be hard, hence only if he is prepared to attribute to it also the predicate 'known to be hard.'"[32] Similarly, "A person will, in general, attribute the predicate 'true' to a given sentence (or proposition) only if he knows it to be true, hence only if he is prepared to attribute to it also the predicate 'known to be true' or 'established as true' or 'verified.'"[33] These claims, citing what a person "knows" and taking no account of even the firmest, most rational belief that falls short of knowledge, would be striking were they not so typical of Carnap's obiter dicta about everyday discourse. These particular assertions may be made more understandable by Carnap's allusion elsewhere to "*imperfect knowledge*, that is, knowledge which has only a certain degree of certainty, not absolute certainty, and which therefore may possibly be refuted or weakened by future experience."[34] For Carnap, "knowledge" may be false! This expansive conception of "knowledge" further illustrates Carnap's slight attention to usage and usage's consequent weakness in competition with rival ideological or theoretical pressures. Though accorded some authority in theory, existing word uses may exert little restraint if a theorist, intent on matters of greater moment, is not in the habit of seriously considering those uses.

"Sense," "nonsense," "meaningless," "assert," "statement," "knowledge"—term after term suggests Carnap's limited awareness of everyday expressions and their everyday employment (not only in English but also in German). However, these are piecemeal indications of his inattentiveness. Of more general interest is Carnap's account of truth, with all it implies for linguistic normativity. In "Truth and Confirmation" and "Remarks on Induction and Truth," he proposes these two sentences (with others) for consideration:

1. "The substance in this vessel is alcohol."
2. "The sentence 'the substance in this vessel is alcohol' is true."[35]

On these Carnap comments: *the sentences (1) and (2) are logically equivalent;* in other words, they entail each other; they are merely different formulations for the same factual content; nobody may accept the one and reject the other; if used as communications, both sentences convey the same information though in different form."[36] Accordingly, "the question regarding the criterion of truth can be given only a trivial answer, which consists in the statement itself."[37] Language, with its words and sentences, apparently mentioned by sentence (2), vanishes from view in sentence (1), with the result that Carnap here ends up like Plato, viewing reality through words and seeing only the reality.

The content of sentence (2) that disappears in sentence (1) reappears if we note the reason why "nobody may accept the one and reject the other": anyone who accepts (1) accepts the nonverbal fact that the substance in the vessel is alcohol and the verbal fact that such are the words to state that fact. In an utterance, there is no separating the packaging and the content; whoever accepts the words accepts what they state, and vice versa. Yet the two sentences are not "logically equivalent," if by that is meant that they "say the same thing." Sentence (1) says nothing about words but just uses them. Sentence (2) uses other words ("sentence," "true") to talk about those words but says nothing about the new words it employs. Speaking of the words, it thereby surfaces the issue that Carnap's argument buries: why are these the right words to use? what makes sentence (1) "true"? To judge from his account, Carnap would answer: "The substance in the vessel." But that is only half an answer. The substance by itself authorizes no use of words. What does? Where does linguistic authority reside? As Carnap's own practice testifies, the response to this question is no "trivial answer."

His reductive argument, equating sentence (2) to sentence (1), helps explain, indeed appears to legitimize, his practice. When, for instance, he

declares nonempirical statements "meaningless," he pays no more attention to the question of language's authority than he does in the argument.
And the argument suggests that he does well to ignore the words he uses,
or any separate issue of truth. He need only consider whether nonempirical statements are meaningful, not how anyone uses the word "meaningful" or "meaningless." This link between Carnap's theory and his
practice appears with special clarity in a passage worth quoting in full:

> Ordinarily no definite rules are expressly stipulated as to how a
> statement may or must be formulated when certain observations
> have been made. Children learn the use of common language,
> and thereby the correct performance of the operation described,
> through practice, imitation, and usually without the benefit of
> rules. These rules, however, could be specified. But if no foreign
> language or the introduction of new terms is involved, the rules
> are trivial. For example: "If one is hungry, the statement 'I am
> hungry' may be accepted"; or: "If one sees a key one may accept
> the statement 'there lies a key.'"[38]

"In this context," notes Carnap, "the definition of the concept of truth
enters into the question of confirmation; the rules we mentioned originate
from this definition." They do, indeed; this is all the guidance his reductive definition of truth has to offer. If you want to know whether you
should say, "I am hungry," just see whether you are hungry. If you want
to know whether you should say, "Empirical statements are meaningless," just see whether the statements are meaningless. The words will
take care of themselves. After all, you know your mother tongue. "No
foreign language or the introduction of new terms is involved."

Carnap's verbal sample, sentence (1), epitomizes the focus of his
thought, on science and its logic, not on everyday expressions such as he
employed. And this focus typifies much contemporary thinking. Platonic
Forms had their day, as did Aristotelian, Thomistic concepts; and young
Wittgenstein's atomic thinking-out never enjoyed equal vogue. In contemporary philosophizing, another competitor for linguistic authority, represented here by Carnap's thinking (especially in its early stages[39]), may be
language's chief rival. Mere attention to the things to be reported or described—the hunger, the key, the stuff in the vessel—poses no challenge to
language's authority as determinant of truth, but theoretical aspirations
do. Without proposing or justifying explicit explications of key terms,
philosophers, undeterred by current usage, often proceed as though they
had provided such alternative verbal backing for their statements. The verifiability principle is just one instance of a widespread syndrome.

As was noted earlier, inattention to word uses is natural enough. To function efficiently, language must become second nature; and it does. Words become like spectacles that we look through but seldom at. Thus Carnap writes, for example:

> We shall speak of "directly testable statement" when circumstances are conceivable in which we confidently consider the statement so strongly confirmed or else disconfirmed on the basis of one or very few observations that we would either accept or reject it outright. Examples: "There is a key on my desk." Conditions for the test: I stand near my desk, sufficient illumination is provided, etc. Condition of acceptance: I see a key on my desk; condition of rejection: I don't see a key there.[40]

As it stands, this account is no more satisfactory than Plato's in the *Phaedo*. Carnap views the nonlinguistic reality—the key on the desk—and knows straight off what to *say*. His position near the desk, the lighting, what he sees—these suffice to validate the *statement*. For, like Plato, he has learned his mother tongue, and that appears unproblematic. Everyone knows the word for seeing, keys, or desks, as everyone knows the word for Goodness, Beauty, or Equality. And yet, for linguistic reasons, Russell, for example, denied that anyone ever sees a key (cf. chapter 11). And the only way to deal with such a claim, and countless similar ones, would be to engage the question Carnap here passes over in silence. He would have to consider the *linguistic* conditions of acceptance for "I see a key," "There is a key on my desk," or any other assertion, and not just nonlinguistic conditions, such as those he cites.

To the common, natural explanation of linguistic inattention, theorists often add another: What note they do take of existing language suggests what an imperfect instrument it is, so one whose guidance they cannot safely accept. Not only, it seems, is familiar word usage regrettably imprecise for scientific, theoretical purposes, but, worse still, it is incoherent and leads to contradictions. Alfred Tarski's account of truth, to which we shall now turn, has been widely viewed as a paradigmatic demonstration of this deficiency.

7

Tarski, Truth, and Claims of Linguistic Incoherence

"As is well known," wrote Carnap in the 1930s, "the concept of truth, when used without restrictions (as in conversational language), leads to contradictions (the so-called antinomies)."[1] Alfred Tarski, however, "succeeded in establishing an unobjectionable definition of truth which explicates adequately the meaning of this word in common language (but of course is also bound to restrict its employment, as compared with common usage, in order to eliminate the contradictions)." Carnap does not here assert that there is anything wrong with "common language" for its customary purposes, for instance in philosophy. He does not say that its concepts, unamended, lead to contradictions in actual discourse. He does not say that there is any reason to mistrust "conversational language" or to reject its guidance. However, what he does not explicitly assert, his words could easily suggest. And indeed such a critical viewpoint has been widespread. "Conversational language," many suppose, leads to contradictions not only in this instance, but in others; it is "inconsistent," "contradictory," "logically unreliable." Accordingly, for such thinkers, Tarski's remedy represents a salutary turn away from "common usage" to formalized, disinfected forms of expression. "If the rules of ordinary language are confused and ridden with cancerous inconsistency," they would agree, "then the rules must be reformed rather than followed more scrupulously."[2]

Positive as well as negative reasons motivated this turn toward new, improved linguistic systems. Speaking of the split in analytic philosophy between those who favor natural languages and those who favor constructed ones, Carnap commented: "It seems to me that one explanation of this divergence is the fact that in the Vienna Circle mathematics and empirical science were taken as models representing knowledge in its best, most systematized form, toward which all philosophical work on problems of knowledge should be oriented."[3] Tarski's explication of truth appeared an important step in this desired direction. On the other side of the naturalist-constructionist divide, Peter Strawson noted that "if the clear mode of functioning of the constructed concepts is to cast light on problems and difficulties rooted in the unclear mode of functioning of the unconstructed concepts, then precisely the ways in which the constructed concepts are connected with and depart from the unconstructed concepts must be plainly shown. And how can *this* result be achieved without accurately describing the modes of functioning of the unconstructed concepts?"[4] How, for instance, can the merits or demerits of Tarski's explication be judged without an accurate understanding of how the term "true" functions at present, and why?

Rather than enter the debate between naturalists and constructionists, we can simply note its implications for the Issue of Language's Authority. Since the ideal linguistic forms envisioned by Tarski, Carnap, and others are seldom employed in actual discourse, they do not directly compete with more familiar forms of speech. Even were they to do so, they would pose no challenge to the authority of language as such, but at most to these alternative, customary forms of speech. If, however, the ideal forms remain merely ideal, as they typically do, and the authority of the familiar, allegedly incoherent forms of everyday speech is ignored or rejected, as it often is, a linguistic vacuum results. Therewith, language in general is indeed profoundly challenged as a determinant of truth or assertability. Other forces, for instance those noted in the last chapter, move into the vacuum. Bound neither by the ideal languages they do not speak nor by the actual languages they do speak but do not trust or respect, theorists do not feel constrained by the authority of language. Such are the issues—in particular the alleged incoherence of everyday language—on which consideration of Tarski and his treatment of truth will allow us to focus.

Truth

"We begin," writes Tarski in "The Semantic Conception of Truth," "with some remarks regarding the extension of the concept of truth which we have in mind here. The predicate '*true*' is sometimes used to refer to psychological phenomena such as judgments or beliefs, sometimes to certain physical objects, namely, linguistic expressions and specifically sentences, and sometimes to certain ideal entities called 'propositions.'"[5] Significantly absent from Tarski's list is the application of "true" to statements, in the sense of speech acts employing the linguistic expressions he mentions. Remarking merely that the meaning of the term "proposition" is notoriously the subject of lengthy disputations and seems never to have been made quite clear and unambiguous, Tarski concludes, momentously:

"For several reasons it appears most convenient to *apply the term 'true' to sentences* [Tarski's emphasis], and we shall follow this course."[6] This focus on sentences rather than on statements crucially affects Tarski's assessment of ordinary language and its "anomalies" or "paradoxes," as also his proposed remedies.

The "liar paradox," Tarski's favorite specimen, takes its name from the Cretan's utterance, "All Cretans are liars," which generates no paradox (since liars need not always lie), but which can readily be given a more troublesome form—for example, "I am telling a falsehood." In Tarski's versions we are asked to contemplate not an utterance or statement, but a sentence, for instance this one: "The sentence printed in this paper on p. 58, *l.* 19, is not true." Since this sentence is printed on that line and page in his text, it appears that if it is true, then it is not true, and if it is not true, then it is true. "We have arrived," concludes Tarski, "at an obvious contradiction."[7] It is not evident, however, that such a verdict follows. This and other modern variants of the liar paradox center on a sentence (e.g., "This sentence is false") rather than an utterance; and paradox results from the initial assumption that the sentence "says" something (e.g., "says of itself that it is false"). With the help of further premises, this assumption then leads to the conclusion that "the liar sentence is true and false."[8] Whereas some solutions challenge later premises in such a derivation, I would draw attention to the first. For a mere sentence, though it may be used by a speaker or writer on some occasion to say something, and may then be either true or false, of and by itself makes no assertion and is neither true nor false.

What, then, of the utterance (not the mere sentence), "I am telling a falsehood"? Has the speaker made a statement, and is that statement true if false and false if true? Dummett's observation is pertinent here: "Independently of his personal motives, a speaker makes an assertion by uttering an assertoric sentence in the appropriate circumstances and manner; his asserting a sentence is to be taken as expressing his recognition of it as true. Hence we may simply equate a speaker's recognition of a sentence as true with his willingness to assert it."[9] Now, who is ready to *assert*, and not merely utter, any such sentence as "I am telling a falsehood"? Not any real-life Cretan. Not Tarski and others who have discussed variants of the liar's paradox. They were just formulating puzzles. Hence, one way out of the puzzles is to reserve truth and falsehood for genuine assertions and exclude such idle utterances.[10]

Suppose, though, that the speaker has indeed succeeded in making a self-contradictory statement. Then his achievement does not differ, in this respect, from the utterance, "I have drawn a square circle." Thus juxtaposed within the same utterance, "square" contradicts "circle" and "circle" contradicts "square." Such a possibility does not discredit any language or its authority. The linguistic medium should not be blamed for the vagaries that can be perpetrated in it, nor should it be imagined that any usable language might be immune to misuse. Languages, like hammers, are instruments, and doubtless no hammer will ever be devised that can effectively be used to drive nails and that cannot be misused—to hit a thumb, punch a hole in a wall, or crack a skull.

Focusing, as we have seen, on mere sentences rather than on their employment to make assertions, Tarski reached a more negative assessment. With respect to "colloquial language," he asserted that "not only does the definition of truth seem to be impossible, but even the consistent use of this concept in conformity with the laws of logic."[11] In his view, the semantic antinomies "prove emphatically that the concept of truth (as well as other semantical concepts) when applied to colloquial language in conjunction with the normal laws of logic leads inevitably to confusions and contradictions."[12] Tarski therefore undertook to refine both the concept "true" and the language to which it applies, in a manner that excluded semantic paradoxes such as that of the liar.

With regard to the concept "true," Tarski explained, "We should like our definition to do justice to the intuitions which adhere to the *classical Aristotelian conception of truth*—intuitions which find their expression in the well-known words of Aristotle's *Metaphysics: To say of what is that it is not, or of what is not that it is, is false, while to say of what is that it is, or of what is not that it is not, is true.*"[13] Here Aristotle speaks of statements—of "saying that." Yet, in formulating Aristotle's point, Tarski proceeds to speak only of sentences; for example: "We regard the truth of a sentence as its 'correspondence with reality.' This rather vague phrase, which can certainly lead to various misunderstandings and has often done so in the past, is interpreted as follows. We shall regard as valid all such statements as: *the sentence 'it is snowing' is true if and only if it is snowing; the sentence 'the world war will begin in the year 1963' is true if and only if the world war will begin in 1963.*"[14] Why such statements should be regarded as "valid" is not immediately evident. The truth of the *utterance* "It is snowing" may bear no relation to the state of the weather, and the truth of the *words* "It is snowing," abstracted from any utterance (as in Tarski's account), remains indeterminate. "What did he then say?" someone asks. "It is snowing," another person may reply, truly, though no snow is falling.[15] "What is your favorite color?" one person inquires. "It is snowing," another person replies—neither truly nor falsely, since, as a reply, his words make no sense. Again, identical words may have different senses, hence different truth-conditions, from setting to setting. "For instance," suggests Hartry Field, "different tokens of 'John takes grass' can differ in 'sense'—e.g., one token may be uttered in saying that John Smith smokes marijuana, and another may be uttered in saying that John Jones steals lawn material, and these differences may give rise to differences of truth value in the tokens."[16] Thus the mere sentence "John takes grass" furnishes no clue as to how to complete Tarski's biconditional ("if and only if") formula, unambiguously. It is evident, then, why Tarski restricts his account to "formalized languages," in which "the sense of every expression is unambiguously determined by its form"[17]—that is, to languages very different from any we customarily speak. Aristotle's correspondence formula, though not very enlightening, at least applies to the things people say in the languages they employ. Tarski's, deliberately, does not.

Tarski's formal definition of truth reveals as little interest in the actual workings or functioning of language as does his biconditional formula. We must distinguish, he first suggests, between object-language, containing such sentences as "Snow is white," and metalanguage, containing such sentences as "The sentence 'snow is white' is true," and meta-metalanguage, containing sentences about second-level sentences, and so forth. In such a hierarchy, an antinomy such as that of the liar is not possible, for no sentence can refer to itself and call itself true or false. The truth of sentences all the way up the ladder can be determined by that of sentences at the bottom, and bottom-level truth can be determined in terms of "satisfaction." If, for instance, snow is white, then it satisfies the function "x is white."[18] Were we to inquire about this "simplest and clearest case" (as Tarski terms it[19]) and ask, "But *is* snow white? Does it satisfy that function?" Tarski might reply, "Well, just use your eyes; look at the snow and observe its color. Where is your problem?" The problem is the one we have noted from the start. Neither Beauty nor snow nor any other nonlinguistic reality determines, by itself, the truth or falsehood of any statement made about it. What else is needed? What, besides the snow and its color, makes "Snow is white?" (or "Der Schnee ist weiss," "La neige est blanche," etc.) the right thing to say? On this question, Tarski has nothing to offer. His formal account leaves off at the point where it would have to begin in order to clarify the issue of truth or assertability in a natural language. As Tarski himself recognized,[20] proponents of the most diverse accounts of truth—pragmatists, correspondence theorists, coherence theorists, no-truth theorists, and others—might all agree that snow is white, that snow satisfies the function "x is white," and that the statement "Snow is white" is true, but they would give very different accounts of what such truth or satisfaction consists in.[21] And their differing accounts might result in differing verdicts in other instances, if not with regard to the whiteness of snow.

Thus Tarski's positive account—his definition of truth and his biconditional scheme—leaves the Issue of Language's Authority wide open. However, his critical account of the everyday concept "true" and of the languages we (Tarski included) actually employ tends to undercut the linguistic contenders for authority. What authority can existing languages claim if they are ridden with incoherence?

Linguistic Coherence

Focusing, with Tarski, on the liar paradox, I have questioned his verdict of incoherence. Sentences may be true or false or neither, depending on their use. The liar's sentence and others like it, which are not used to make assertions, appear good candidates for the verdict "neither." If they still look objectionable, that is the fault of the speakers, not of the language they speak. Any language can be misused, as can any instrument, however well suited to its intended purposes. From this instance, therefore, I suggest that we may learn a certain skepticism concerning claims of natural languages' incoherence.[22]

True, I have considered only the favorite example of the thinker best known for this type of critique and most responsible, perhaps, for its widespread acceptance, and claims of language's incoherence take widely varied forms.[23] However, the words of the later Wittgenstein seem broadly relevant. "In language," he remarked, "we often *compare* the use of words with games and calculi which have fixed rules, but cannot say that someone who is using language *must* be playing such a game."[24] Wittgenstein did not believe that, in fact, "if anyone utters a sentence and *means* or *understands* it he is operating a calculus according to definite rules."[25] In response, therefore, to allegations of incoherence in natural languages, he might have responded in words I find apt: "If I had to say what is the main mistake made by philosophers of the present generation, including Moore, I would say that it is that when language is looked at, what is looked at is a form of words and not the use made of the form of words."[26]

Suppose that we do attend to the actual use made of words: how might our languages, as they actually function, be incoherent? Individual speakers may say incoherent things. (I recall the lady who, when asked about her television viewing, replied, "Oh, I turn it off more than I turn it on.") Perhaps (though no illustrations come to mind) the whole population might say equally incoherent things. But that would imply no incoherence in the language spoken. Perfectly good words would have been put to a bad use. The question, then, is this: how might languages—how might their concepts or word meanings—harbor contradictions? They might do so, I suggest, only if standard usage employed the terms both to assert and negate the same thing. But it is not readily conceivable that standard usage—that is, the practice of a whole linguistic community— might do such a thing. Consider the case of fetal status. Many people assert the humanity of the fetus, many people deny it, and many people do neither. It is this lack of agreement that accounts for the absence of any precise dictionary entry for "human being" (comparable, say, to that for "zinc") and that deprives both the assertion and the denial of verbal backing. The only situation that might convict the concept "human being" of incoherence would be its application and refusal, with respect to the same referents (e.g., fetuses), not merely by many speakers on one side and many on the other, but by practically the whole English-speaking population. It would have to be customary practice both to affirm that fetuses are human beings and to deny that they are human beings. Not surprisingly, no such usage can be found, either for this term or for any other I know of. What would be the point? What utility would such a term retain, or a language composed of such "concepts"?

Those who, like Tarski, urge the incoherence of everyday concepts do not allege that the speakers of any language do collectively both assert and deny the same thing. They do not contend, for example, that the English-speaking population asserts both the truth and the falsehood of utterances like the liar's (or tightened versions thereof). Thus, their arguments do not appeal to usage and its evident contradictions, but to those revealed by "logic." It is not possible, says Tarski, to make consistent use of the natural concept "true" in conformity with the laws of logic. But it is. It is just as possible as making consistent use of the words "square" and "circle" in conformity with the laws of logic. In the first case, we can refrain from saying, "What I am saying is not true." In the other, we can refrain from saying, "I drew a square circle." And such avoidance is neither arbitrary nor inconsistent, but is perfectly in accordance with the laws of language—that is, of living language, functioning communicatively, not formalized language.

These general remarks are no substitute for a detailed examination of varied semantic paradoxes, to see how well the remarks apply to them. However, this is not the place for such a thorough review. In conclusion, then, I shall just note the multiple significance of the present discussion. It concerns the need or desirability of languages that, as Wittgenstein put it, are "better, more perfect, than our everyday language."[27] It concerns, still more significantly for the present study, the reliability of existing languages as arbiters of truth or assertability. If such languages are "ridden with cancerous inconsistency," that is a more serious challenge to their authority than, for instance, their alleged imprecision. If, furthermore, accusations such as Tarski's are too readily accepted, they may beget the kind of closed circle discernible, perhaps, in Tarski's thinking. Those who view the languages they speak as incoherent, so accord them slight authority, may see no reason to examine their workings very carefully; not examining their workings very attentively, they may see no reason to question or reassess their original judgment of incoherence.

8

Wittgenstein's Acceptance of the Authority of Language

NO WONDER MANY philosophers accord little authority to the natural languages they speak. Such languages, they hold, are vague (chapter 5), incoherent (chapter 7), and error-filled (chapter 11). Of these alleged defects, the vagueness of everyday expressions concerned young Wittgenstein, but not greatly; though he exaggerated the need for exactness, he believed the need was met by the way we think out the sense of our words. However, both early and late he was seriously concerned about a further problem, the power of existing idioms to confuse and deceive us through their misleading surface features. "In everyday language," he wrote in the *Tractatus*, "it very frequently happens that the same word has different modes of signification, and so belongs to different symbols—or two words that have different modes of signification are employed in propositions in what is superficially the same way."[1] For example, the single word "is" has three distinct modes of signification—as the copula (e.g., in "The day is sunny"), as a sign for identity (e.g., in "The president is Bush"), and as an expression for existence (e.g., in "Troy is no more"). "In this way," Wittgenstein observed, "the most fundamental confusions are easily produced (the whole of philosophy is full of them)."[2] In order to avoid such errors, he envisaged employing "a sign-language that excludes them by not using the same sign for different symbols and by not using in a superficially similar way signs that have different modes of signification."[3]

Misleading surface analogies still preoccupied the later Wittgenstein, but at a deeper level. He saw the *Tractatus* itself as their victim, and he proposed a very different remedy. The story of this shift has multiple interest. It explains why and in what sense—what strong sense—Wittgenstein became a linguistic philosopher. It explains the authority he came to confer on language rather than on rivals such as those in the *Tractatus*.

And it thereby explains the challenge that his later thought still poses to less linguistic approaches in philosophy. I shall start with a brief account of the shift, then note its significance.

An Irremediable "Defect"

The elementary propositions envisioned by the *Tractatus* would have nicely satisfied the demand for unambiguous expression. Not only would each name stand unmistakably for a single atomic object, but the names would not have "different modes of signification." Names would always stand for objects, never, for instance, for relations: the names' relations would represent the objects' relations. Disanalogies would still remain; the propositions would not perfectly mirror reality (for example, the written or spoken names would not resemble their logically simple referents). But this did not trouble young Wittgenstein. His attitude, it seems, was that suggested by the comparison implicit in talk about "mirroring." Animals are often fooled by mirrors, and humans may not notice how mirrors reverse the figures they reflect. No one, however, concludes that mirrors, as presently constructed, should be replaced by ideal mirrors that lack these defects. The possibility of such deception comes with the nature of mirrors; they could not fulfill their function in any other way. If, however, distortions result from imperfections in the glass, then we had better replace the mirror—especially if the defects are numerous and pervasive. Only thus can we hope to get a clear picture of reality. Such was Wittgenstein's early attitude toward existing languages and the logical pictures that, in his view, we construct by their means. Philosophical clarity demanded something better.

In chapter 5, we have already noted one difficulty that Wittgenstein encountered in his search for a reliable, logically perspicuous notation. Even empirical objects as simple as Russell's color patches could not figure in logically independent elementary propositions such as the *Tractatus* supposed, and Wittgenstein could discover no simpler objects to replace them. Shade would conflict with shade, tone with tone, spot with spot. So by 1929 he had given up the search for Tractarian objects, but not his overall project. "If, now," he wrote, "we try to get an actual analysis, we find logical forms which have very little similarity with the forms of ordinary language. We meet with the forms of space and time with the whole manifold of spatial and temporal objects, as colours, sounds, etc., etc., with their gradations, continuous transitions, and combinations in various proportions, all of which we cannot seize by our ordinary means of expression."[4] What we need, he believed, was a "phenomenological" or "primary" language[5]—that is, a language that would represent phenomena as they really are, without distortion, and that would do so without any reliance on, or contamination by, existing languages. With respect both to the phenomenological fidelity of such a language and to its independence, Wittgenstein came to recognize serious problems.

First, the "logical forms" of experienced reality could not dictate the logical forms of his ideally perspicuous language, since reality, as experienced, has no such forms—or rather, has as many as we care to impose on it. The *Investigations*' discussion of simplicity and complexity illustrates the point. Reality—a chair, say, or the visual image of a chair— does not determine what is simple and what is complex; it does not chop itself up for inspection. "But isn't a chessboard, for instance, obviously, and absolutely, composite?" asked Wittgenstein. "You are probably thinking," he replied,

> of the composition out of thirty-two white and thirty-two black squares. But could we not also say, for instance, that it was composed of the colours black and white and the schema of squares? And if there are quite different ways of looking at it, do you still want to say that the chessboard is absolutely "composite"?— Asking "Is this object composite?" *outside* a particular language-game is like what a boy once did, who had to say whether the verbs in certain sentences were in the active or passive voice, and who racked his brains over the question whether the verb "to sleep" meant something active or passive.[6]

Wittgenstein had supposed that there was "something like a final analysis of our forms of language,"[7] and that to this analysis, revealing the single structure of the reality described, a single form of expression might correspond. But this, he now realized, was a delusion.

A second difficulty related to the language's description as "primary," that is, as independent, nonderivative. "When I talk about language (words, sentences, etc.)," Wittgenstein later remarked, "I must speak the language of every day. Is this language somehow too coarse and material for what we want to say? *Then how is another one to be constructed?* . . . In giving explanations I already have to use language full-blown (not some sort of preparatory, provisional one)."[8] Implicit in this comment is the dilemma on which Wittgenstein had found himself impaled when he tried to give direct, pure expression to phenomena. If, on the one hand, he introduced the expressions of his phenomenological language by means of explanations using German, English, or the like, the new symbolism would not be primary, but secondary and derivative. In order to understand it, one would have to understand everyday language, not vice versa. The language to be clarified would be used to clarify. On the other hand, if he tried to introduce the new notation without any such explanations, even to himself, the signs would have no meaning, even to himself. There can be little doubt, therefore, that Wittgenstein had himself, too, in mind when he wrote: "So in the end when one is doing philosophy one gets to the point where one would like just to emit an inarticulate sound.—But such a sound is an expression only as it occurs in a particular language-game, which should now be described."[9]

New Object, New Medium

The demise of Wittgenstein's ideal-language project had a double implication: therapeutic phenomenology could not be "pure" either in its object or in its medium, but would have to be linguistic from the start, as in the *Investigations*. By themselves, nonlinguistic phenomena could not reveal the one true analysis of expressions, and no ideally perspicuous notation could replace existing languages as an instrument of analysis. Using his native German or acquired English, Wittgenstein would have to focus directly on the linguistic confusions that concerned him—starting, now, with his own.

The *Tractatus* warned against words such as "is," which have "different modes of signification." The later Wittgenstein warned against the greater but less evident danger posed by words such as "name," "proposition," and "language" ("*Name*," "*Satz*," "*Sprache*") that figured in the *Tractatus*'s central claims. These claims mount to a climax in 4.5: "It now seems possible to give the most general propositional form: that is, to give a description of the propositions of *any* sign-language *whatsoever* in such a way that every possible sense can be expressed by a symbol satisfying the description, and every symbol satisfying the description can express a sense, provided that the meanings of the names are suitably chosen." Any and every sign-language consists of propositions (*Sätze*), and the propositions all have the general form: "This is how things stand."[10] Such is the essence of language, and such is the essence of propositions.

In Wittgenstein's later judgment, such claims exemplify the "craving for generality" mentioned earlier, which has as one of its chief sources the "tendency to look for something in common to all the entities which we commonly subsume under a general term." Thus, "We are inclined to think that there must be something in common to all games, say, and that this common property is the justification for applying the general term 'game' to the various games; whereas games form a *family* the members of which have family likenesses."[11] The like holds for the term "language": "Instead of producing something common to all that we call language, I am saying that these phenomena have no one thing in common which makes us use the same word for all,—but that they are *related* to one another in many different ways. And it is because of this relationship, or these relationships, that we call them all 'language.'"[12]

Young Wittgenstein had recognized three kinds of utterances, but had forced them into a single mold: "Judgment, command and question all stand on the same level; but all have in common the propositional form, and that alone interests us."[13] One speaker asserts a propositional content (e.g., "The door is closed"), a second orders it (e.g., "Close the door"), a third questions it (e.g., "Is the door closed?"); but these differences he dismissed as merely psychological.[14] Only the propositional content interests the logician, and that has a single form. In the *Investigations*, Wittgenstein counters: "But how many kinds of sentence are there? Say assertion, question, and command?—There are *countless* kinds: countless different kinds of use of what we call 'symbols,' 'words,' 'sentences.' And this multiplicity is not something fixed, given once for all; but new types of language, new language-games, as we may say, come into existence, and others become obsolete and get forgotten."[15]

This critique of his earlier essentialism illustrates and further explains Wittgenstein's shift, not only to natural language (e.g., German) but to familiar, everyday forms of natural language as the object of his philosophical scrutiny. Natural-language utterances such as those in the *Tractatus* were not the cause of philosophical problems but their symptoms. Their source lay elsewhere, in familiar forms of speech. It was not enough, Wittgenstein now realized, to warn against terms like "is" that have "different modes of signification." More deceptive were innocent-looking expressions such as "language" and "proposition" that, though they might not have different modes of signification, did not pick out any common essence, as their surface sameness and their similarities to proper names suggested and as young Wittgenstein (influenced perhaps by Frege[16]) too readily supposed. When Wittgenstein finally looked, attentively, at what a term such as "language" or "game" designates, he found no common essence shared by members of that class and it alone.

Along with the object of his reflection, his medium also shifted. Not only did the later Wittgenstein employ no artificial substitute for ordinary language—no "logical," "phenomenological," "primary" language; but neither did he employ any theoretical substitute. He did not speak the language of the *Tractatus*. That is, he did not employ everyday expressions (German, English, or other) and disregard the meanings they had in the language he was speaking. Names were what people called names, statements were what people called statements, language was what people called language, and so forth. Though perhaps jejune in appearance, this acceptance of language's authority to determine what we say has such significance for Wittgenstein's later thought, for the present inquiry, and for philosophy in general that it calls for fuller documentation, clarification, and explanation.

Language's New Authority

As we have seen, the author of the *Tractatus* had believed that the expressions we utter acquire their precise meanings, not from context, or from the language spoken, but from the way speakers think them out. The same held, no doubt, for the terms he himself employed philosophically—for "*Sprache*," "*Satz*," and the rest. They had the sense he gave them in the *Tractatus*. For him, there would be nothing idiosyncratic about that; it was the way all utterances functioned, how meaning was established, how truth was determined. In this perspective, what point could there be in examining German or English usage? "My *whole* task," Wittgenstein had declared, "consists in explaining the nature of the proposition."[17] German usage could be left to lexicographers.[18]

Reminiscing on his early attitude, Wittgenstein later wrote: "We ask: '*What is* language?', '*What is* a proposition?' And the answer to these questions is to be given once for all; and independently of any future experience."[19] And independently, to be sure, of any variations or eventual shifts in linguistic usage. The essence is "something that lies *beneath* the surface. Something that lies within, which we see when we look *into* the thing, and which an analysis digs out."[20] We have seen where this "analysis" led—to atomic objects of which neither speakers nor hearers have any reflective awareness, picked out by the trillion even for such statements as "Germany invaded Russia" and "The universe is expanding." How extraordinary! As the later Wittgenstein aptly remarked: "our forms of expression prevent us in all sorts of ways from seeing that nothing out of the ordinary is involved, by sending us in pursuit of chimeras."[21] The Tractarian rival for linguistic authority—its "pure intermediary between the propositional signs and the facts"—was indeed chimerical.

"*Essence*," the *Investigations* declares epigrammatically, "is expressed by grammar."[22] Less cryptically, "Grammar [word use] tells what kind of object anything is."[23] Things are what they are, independently of language; but they do not count as "names," "propositions," "languages," or the like independently of language. More fully, §116 advises: "When philosophers use a word—'knowledge,' 'being,' 'object,' 'I,' 'proposition,' 'name'—and try to grasp the *essence* of the thing, one must always ask oneself: is the word ever actually used in this way in the language-game which is its original home?—What *we* do is to bring words back from their metaphysical to their everyday use."[24] The *Investigations* is full of such "bringing back." For example, in §65 we hear Wittgenstein's Tractarian ghost object, "You talk about all sorts of language-games, but have nowhere said what the essence of a language-game, and hence of language, is." In response Wittgenstein now focuses, as he never did in the *Tractatus*, on "what we *call* language"[25] (emphasis added), illustrates that by examining "the proceedings that we *call* 'games'"[26] (again, emphasis added), and concludes that games, like languages, "form a family."[27] Such is their "essence," their nature, revealed and determined by the familiar use of the word. Language is accorded this authority.

Why? The underlying reason surfaces in another apt illustration of §116. Russell had declared that the proper nouns we customarily call names (e.g., "Socrates," "Everest," "Cincinnati") are not names, whereas words such as "this" and "that," which we do not call names, are indeed names. For they, he held, and not the so-called names, satisfy the essence of a name, which is to pick out some particular object without describing it. To this, Wittgenstein objects: "If you do not want to produce confusion you will do best not to call these words names at all."[28] For the same pragmatic reason, you had better not deny that "Socrates," "Everest," and "Cincinnati" are names. ("Her middle name is 'Ann,'" someone says. "No it isn't," a Russellian replies; "for 'Ann' is not a name, and indeed she has no name—not in the proper, strict, logical sense of the term.") Granted, you need not parrot others' opinions (you may, if you wish, contest that a person's name is the one they suppose); but at least speak their language when you state your own views. For, as Wittgenstein remarked and this example illustrates, "If language is to be a means of communication there must be agreement not only in definitions but also (queer as this may sound) in judgments."[29] If you wish to communicate with English-speaking people, call names names and pronouns pronouns. Widespread acceptance of Russell's attitude toward the authority of language (examined more fully in chapter 11) would lead to Babel.

Doubtless concern for effective communication explains Wittgenstein's strongly prescriptive verdict in another place where he restores a key term to its everyday use:

> It is important to note that the word "meaning" is being used illicitly if it is used to signify the thing that "corresponds" to the word. That is to confound the meaning of a name with the *bearer* of the name. When Mr. N. N. dies one says that the bearer of the name dies, not that the meaning dies. And it would be nonsensical to say that, for if the name ceased to have meaning it would make no sense to say "Mr. N. N. is dead."[30]

What, then, is the meaning if it is not the thing the word refers to? We have seen Wittgenstein's answer: "For a *large* class of cases—though not for all—in which we employ the word 'meaning' it can be defined thus: the meaning of a word is its use in the language."[31] Such being the use of the word "meaning" in the language, such is meaning: "grammar" determines its essence, its nature—in these instances.

Why, though, must we always ask how a word is "actually used" in the language-game that is its home? Can its familiar use never be improved on? Certainly it can. Wittgenstein sometimes introduced special senses for terms[32] and envisioned others.[33] However, not only do stipulations of sense, or their possibility, lend no backing to the kind of "metaphysical" word use exemplified by the *Tractatus* and targeted by the *Investigations*; they are antithetical to such use. Had young Wittgenstein simply stipulated, "I shall reserve the term 'proposition' (or '*Satz*') for utterances that state how things stand," no one would have taken any interest in the announcement. Indeed, it would not have interested Wittgenstein himself, for it would not have revealed "the nature of the proposition." So, guided neither by standard nor by stipulated senses, "metaphysical" word use floats in a linguistic limbo. That is what is wrong with it. Reality alone cannot endorse any statement or make it true; the backing of language is also required. But metaphysical claims such as those in the *Tractatus* lack linguistic support.

Individual texts, taken out of context, could obscure Wittgenstein's balanced stance in the *Investigations*. On the one hand, his declaration that "Philosophy may in no way interfere with the actual use of language,"[34] which sounds dogmatically restrictive, must be read together with his concession that linguistic reform "for particular practical purposes, an improvement in our terminology designed to prevent misunderstandings in practice, is perfectly possible."[35] On the other hand, he must also be rightly understood when, having noted that names such as "Moses" have no fixed meaning, he writes with apparently excessive permissiveness: "Should it be said that I am using a word whose meaning I don't know, and so am talking nonsense?—Say what you choose, so long as it does not prevent you from seeing the facts. (And when you see them there is a good deal that you will not say.)"[36] Usage would hardly sanction asserting that, since our words' meanings are not fixed, we do not know their meanings, hence talk nonsense when we use them. And if Wittgenstein believed, as he doubtless did, that these are things a person would not say if sufficiently aware of the typical, effective functioning of words, what is the point of his observation "Say what you choose"? It reflects, I suggest, his therapeutic intent, which required a nonconfrontational approach. Thus when the Cambridge philosopher John Wisdom told him about an unsuccessful philosophical discussion Wisdom had had, Wittgenstein remarked: "Perhaps you made the mistake of denying what he said."[37] Here in the *Investigations*, Wittgenstein did not wish to make that mistake. But his unwillingness to contradict another's saying indicates no willingness to accept what he did not deny. We do know the meaning of adaptable expressions such as "Moses" and we do not speak nonsense when we utter them.

A Paradoxical Stance

From this account of Wittgenstein's transition from the *Tractatus* to the *Philosophical Investigations*, a paradox emerges: even as Wittgenstein became more fully aware of the tricks that existing language plays on us (including, first and foremost, himself), he became far more accepting of language's authority. This paradox, which is still stronger than so far suggested, demands fuller consideration.

For the later Wittgenstein as for the earlier, language was the primal source of philosophical puzzlement and confusion. "What interests us," he said, "is the contrast between the real state of affairs and that which our mode of expression inclines us to expect."[38] Of the resulting misconceptions, four kinds figure prominently in the *Investigations*:[39] (1) *Sense Fallacy*: a meaningless word group that superficially resembles meaningful sentences is taken to have sense. "It is not every sentence-like formation," Wittgenstein warns, "that we know how to do something with, not every technique has an application in our life; and when we are tempted in philosophy to count some quite useless thing as a proposition, that is often because we have not considered its application sufficiently."[40] (2) *Description Fallacy*: an utterance that sounds like many a description or report is mistakenly taken for one. *Investigations* §585 can serve as illustration: "When someone says 'I hope he'll come'—is this a *report* about his state of mind, or a *manifestation* of his hope? . . . If I tell someone 'I can't keep my mind on my work today; I keep on thinking of his coming'—*this* will be called a description of my state of mind." (3) *Reference Fallacy*: an expression which parallels referring ones is provided with a nonexistent reference. For instance, the surface similarity between "to say something" and "to mean something" tempts us to conceive meaning one's words as a process that accompanies the words.[41] Similarly, as "walk," "talk," "jump," and the like report external acts, so "love," "hope," "will," "desire," and the like are taken to report internal acts. Some psychological verbs do report inner occurrences, at least on some occasions, but of such assimilations as these Wittgenstein remarked: "A false—falsely simplified—conception of their meaning, that is of their grammar, seduces us into thinking that a specific, characteristic experience must correspond to the word."[42] (4) *Essence Fallacy*: from the sameness of a word on various occasions we mistakenly infer the sameness of the word's reference on all those occasions. "I cannot characterize my standpoint better," Wittgenstein explained, "than by saying that it is opposed to that which Socrates represents in the Platonic dialogues. For if asked what knowledge is I would list examples of knowledge, and add the words 'and the like.' No common element is to be found in them all."[43] That is, no one feature is found in all the cases covered by the term, and in them alone, so that the presence of this feature accounts for our use of the term.

Such illustrations, pointing constantly to misleading surface analogies as the source of error and confusion, show how mistaken is the common account that has Wittgenstein trace most philosophical ills to deviant uses of language. The pertinence of this misinterpretation for our topic can be sensed from a comment such as the following, from the 1960s: "What ordinary language philosophy urged . . . was that natural languages are perfectly all right as they stand so long as they are used properly, i.e., in the ordinary way. Conceptual confusions are consequences of aberrations in usage. The restoration of normal, ordinary usage automatically clears them up."[44] The author of these words had Wittgenstein primarily in view;[45] yet such, certainly, was not Wittgenstein's position, either with regard to the source of philosophical perplexities or with regard to their solution or with regard to the reason for employing, for the most part, ordinary terms with their ordinary senses. In Wittgenstein's view, the source of our difficulties is the whole conceptual system in which we live and move and have our being from the moment we are born; this second nature; this air we breathe. The difficulties with which Wittgenstein deals are correspondingly widespread, deep-rooted, and tenacious. "They are deep disquietudes; their roots are as deep in us as the forms of our language and their significance is as great as the importance of our language."[46]

Consider a quotation from Moore. In striking illustration of what I have labeled the "Reference Fallacy," Moore wrote:

> One of the chief things which we mean, by saying we have minds, is, I think, this: namely, that we perform certain mental acts or acts of consciousness. That is to say, we see and hear and feel and remember and imagine and think and believe and desire and like and dislike and will and love and are angry and afraid, etc. These things that we do are all of them mental acts—acts of mind or acts of consciousness: whenever we do any of them, we are conscious of something.[47]

Wittgenstein would question this blanket assimilation of psychological verbs, induced in large part by their surface similarities. All of the verbs in Moore's list, plus others, can be employed in the active voice, with personal subject terms: A hears x, feels x, desires x, fears x, means x, and so forth. From such similarity of appearance, we may too readily assume similarity of function. Thus, if feeling a fabric is an act, so too, we may think, is feeling an itch. If observing a spider or imagining a solution is an act, so too is hearing an explosion or knowing Esperanto. If "imagine," "contemplate," and "feel" signal conscious occurrences, doubtless "believe," "will," "expect," "understand," and "mean" do, too. Such is language's ability to veil important differences and generate nonentities from mere verbal appearances.

So, should psychological verbs be recast, with one form for acts (e.g., imagining), another for dispositions (e.g., liking), another for capacities (e.g., understanding), and so forth? Indeed, since acts, dispositions, capacities, and other mental referents are not all of one piece, should there be different verb forms for different varieties of each (e.g., one form for voluntary mental acts and another for involuntary)? And if these more refined linguistic forms still veiled inner diversity, should more fine-grained expressions replace them? Ultimately, should names for individual acts, dispositions, capacities, and the rest, of individual people at specific moments, replace all general terms, with their deceptive suggestion of identity from instance to instance, person to person, moment to moment? No, Wittgenstein had been down this road and knew where it led. No conceivable language, let alone any handy or usable language, could be perfectly isomorphic with reality. Existing language may be still more deceptive than young Wittgenstein had realized, but the solution, on most occasions, is not to replace the language but to observe it—and to speak accordingly.

In this connection, Moore's passage suggests a further point worth noting. Russell, say, may have misused the word "name" when, conceiving the difference between "this" and "Socrates" much as the rest of us do, he called the former a name but not the latter. Moore, however, did not similarly misuse "conscious," "act," or any of his verbs when he ran through his listing of conscious mental acts. Had he taken a closer look and spotted how notably some of these verbs differ from others, perhaps, according language some authority, he would have spoken differently than he did. However, given his homogeneous conception, he used the right words to express it. Conscious mental acts are rightly described as conscious mental acts. Wittgenstein did not deplore Moore's use of words, but the viewpoint they expressed. And he deplored it because, in many cases, there are no such conscious acts as Moore supposed. We do not use the verbs that way.

"One cannot guess how a word functions," Wittgenstein observed. "One has to *look at* its use and learn from that. But the difficulty is to remove the prejudice which stands in the way of doing this. It is not a *stupid* prejudice."[48] The author of the *Tractatus*, Wittgenstein's chief target, surely was not stupid, but he does not appear to have even been tempted to examine how German-speakers employ expressions such as "*Name*," "*Satz*," and "*Sprache*" or how English-speakers employ expressions such as "name," "statement," and "language." What would be the point? He was interested in the nature of names, statements, and language, not in the vagaries of German or English usage. The attitude of many, perhaps most, nonlinguistic philosophers has been basically so similar that Wittgenstein's later critique has far-reaching significance.

With respect to any of their claims, theorists like young Wittgenstein have three methodological options: (1) They can let usage be their guide, and speak the language as it is spoken. If, for example, English-speakers call "Churchill" and "Chicago" names, the theorists, too, will call them names; they will not, like Russell and young Wittgenstein, pronounce them "pseudonames" or exclude them as veiled propositions. (Fuller characterization of this first option will occupy later chapters.) (2) When it seems opportune, they can stipulate new senses for their terms. For example, rather than declare that all names or propositions function in some single way, they can (if they see the need) identify that one way as the sense they will give the expression "name" or "proposition," then abide by this stipulation in their application of the expression. (3) Ignoring usage and seeing no need for stipulation, they can bypass the preceding two options and simply declare, for example, what names are or propositions are.

Young Wittgenstein's reasons for adopting this third alternative appear typical. He was not interested in details of word usage but in the great questions of philosophy as he conceived them—in the relationship between language, thought, and world. Not only did usage appear irrelevant to his theoretical purposes, but, if accepted as a norm, it would have cramped his style: it would have inhibited the generalizing urge behind such theories as fill the *Tractatus*. The second option, stipulation of new senses, held no more charm, irrelevant as it appeared to his aims. Mere definitions of words say nothing about reality. If, then, with the first two options rejected or ignored, young Wittgenstein's claims lacked linguistic backing, that did not much concern him: as determinants of truth, he could consult either the logic of reality (for his ideal language) or the senses determined by personal projection (for his theoretical claims). When, however, the later Wittgenstein rejected these Tractarian rivals, as well as more traditional ones (in Plato, Aquinas, and others), there remained only options one and two. Now in one form, now in the other (linguistic usage or linguistic stipulation), language would have to be recognized as a principal determinant of truth and assertability. Accepting this verdict (unstated but implicit in ways here suggested), Wittgenstein became a linguistic philosopher in a stronger sense than any of his predecessors. Given its significance both for his own thinking and for philosophy generally, the misconceptions and objections to which it has given rise, and the problems that it does in fact leave unresolved, it is a pity that Wittgenstein did not say more about this development in his thought.

9

Wittgenstein versus Theoretical "Intuitions"

ACCORDING TO THE later Wittgenstein, "If one tried to advance *theses* in philosophy, it would never be possible to debate them, because everyone would agree to them."[1] This assertion itself sounds like a thesis. What did Wittgenstein have in mind? In simple illustration, consider games. If the familiar use of the word "game" reveals no essence, one will advance no thesis asserting an essence of games. Blocked in this direction, one may attempt to state at least sufficient or necessary conditions for being a game. Sufficient conditions look easy: to qualify as a game it suffices, for example, that an activity be poker or football. Whatever is poker or football is ipso facto a game. No one will disagree with that; neither, however, will anyone think it worthwhile to propose such an obvious "thesis." What, then, of necessary conditions? To be a game, one might suggest, an activity must have competition, or winning and losing. But then Wittgenstein cites patience (solitaire), which has neither and which, nonetheless, we call a game. Such is usage. So one resorts, perhaps, to "conducted by people" as a necessary feature of games—only to recall the "games" played by otters or computers. Again, such is usage. Well, then, mustn't games at least be *activities*? To be sure, but once all doubt disappears and everyone agrees, what is the point of advancing such a "thesis"?

Such being the apparent implications of accepting the authority of the languages they speak, some philosophers have desisted from theorizing in the popular manner of stating sufficient and/or necessary conditions. Others (for reasons seen and to be seen) have ignored usage and continued their theorizing. Still others, however, have spotted a possible compromise solution that neither flouts usage nor takes its word as final: usage leaves cracks that theory can fill. Thus, to continue our simple illustration, people may readily speak of otters or dogs playing "games," but what about earthworms? (The question is not sillier than those sometimes posed.) To be sure, no one has observed earthworms playing games, but might they? Is that a possibility? Here "intuitions" may diverge, and theses may seem worth advancing and defending on one side or the other. Or rather, they may if the verdict concerns something of greater apparent significance than the nature of games—if, say, it concerns the nature of meaning, knowledge, truth, life, or personal identity. The question that the Issue of Language's Authority then raises is this: If usage does not back these "intuitions," what does? Does language here have a new rival for authority? Wittgenstein's famed discussion of rules connects importantly with these queries, but first let us develop them more fully, using as illustration the lively, continuing debate concerning the nature of knowledge.

An Illustration: "Knowledge"

We can start with a representative exchange some decades ago between Bernard Williams and A. J. Ayer. "I shall be concerned," Williams explained, "only with what I shall call *propositional* knowledge, knowledge whose paradigmatic expression in language-users is the confident assertion of truths, and where the claim that it is knowledge that is being expressed involves as a necessary condition that what is asserted is true."[2] In addition,

> What is necessary—and what represents the undoubted fact that knowledge differs from mere true belief—is that one or more of a class of conditions should obtain, which relate the fact that A has this belief to the fact that the belief is true: conditions which can best be summarised by the formula that, given the truth of p, it is no accident that A believes p rather than not-p. This formula is vague and over-generous, but it gets us, I think, on the right line.[3]

That the formula is "vague and over-generous" as an analysis of knowledge appears, Williams suggested, from an example like the following:

> suppose that A, being from Guinea, tells B falsely that he is from Ghana; but (let us fancifully suppose) owing to features of A's spoken English which are peculiar to Guineans, B takes him to have said "Guinea" when he said "Ghana." Then B has come truly to believe that A is from Guinea, and (in an obvious sense) it is no accident, relative to A's being from Guinea, that this has come about; but B can scarcely be said to have acquired knowledge in this way, as opposed (for instance) to a situation in which, familiar with the Guinean accent, he sees through the pretense.[4]

From this and similar counterexamples, Williams did not conclude, with the later Wittgenstein, that precise, definitional analysis should be abandoned. Instead, he expressed the hope that further investigation might indicate some appropriate types of restriction. In their absence, he offered the "no accident" clause "not as part of an analysis but (as I said before) as a label for a class of conditions, the general requirements on which need to be spelled out with greater precision."[5]

Ayer responded as Wittgenstein might have. He agreed with Williams, he said,

> that there are various different grounds on which claims to knowledge can be accredited, and I therefore suspect that if one is trying to define knowledge, in its personal aspect, one may have to be content with some such vague formula as my own "having the right to be sure." If one ventures on anything more precise, one is likely to be faced with counter-examples . . . We are usually able to decide the question in particular cases, though even here there may be differences of opinion, but I have some doubt whether these particular decisions can be fitted tidily under any general rule.[6]

In view of difficulties for even his own formula, Ayer's response looks realistic, both a priori and a posteriori. A priori, neither personal redefinition of the term "knowledge" nor accurate analysis of the existing concept is likely to yield the result Williams sought. Freed from the constraints of usage, theorists may define terms as they please, and no uniformity is likely to result. If, however, they consult usage, they are not likely to discover any consistent pattern more definite than the vague one Williams indicated. For the usage in question supposedly is that of the English-speaking population—young and old, literate and illiterate, dogmatic and skeptical, tugged this way and that by the most varied evidence, in the most varied contexts, with the most varied interests, purposes, and standards. ("I *know* my boy didn't do it," declares the mother; "You know no such thing," counters the epistemologist.) Again, how likely is it that, whereas philosophers have played fast and loose with the concept "know," the general population has resisted any temptation to depart from a precise application of the term as rigidly consistent from case to case as any epistemologist might desire? How likely is it that philosophers such as Williams and Ayer, who knew the English language and had employed the terms "know" and "knowledge" countless times, consistently employed them according to a pattern that they could not detect, despite their best efforts?

Thus, a priori, as I say, theorists are not likely to discover in common usage any more exact delimitation of what counts as knowledge.

A posteriori, they in fact have not. Theory clashes with theory, "intuition" with "intuition," and no consensus is anywhere in sight. Consider, for example, the case proposed by Keith Lehrer and summarized thus by Peter Klein: "a certain Mr Truetemp has a thermometer-with-temperature-belief-generator implanted in his head so that within certain ranges of temperatures he has perfectly reliable temperature beliefs. When it is 50 degrees, he comes to believe that it is 50 degrees. When it is not 50 degrees, he does not come to believe that it is 50 degrees. He holds these beliefs without knowing why he does."[7] Since Mr. Truetemp's beliefs are reliable, some epistemologists assert that he knows the temperatures. Since he has no clue why he holds the beliefs, other epistemologists deny that he knows the temperatures. "Here," Klein concludes, "we can detect a fundamental clash of intuitions. . . . There appears to be no way to satisfy both."[8]

What, we may now ask, is the status of these conflicting "intuitions" and countless others that they represent, on this and other issues? Mr. Truetemp and his beliefs carry no identifying label ("knowledge" or "mere belief") any more than does a Platonic Form. To bridge the gap between nonverbal reality and verbal classification, something more is needed—some codeterminant of truth, as I might call it. Typically, as here, theorists who allege such intuitions offer no clue what the codeterminant might be: they just contemplate their cases and countercases, and issue their verdicts. It is clear, however, that familiar word usage knows nothing about Mr. Truetemp and his innumerable far-fetched kin. So what verbal backing can such intuitions claim, and without such backing, what support do they have other than the mere preferences or inclinations of the rival claimants?

Wittgenstein on Rules

The most plausible claim to verbal backing that I can envision would go something like this.[9] As the English-speaking population has never encountered or envisaged a Mr. Truetemp and accorded or refused the classification "knowledge" to his temperature beliefs, so the mathematical community has never counted up to 7,003,677 and agreed that the next number is 7,003,678. Nonetheless, it is; on that we agree. So might not the classification of Mr. Truetemp's beliefs be equally veridical? Might it not lie implicit in the rules of language, and specifically the rules for applying "know," much as the as-yet-uncounted number lies implicit in the rules of mathematics, and specifically the rules for counting integers?[10]

And just how, asked Wittgenstein, is that number's implicit presence to be conceived? If we examine the written number 7,003,677, we do not spot 7,003,678 there; one set of digits is not hidden in the other (written in invisible intellectual ink, as it were). Neither do the laws of physics or physiology lead us from one set to the other. However, we meet again and again, the later Wittgenstein remarked, "with this curious superstition, as one might be inclined to call it, that the mental act is capable of crossing a bridge before we've got to it. This trouble crops up whenever we try to think about the ideas of thinking, wishing, expecting, believing, knowing, trying to solve a mathematical problem, mathematical induction, and so forth."[11] It arises with paradigmatic simplicity with regard to counting. "Keep on adding one," someone says, "till you reach five thousand." Now the tracks are laid; each step is predetermined. "I also," Wittgenstein concedes, "should carry on the series 'Add 1' in the way 101, 102, etc., but not—or not necessarily—because of some other justifying mental act."[12] Not because I read each number off from some rule that takes all the steps before I do. Every rule formulation can be differently interpreted, but interpretations finally come to an end, and then we simply act. Agreement in our counting makes mathematics possible. Agreement in our use of words makes communication possible. "It is what human beings *say* that is true and false," wrote Wittgenstein; "and they agree in the *language* they use. That is not agreement in opinions but in form of life."[13]

Wittgenstein went further. Not only did he resist the idea of logical precontainment in mathematics, but he resisted the comparison of speech with mathematics. He no longer supposed, as earlier, "that if anyone utters a sentence and *means* or *understands* it he is operating a calculus according to definite rules."[14] Thus,

> How should we explain to someone what a game is? I imagine that we should describe *games* to him, and we might add: "This *and similar things* are called 'games.'" And do we know any more about it ourselves? Is it only other people whom we cannot tell exactly what a game is?—But this is not ignorance. We do not know the boundaries because none have been drawn.[15]

Neither have any boundaries been drawn for "knowledge." Reading a reliable thermometer, hearing a weather report—these and "similar things" warrant the claim that one "knows" the temperature.

Then there are borderline cases. Mr. Truetemp is an unusual specimen, resembling paradigm instances of knowledge in one respect (reliability) and paradigm instances of nonknowledge in another (lack of reasons). This bizarre configuration explains epistemologists' conflicting "intuitions" about him, similarity eliciting one verdict and dissimilarity the other. Typically, reasons and reliability go together, and borderline cases of knowledge have a different look. At one extreme, say, lies a bit of evidence from a not very reliable informant; at the other extreme lie masses of evidence from varied, highly reliable sources of information; and in between stretch a continuum of cases. Now where, precisely, along this continuum, does usage or linguistic agreement draw the line between knowledge and justified true belief? At three witnesses of grade-3 reliability providing grade-2 evidence; at five witnesses of grade-2 reliability providing grade-4 evidence; at . . . ? No, this is obvious nonsense. But the game of intuition and counterintuition makes no better sense. Specifically, the assertion or denial that Mr. Truetemp *knows* the temperatures enjoys no better backing than the assertion or denial that a true belief qualifies as knowledge provided that its combination of witness number, witness reliability, and evidence quality satisfies some specific formula (e.g., $WN \times WR \times EQ > 20$). Neither explicitly nor implicitly does usage draw any such line. ("My aim," wrote Wittgenstein, "is: to teach you to pass from a piece of disguised nonsense to something that is patent nonsense."[16])

A key premise in this critique is the relevance of language, but that is often not noted by intuitionists. Take, for example, the question of fetal status. From zygote to newborn infant a continuum stretches, and there, too, intuitions diverge, with some asserting and some denying that the being in the womb is a person or a human being. To resolve the impasse, John Noonan invites us "to consider the organism kicking the mother, swimming peacefully in amniotic fluid, responding to the prick of an instrument, being extracted from the womb, sleeping in death. Is the kicker or swimmer similar to him or to her? Is the response to pain like his or hers? Will his or her own face look much different in death?"[17] The answer seems clear enough: Somewhat similar, somewhat dissimilar, and the dissimilarity increases the less developed the fetus. But at no stage, along with the kicking, swimming, or the like, do we observe the word "person" or "human being" authoritatively attached by God or by nature. And in every case we may ask, in the manner of Wittgenstein: "Does it *follow* from the description that the fetus is a human being? How can a *proposition* (e.g., 'The fetus is a human being') follow from the observation of the *fetus*?"[18] Were fetuses, or fetuses at this or that stage of development, standardly called human beings, there would be no problem. But they are not. Application of the expression "human being," or "person," like that of most words, has an imprecise border, and that is where these cases fall: on, or in, the border.

Gilbert Harman, who adverts to the possible relevance of linguistic usage for the question of knowledge, may have revealed the mentality of many other participants in this and similar debates when he wrote:

I take an analysis to be any interesting set of necessary and sufficient conditions. Although I shall not offer an analysis of the

meaning of "know" (whatever that would be), I shall appeal to
your intuitions about hypothetical cases. I shall claim, for example, that a person can come to know something when he is told
it, or when he reads it in the newspaper. Although I may seem to
appeal to what one would ordinarily say about such cases and
for this reason may seem to be doing "linguistic analysis," I am
interested in what is true about such cases and not just in what
we say about such cases.[19]

yup

Harman's comments resemble Moore's, in chapter 1, and invite a similar
response. We do not ordinarily say anything about such hypothetical
cases as Lehrer's Mr. Truetemp, and no verdict on those cases lies implicit
in what we say about familiar cases. It is therefore understandable that
Harman and other theorists should look elsewhere than to "what one
would ordinarily say" to back their "intuitions." But what is "true about
such cases" is, for example, that Mr. Truetemp is reliably programmed
and that he has no reasons for his judgments; and how do these stipulated
facts yield the further fact that Mr. Truetemp does or does not "know"?
What makes that term the right or wrong one to apply? In what does the
"truth" of the assertion or negation consist? Harman dismisses any linguistic determinant of truth but does not substitute any alternative, nonlinguistic determinant, to complement the reality described; his position
therefore resembles that of Moore gazing upon the good, Plato's soul
contemplating the pure Forms, or Noonan scrutinizing the fetus and
thereupon, from the object alone, knowing what to *say*.

Further Problems

Reflection reveals further problems for the statement of precise sufficient
or necessary conditions. One concerns the precision, the other the utility,
of the enterprise.

First, with regard to precision, it might be conceded that neither explicitly nor implicitly does everyday usage draw precise borders for a concept such as "know." However, perhaps a different sort of precision is
attainable, not affected by the indefiniteness of usage or by the uncertainty of what we would say in unusual circumstances. Theorists might
aspire, not to determine precise boundaries of imprecise concepts but to
discover precise matches between imprecise concepts—that is, between
the vague concepts used to state sufficient or necessary conditions and the
vague concepts thus delineated. "Game," for example, is a vague concept, and so is "activity"; but surely all games are and must be activities:
anything that falls outside the vague concept "activity" falls outside the
vague concept "game." Similarly, "verb" is a vague concept, and so is

"word"; but surely all verbs are and must be words: anything that falls outside the second vague concept falls outside the first. No doubt these examples are obvious and trite, but might not other examples have greater interest: might they not be both less obvious and more significant?

"Knowledge" is deemed a more significant concept, but we have already noted the difficulty of finding other concepts whose indefinite borders coincide with its indefinite borders. Focusing on propositional knowledge, Williams suggested that in order to qualify as such knowledge, the truth of a belief must not be "accidental." His formula, he recognized, was vague, but also "over-generous." It is no accident that B, who misunderstands A's false statement, believes A to be from Guinea, but B can scarcely be said to have acquired knowledge in this way. It is no accident that Mr. Truetemp arrives at his true beliefs about the temperature, but it is not clear that his beliefs count as knowledge. A sure, perfect match for "knowledge" remains to be found. So the search continues, as does the debate. What condition or conditions must true belief satisfy in order to count as knowledge?

I find the following comparison illuminating with regard to both the prospects and the utility of such theoretical aspirations. Shifting with the winds, clouds assume the most varied shapes. What, then, is the likelihood that the border of one cloud, or any considerable stretch thereof, exactly matches that of another, or exactly matches the contours of several other clouds combined, and what would be the interest of the discovery? Analogously, concepts, shifting with different interests and circumstances, from context to context and period to period, assume the most varied shapes. What, then, is the likelihood that the border of one concept, or any considerable stretch thereof, exactly matches that of another, or that of several other concepts combined, and what would be the interest of the discovery? The momentary sameness of cloud borders, before winds refigured them, might be a curious fact but would have no significance that might motivate a search of the heavens for coinciding borders. So too, the momentary sameness of conceptual borders, before the winds of culture and communication refigured them, might be a curious fact of language but would have no evident significance that might motivate a search of the conceptual heavens for coinciding borders. The search might uncover interesting distinctions or considerations along the way, but these might be spotted independently of the search for precise defining conditions, or its success.

Let us consider this question of utility still more closely. Suppose everyone, if presented with the strange case of Mr. Truetemp, agreed that he knows the temperature. That would tell us nothing new about his stated capacities; it would simply attach a label. The only interesting discovery would be the subjective, psychological one: how strange, how inexplicable, that all these people, despite their different backgrounds, experiences, tendencies, interests, and circumstances, agree in attaching the label "knowledge" to a case that differs so notably from those familiarly so labeled! This lack of objective interest is veiled by the analogy between this inquiry and other, more familiar cases. A linguist, say, who knows their language, asks numerous natives the name of a plant he has found, and all agree that the familiar plant is a "vagage." Now he knows something new, not about the plant but about the language—about existing linguistic practice. Again, art experts all examine a painting and reach the common verdict that it is a forgery. Now the new fact is objective, not linguistic: the painting they have studied was not painted by the man whose name appears on it. Our imagined case, where for some reason the disputants all agree and apply the label "knowledge," resembles neither of these analogs. There is agreement in applying an expression: here is the similarity. But this agreement reveals neither some new fact about existing linguistic practice, as for the plant, nor some new fact about the thing labeled, as for the painting. The contrary impression, which motivates the attempt to delimit knowledge precisely (and countless similar efforts), appears illusory.

These critical remarks may all sound wrongheaded. Knowledge is important; so philosophers wish to know what it is. Being philosophers, they wish to know *exactly* what it is. What is wrong with that? First, the assumption that knowledge is precisely defined; second, the assumption that something other than language defines it—that the precise nature of Knowledge (with a capital "K") is unaffected by the imprecision of the word "know" or "knowledge." In our post-Platonic, scientific age, thoughts may flit through our minds of hidden brain states, say, that, once discovered, may more exactly determine the nature of knowledge, much as chemical analysis has revealed the precise composition of water. However, knowledge, in all its varieties, admixtures, and degrees, is not comparable to a natural kind. And even for water it is important to distinguish between the scientific task of analyzing the stuff that flows in our rivers and the much murkier task of determining what stuff, real or imaginary, should be labeled "water" (see chapter 15). Similarly, it is important to distinguish between the scientific task of determining possible neural correlates of clear instances of knowledge and the much murkier task of deciding, for example, whether Mr. Truetemp should be credited with "knowledge." If, as Wittgenstein remarked, essence "is expressed by grammar," and the grammar of "knowledge" is imprecise, so is the nature of knowledge: no precise account of its nature can be given without ignoring the word's familiar use, or contesting it.

In this chapter and in chapter 8, we have seen why philosophers might want to contest Wittgenstein's linguistic turn, acknowledging the authority of language. "Philosophers," we have seen him say, "constantly see the method of science before their eyes, and are irresistibly tempted to ask and answer questions in the way science does."[20] They state conceptual (not physical) necessities, possibilities, and impossibilities. They state—precisely, as scientists do—what knowledge is, what reference is, what truth is, and so forth. This way, Wittgenstein warned, lies darkness—the darkness, for example, of supposing that precise philosophical verdicts follow from imprecise linguistic usage, or that the discovery of concepts whose borders happen momentarily to match would hold ontological or epistemological significance.

Zettel 458 encapsulates Wittgenstein's later viewpoint: "Philosophical investigations: conceptual investigations. The essential thing about metaphysics: it obliterates the distinction between factual and conceptual investigations." Doubtless Wittgenstein would judge that much contemporary philosophical practice is still metaphysical in this sense. Using language but ignoring or contesting its authority, philosophers often advance theses whose truth doubtless depends somehow and to some extent on the words employed; but in the absence of any clear indication of how and to what extent it does, there is no telling whether or to what extent the claims advanced are factual or conceptual. This unclarity characterizes both essentialistic theories such as those discussed in the last chapter (e.g., concerning language and propositions) and "intuitions" such as those discussed here (e.g., concerning knowledge and fetal status). One explanation for this continuing manner of philosophizing is some thinkers' slight acquaintance with Wittgenstein's thought or their imperfect grasp of its implications.[21] Another is resistance to these implications, which call into question ingrained habits and aspirations and which, contesting them, may appear to call into question the whole philosophical enterprise. However, more than unpalatable implications account for the resistance to Wittgenstein's later thought. For various reasons, which the next chapter will start to examine, the sort of favorable response he evoked to the Issue of Language's Authority has appeared excessive, inadequate, or fundamentally mistaken.

10

Flew and Paradigm-Case Arguments

"W HERE DOES OUR investigation get its importance from," asks Wittgenstein in the *Investigations*, "since it seems only to destroy everything interesting, that is, all that is great and important?" His reply: "What we are destroying is nothing but houses of cards and we are clearing up the ground of language on which they stand."[1] Such was Wittgenstein's judgment on the *Tractatus*'s theses, and, by implication, on many others like them.[2] Yet the questions to be clarified often do seem "great and important," and any approach that clarifies them has corresponding interest. Interest attaches, for example, to the questions of which Max Black wrote: "After centuries of discussion, philosophers are still embarrassed by the resurgence of doubts about free will, the reality of time, the existence of other minds and the external world, the possibility of knowledge about the future or matters of fact; and any method which promises to give a satisfactory and permanent answer to such sceptical questionings deserves careful examination."[3] The promising approach Black had in mind was linguistic and took varied forms of what was termed (in the singular) "the paradigm-case argument." This approach, of Wittgensteinian inspiration,[4] is a principal reason for the impression noted at the end of chapter 9, that the linguistic turn which Wittgenstein promoted accorded excessive authority to language. To assess the method's merits, and its relevance for the Issue of Language's Authority, we can focus on a single representative example.

Flew on Freedom

Reviewing the findings of *The Idea of Freedom*, issued by the Institute for Philosophic Research, Roger Hancock noted three major conceptions of freedom in authors from Plato to the present: a "circumstantial freedom of self-realization," an "acquired freedom of self-perfection," and a "natural freedom of self-determination."[5] One use of such a listing, he suggested,

> is to show the extent to which philosophers are "talking about different things" when, for example, the subject is freedom. Another use is that, after reading *The Idea of Freedom,* it is hard to dismiss any of these conceptions as simply a kind of perverse or illegitimate use of the word "freedom"; each conception seems to have a kind of plausibility, and they all seem to be meaningful, in the sense that they can each be used to distinguish actions which are free from actions which are not free.[6]

As much might be said for most competing theories in philosophy: they all seem to be meaningful, and can be used to distinguish cases that qualify and those that do not. But what "kind of plausibility" do they possess? Hancock has little to offer in reply. How, he asks, "could anyone hope to refute a conception of freedom; on what grounds could one argue that a certain type of act 'ought not' to be called a free act? The most one could do in attacking a conception of freedom would be to argue that, according to it, there are few or no actual cases of acting freely, so that the conception fails to make a useful distinction."[7] Significantly, Hancock does not mention everyday, nonphilosophical linguistic usage, familiar to all, or any claims it might have. No authority is accorded to language as a determinant of what to say. By contrast, Antony Flew, in apparent conformity with Wittgenstein's advice to return contested concepts to the language-game that is their original home, resolved the issue of freedom by means of a paradigm-case argument.

A philosophical dictionary for which Flew was a consultant described such an argument as one "that infers from the fact that a word is taught by reference to clear (paradigm) cases, the conclusion that examples of the thing referred to by the word must exist."[8] In a paradigmatic exposition and illustration of the genre, which provoked much comment, Flew himself wrote:

> Crudely: if there is any word the meaning of which can be taught by reference to paradigm cases, then no argument whatever could ever prove that there are *no cases whatever* of whatever it is. Thus, since the meaning of "of his own freewill" [*sic*] can be taught by reference to such paradigm cases as that in which a man, under no social pressure, marries the girl he wants to marry (how else *could* it be taught?): it cannot be right, on any grounds whatsoever, to say that no one *ever* acts of his own freewill [*sic*].

For cases such as the paradigm, which must occur if the word is ever to be thus explained (and which certainly do in fact occur) are not in that case specimens which might have been wrongly identified: to the extent that the meaning of the expression is given in terms of them they are, by definition, what "acting of one's own freewill" [*sic*] is. As Runyon would say: If this isn't an x, it will at least do till an x comes along. A moment's reflexion will show that analogous arguments can be deployed against many philosophical paradoxes.[9]

Flew furnished an agenda for the present chapter when he added: "To see the power, and the limitations, of the Argument of the Paradigm Case is to realize how much of common sense can, and how much cannot, be defended against philosophical paradoxes by simple appeal to the ordinary use of words; and why."[10] Something of the argument's power and limitations can be discerned by examining Flew's own sample specimen.[11]

Even thinkers sympathetic to an ordinary-language approach have had problems with his quoted argument. They have wondered, for example, how we know that the meaning of "freely" or "of his own free will" can be taught by means of paradigm-cases and that such cases therefore exist. A first response is implicit in Flew's parenthetical query, "how else *could* it be taught?" As we could not know the meaning of "yellow" or "hot" (or could not know it fully) if nothing was ever yellow or hot, so too, Flew apparently supposed, we could not learn the meaning of "of his own free will" if no one had ever acted of his own free will. To this, a common objection has been to distinguish, as Norman Malcolm did, between two classes of expressions: those that could be learned through descriptions and those that must be learned by reference to cases. "Ghost" exemplifies the former category. People can learn the meaning of the word "ghost" without encountering any ghosts; so the existence of ghosts can be questioned without any inconsistency or implicit self-contradiction. The term can have the meaning intended without there being any such thing. In illustration of the second category, Malcolm notes, "People could not have learned the meaning of the expressions 'to the left of,' or 'above,' unless they had actually been shown instances of one thing being to the left of another, and one thing being above another. . . . Likewise, people could not have learned the use of expressions describing temporal relations, like 'earlier' and 'later,' unless they had been shown examples of things standing in these temporal relations."[12] With respect to this second category of expressions, Malcolm concludes: "In the case of all expressions the meanings of which must be *shown* and cannot be explained, as can the meaning of 'ghost,' it follows, from the fact that they are ordinary expressions in the language, that there have been *many* situations of the kind which they describe; otherwise so many people could not have learned the correct use of those expressions."[13] It also follows that such expressions as these cannot coherently be employed to state general doubt about the existence of *any* such cases as the ones described.

Flew's own account suggests on which side of the descriptive-ostensive divide an expression such as "of his own free will" falls. The expression's meaning can only be taught, he contends, by reference to such paradigm cases as that in which a man, under no social pressure, marries the woman he wants to marry. Yet such cases, it seems, might be as imaginary as unicorns; they need not be actual in order for us to be able to describe them as Flew does (by reference to wants, intentions, pressures, and the like) or to indicate thereby the meaning of the expression "of his own free will." That might be taught descriptively. Conceivably, the like might hold for at least some of the other items in Black's list—"the reality of time, the existence of other minds and the external world, the possibility of knowledge about the future or matters of fact." Whatever the item, the impossibility of purely descriptive learning would have to be shown in order for a paradigm argument like Flew's, read in this manner, to succeed.

However, Flew's remarks on this and subsequent occasions suggest a different way to take his argument and paradigm-case arguments generally, focusing less on the learning of words and what that implies and more on "the ordinary and everyday uses of the key words and expressions."[14] As those who doubt the reality of physical objects usually do not doubt the existence of hands and those who doubt the reality of time usually do not doubt that some events precede or follow others, so those who doubt free will usually do not contest Flew's paradigm case: they do not doubt that a man may, under no social pressure, marry the woman he wants to marry. The real issue, therefore, is whether on such occasions the man may or should be said to have acted "freely" or "of his own free will." And this question, it seems, brings us back to Wittgenstein's point about honoring the standard use of words. No one contests the customary application of "right" or "left," "earlier" or "later," in Malcolm's list. Why contest the customary application of "freely" or "of his own free will"?

Alternatives

At this point, our study of the Issue of Language's Authority can enter a new phase. After reviewing various rivals to language's authority, our quick tour through the centuries reached the later Wittgenstein, who accepted the authority of language more unreservedly than did any of his predecessors. However, Wittgenstein did not fully articulate or systematically develop this major shift from traditional thinking, and neither have

I. So the next eight chapters, starting with this one, will switch from challenge to articulation. The moment has arrived to start considering more
closely how and to what extent language might or should determine what
to say. Positions taken vis-à-vis Flew's argument reveal three different
ways in which the authority of language might be understood. Schemati-
cally stated: one position reads the linguistic evidence nontheoretically,
another reads it both theoretically and nontheoretically, and a third reads
it theoretically.

Initially, Flew viewed the linguistic evidence in the popular, nontheoretical manner we have noted. To counter such claims as that people
never act of their own free will, two steps sufficed: "the first is to bring to
mind certain very familiar facts, and the second is to insist that these are
paradigm exemplars of the concepts in question."[15] If, for example, a
bridegroom goes gladly to the altar, uncoerced by parents, lawsuits, or
the like, and this is a paradigm of what it means to do something "of
one's own free will," then that is how his action should be described. If
we believe that even such actions are causally determined, we should conclude that freedom is compatible with such determination, not that the
actions are unfree.

Others endorsed both affirming and denying human freedom, depending on the context of discussion.[16] Arthur Danto, for example, first
envisaged a nontheoretical sort of setting in which the question might
arise whether someone (e.g., the bridegroom) acted of his own free will.
"Suppose now," he wrote,

> we have made such an assertion and are declared wrong. And
> suppose the reason offered is the following one: nobody ever
> does anything of his own free will. We would, I think, be impa-
> tient; we would regard the person who says this as altogether
> facetious. When we were declared wrong, we were primed to
> hear a *fact*, were prepared for a piece of history or a bit of gossip;
> and what we received instead could not have been more beside
> the point.[17]

In a metaphysical context, however, it may be perfectly appropriate for a
determinist to say that nobody ever acts freely. For there, notes Danto,
"The determinist is surely not arguing the patently false proposition that
we always act unwillingly, *contrary* to our will."[18] Rather, "the determinist's thesis is this: given any act whatsoever, there exists some set of
conditions such that information about these conditions, together with
certain laws, would enable us accurately to predict that act."[19]

For the early Flew, quoted above, and for like-minded thinkers, such
a denial of all free human actions might not express an erroneous opinion

but it would be a verbal aberration. For Danto, it would be an aberration only if proffered in the wrong setting. For others, it might be mistaken but would never be an aberration, since even in familiar, nontheoretical contexts, terms such as "free" and "freely" are theoretically loaded—or, as Charles Taylor puts it, are metaphysically "infected."[20] Thus, according to Richard Purtill, "if most non-philosophers were asked whether a man 'controlled by direct physiological manipulations' so that he 'performed whatever actions [another] determines' were free they would, I am sure, answer that such a man was not free."[21] Such would be their verdict, regardless of context. A determinist, then, who holds a similar view of human actions, may deny their freedom without any linguistic impropriety or fear of diverging from "what we would ordinarily say."

Reviewing these three positions, we can see that no one account exemplifies more obviously than the others Wittgenstein's injunction to return contested terms to the language-game that is their home. Each position does that in its own way, with more or less attention to context and more or less attention to theoretical content. In the first position, the language-game is not viewed as theoretical; in the third it is; and in the second it is taken to be either theoretical or nontheoretical, depending on the setting. And the meaning of the terms varies accordingly. Thus all three positions accept the authority of language; all three recognize it as relevant for a verdict. They simply read its relevance differently, with different results.

Each reading has some plausibility: the first, because even determinists are likely to say such things as "He freely admitted his crime" or "You didn't *have* to do it"; the second, because contexts do differ and affect the understanding of expressions; the third, because even the most familiar expressions are, indeed, theory-laden. However, each reading also has its difficulties. For instance, the relevance of Purtill's imagined person, manipulated from without, might be questioned, and so might the relevance and reliability of his surmise about what "most nonphilosophers" would say. Even if the majority responded as predicted, what would make them right? (Recall the previous chapter's discussion of similar "intuitions.") As for the likelihood of their so responding, the everyday verbal practice of determinists calls it in doubt.

So do comparable cases. In ages past, most people who spoke of the sun rising and setting believed that the sun revolved around the Earth rather than vice versa. Their sayings were infected with this theory. One might therefore surmise that abandonment of the theory would bring abandonment of the sayings, but it did not. To this day, people still speak of the sun rising, setting, moving across the sky, and the like. Some theorists decry this survival of what they regard as outdated, unscientific ways of speaking. They do not, however, suggest more suitable, equally handy ways of stating the same facts. In like manner, neither do determinists suggest more suitable, equally convenient ways to state the facts and draw the distinctions that our familiar, libertarian-sounding expressions do. One employee "freely" opens a bank vault for accomplices; another, at gunpoint, opens it "under compulsion." One person is "free to do as he pleases"; another is bound by contract. And so forth. How would the determinist as readily state such differences? Here Wittgenstein's words seem applicable: "When as in this case, we disapprove of the expressions of ordinary language (which are after all performing their office), we have got a picture in our heads that conflicts with the picture of our ordinary way of speaking. Whereas we are tempted to say that our way of speaking does not describe the facts as they really are. . . . As if the form of expression were saying something false even when the proposition *faute de mieux* asserted something true."[22]

As Keith Donnellan has noted, "The idea that philosophy cannot cast doubt on the applications ordinarily made of everyday expressions is not a new one. It can be seen, for example, in Berkeley's refusal to draw skeptical consequences from his radical thesis that nothing exists apart from the mind. He did not conclude that we are mistaken in talking of material objects such as trees and tables; instead, he attempted to show how his thesis could be used to analyze the meaning of statements about these things."[23] Expressions such as "tree" and "table" do their job, and indeed, are irreplaceable. But their job is not to state some metaphysical theory. There *is* a tree out front, there *is* a table in the drawing room. On that the realist and the idealist can agree, while differing in their analyses of what a tree or a table is. So too, Flew might have said, the man does marry the woman of his own free will, let the libertarian and the determinist analyze the man's action as they will. To confuse metaphysical distinctions with everyday distinctions and exclude familiar expressions for the latter would impoverish our language and deprive it of expressions it needs for its everyday purposes.

Much, then, can be said—at least in everyday settings—for a nontheoretical reading of language's authority such as Flew exemplified. However, Flew himself came to view matters differently.[24] And the recommendation to abide, for the most part, by familiar word usage has appeared to many an endorsement of mere common sense and has therefore been rejected. As perhaps the foremost representative of this critical attitude, we can pass to Bertrand Russell, so as to continue the present discussion in somewhat greater breadth and depth.

11

Russell's Critique of "Common Sense"

OF HIS PARADIGM-CASE approach, Flew wrote: "what could be more elementary and more prudent, when confronted by some apparently bizarre assertion, than to begin by probing the intended meaning with the testing instrument of instances?"[1] Do deniers of freedom, time, or physical bodies really mean to question the occurrence of uncoerced marriages, nights that follow days, or the existence, say, of chairs and tables? Is this what, in all seriousness, they intend to assert? In Flew's judgment, "The philosophical hero prepared to try to take the full logical consequences of his paradoxes with his eyes wide open is largely a figure of legend. Persons of our common human clay will usually begin to hedge or to haver."[2]

Russell, for one, did not hedge or haver; he was, indeed, such a "philosophical hero." "The point of philosophy," he declared, "is to start with something so simple as not to seem worth stating, and to end with something so paradoxical that no one will believe it."[3] True to this conception of his calling, Russell started, for example, with the simple facts of sensation as presently understood and concluded that, contrary to our customary claims, we never see, hear, touch, taste, or smell the things we say we do. No one has ever heard an explosion, touched a table, tasted a pie, smelled a rose, or seen a sunset. True, common sense and naive realism suppose the contrary; they suppose, for example, that we see physical objects. However, science knows better.[4] Physical objects originate impulses, which reach our eyes, stimulate our nerves, and finally reach our brains. The end results, there in the brain, are all we actually see. Thus, "To say that you see Jones is no more correct than it would be, if a ball bounced off a wall in your garden and hit you, to say that the wall had hit you. Indeed, the two cases are closely analogous. We do not, therefore, ever see what we think we see."[5] Common sense is mistaken.

Russell's claims are no mere personal aberration. Many people have
made similar assertions, for similar reasons. They have denied that lights
flash; that objects are red or yellow, hot or cold; that we hear sounds;
that we hear anything but sounds; that light rays are colored; that people
take an interest in their activities; that tables and the like are solid objects;
that the sun rises or sets; that people are buried; that they are agreeable or
useful; that they love one another; that they feel pain in their extremities
or pleasure in their sexual organs; that animals act, or feel pain; indeed,
that there are any such things as animals or human beings; and so on,
endlessly.[6] In each instance, we may question whether those who make
such claims are challenging common sense, as they suppose, or contesting
common language; for they often show little awareness of any such distinction. Shared opinions get conflated with shared word meanings.

Russell sometimes gave the impression of suffering from this confusion, with the result that in rejecting ordinary statements and beliefs he
appeared to be rejecting ordinary language and with it the authority of
language to determine what we should say. However, the explanation he
offered when pressed about his doctrine of sensation gives a different impression: he based his rejection of ordinary statements and beliefs on his
understanding of ordinary language. The ordinary meaning of sensation
words called for the rejection of ordinary statements about sensations.
Viewed either way, Russell's doctrine has great interest for the Issue of
Language's Authority. The conflation of common sense and common
idiom adds another item to the list of important reasons why people have
contested the authority of language, while Russell's reading of sensation
expressions introduces a new way of understanding language's authority.

Common Sense and Common Usage

Russell's judgment on what he termed "The Cult of 'Common Usage'"
was severe. A pungent piece by this title, published in 1953, contains an
entertaining exchange between a policeman and a bedmaker. "'Ere, I
want a word with yer," says the policeman. "What do you mean? 'A
word'?" replies the bedmaker. "I ain't done nothing." "Ah, that's just
it—Yer ought to 'ave done something. Couldn't yer see the pore gentle-
man was mental?" "That I could," answers the bedmaker. "For an 'ole
hour 'e went on something chronic. But when they're mental you can't
make them understand." In this little dialogue, Russell observed,

> "word," "mean," "mental," and "chronic" are all used in accor-
> dance with common usage. They are not so used in the pages of
> *Mind* by those who pretend that common usage is what they be-
> lieve in. What in fact they believe in is not common usage, as de-

termined by mass observation, statistics, medians, standard deviations, and the rest of the apparatus. What they believe in is the usage of persons who have their amount of education, neither more nor less—less is illiteracy, more is pedantry—so we are given to understand.[7]

This criticism seems misdirected. The same considerations that sanction the style of speech effectively employed by the bedmaker and the policeman when speaking with their own kind sanction and recommend the very different style of speech employed by philosophers when writing or discussing philosophy with their peers. One may therefore doubt the general justice of Russell's complaint. Ordinary-language philosophers did not resist Russell because he said, with the bedmaker, "For an 'ole hour 'e went on something chronic." They resisted his saying, for example, that no one has ever heard a nightingale or watched an eclipse, or that all we ever see is our brains.

Russell identified his target as the doctrine, then dominant in "the most influential school of philosophy in Britain," "that the language of daily life, with words used in their ordinary meanings, suffices for philosophy."[8] Such, on the whole, was in fact the view of Wittgenstein, Austin, Ryle, and others. However, Russell confused their stance with reverence for common sense. Thus, in refutation he observed:

> In former centuries common sense made what we now think mistakes. It used to be thought that there could not be people at the antipodes, because they would fall off, or, if they avoided that, they would grow dizzy from standing on their heads. It used to be thought absurd to say that the earth rotates because everybody can see that it doesn't. When it was first suggested that the sun may be as large as the Peloponnesus, common sense was outraged; but all this was long ago. I do not know at what date common sense became all-wise.[9]

Here, it is instructive to observe Russell employ ordinary language—ordinary words such as "people," "earth," "rotates," and "sun" with their ordinary meanings—to criticize common sense. He has no need of new terms or new meanings, nor would he have needed them at the time of the beliefs he reports. Everyday expressions prove adequate for his purpose. The distinction between common sense and ordinary language is starkly revealed by Russell's use of ordinary language to criticize common sense.

Similar criticisms could be made, similarly, of current commonsense beliefs. Indeed, this is the only effective way the criticisms could be made.

If you wish to contest the claim "Life evolved," you had better use the same terms, with the same senses, and say, "Life did *not* evolve." Otherwise your denial is likely to miss its target; the apparent disagreement may be purely verbal. Similarly, if you wish to deny that people see the sun, you had better employ familiar terms and say "People don't see the sun," and, so doing, you had better mean by "people" and "see" and "sun" what others mean by these terms when they claim that people see the sun.

If language is distinguished from discourse—the instrument from the instrument's use, the linguistic components from the statements they compose—the difference between ordinary language and ordinary statements and beliefs may appear obvious. Yet medium and message are easily conflated. The message, after all, comes packaged in the medium. "Commonsense" beliefs are ordinary beliefs expressed in ordinary ways. What is more, the familiar meanings of the words employed largely determine the meaning and truth of the commonsense statements in which the words occur, while, reciprocally, their occurrence in such statements largely determines the words' meanings. As Wittgenstein noted, for there to be agreement in meanings, there must be agreement in judgments. We must agree that these fluffy things are clouds and those lumpy things are toads for the words "cloud" and "toad" to have the meanings they do. Yet we need not agree in all our cloud or toad assertions, just in some—in enough, and of the right kind. It is all rather confusing, even without the details. And I have not mentioned the fact that in all this complex interplay between medium and message, our gaze is typically fixed on just the message, since the medium, our mother tongue, is second nature to us. It is not surprising, then, that critics of commonsense beliefs should frequently fail to discern which aspect of the beliefs they are targeting—the factual or the linguistic—and should take defendants of the latter to be wedded to "common sense."

Common Content and Common Assertions

A related point is important for the present discussion: our beliefs about evaporation, condensation, the composition of water, and the like affect the cognitive content of "cloud"; similarly, our beliefs about genetics, evolution, vital processes, and the like affect the cognitive content of "toad." Such is the content expressed, and such is the content conveyed, thanks to our shared beliefs. It is natural, therefore, to suppose that this cognitive content affects the truth or falsehood of the statements in which the expressions occur—that the falsehood of the beliefs entails the falsehood of the statements or beliefs that they infect. This supposition figured crucially, as we shall now see, among the reasons Russell gave for his claims about sensation.

Ernest Nagel judged these claims to be "incredibly wrong." "There might indeed be a sense of 'see,'" he objected,

> in which I see my own brain, though I have not the slightest inkling as to what that sense is. I do know, however, that I have never seen any portion of my own brain, and that I have seen many physical objects—where the statement that I have not seen one but seen the other is to be understood in the customary sense of "see." To deny the facts expressed by the statement seems to be absurd; and such a denial can be understood only if we suppose that the person making the denial is misusing language.[10]

"Like Mr. Nagel," Russell replied, "I have often had the experience called 'seeing a table.'" However, "what I see when I 'see a table' is simultaneous with my seeing, whereas the table as the physical object connected with my seeing is slightly earlier. (The sun is eight minutes earlier, some nebulae hundreds of thousands of years earlier.)"[11] How, asks Russell, can a sunspot be the thing I see, if the sunspot occurred eight minutes ago and the seeing occurs now? One may wonder where the difficulty lies. Can't I be said to "receive a letter from a friend" if the friend sent the letter three days ago and I receive it only now. Must the sender of a letter be simultaneous with its reception? Mightn't she die in the meantime? Similarly, mightn't the sunspot I see at this moment have ceased to exist several minutes ago, yet still be the thing I see?

The solution to this puzzle may be revealed when Russell continues: "Mr. Nagel is indignant with me because I use the word 'see' in an unusual sense. I admit this. The usual sense implies naive realism, and whoever is not a naive realist must either eschew the word 'see' or use it in a new sense." Several points demand attention here, but notice first the likely explanation that emerges for Russell's claim of simultaneity. "When we 'see' an object," he writes, "we *seem* to have immediate knowledge of something external to our own body."[12] This is how the naive realist conceives visual perception. If, for instance, I see a table, then the table is present in that moment, and my seeing relates me to the table in that moment. Hence (Russell may be taken as concluding), if that is what seeing is, the only object that can fill the bill is the brain; for the viewer's relation to the table is not immediate, but mediated by light waves and neural impulses, and they take time.

One may therefore wonder why Russell concedes that he is using the word "see" in an unusual sense. He is using it to make an unusual statement, but he bases his use precisely on what he takes to be the ordinary sense of the term. If the word meant something else in everyday parlance, he would not deny that we see the table or claim that we see our brains.

To state the situation paradoxically, Russell, the great critic of "ordinary-language" philosophy, reveals himself here as (at least momentarily) an ordinary-language philosopher. He does not challenge the authority of language, any more than does someone who denies the existence of witches. In the ordinary sense of "witch" (sorceress endowed with supernatural powers, etc.), there are no witches. In the ordinary sense of "see," as Russell understands it, we never see physical objects.

With his position in clearer focus, we can first ask whether Russell's understanding of the term "see"—of its current sense in the English language—is accurate, and, more interesting, whether his inferences would be warranted even if his understanding was correct. The chief, though not sole, reason for doubting Russell's analysis of "see" is that current users of the term are as familiar as Russell with the physical, optical, and neurological facts he cites, yet they go right on saying that they see tables, kites, collisions, and the like. How can their usage be infected with a theory they all know is wrong? How can the term fail to be infected by their actual, scientific beliefs? Russell might suggest that they have just failed to notice the contradiction between their scientific and their naive, prescientific beliefs. But in that case, why not deny that anyone ever sees anything, since the concept "see" has now become incoherent? Why take one set of beliefs—the prescientific rather than the scientific—as currently defining the term and conclude, with Russell, that we do not see the things we say we see? Raising our heads above this particular morass, we can inquire more generally: if terms are loaded with theory and the theory may easily be mistaken, how can we or should we take language (the language we happen to be speaking) as our guide?

Russell's response is natural enough. If people's visual claims are defined by a mistaken understanding of what occurs in sight, then their claims are mistaken. No such thing occurs. However, the likely consequences of following Russell's example here should give us pause; paradox might become all-pervasive. Consider, for instance, the initial understanding of the term "atom." For most, atoms were indivisible units; they could not be split. But then they were, in fact, divided. Or rather, the units previously called "atoms" were divided. If we followed Russell, we might have to conclude that there are not and never have been any atoms. And since all physical terms—"table," "mountain," "water," and the rest, for things composed of atoms—were infected with the same basic error, we might have to conclude that there are no physical objects—no tables, mountains, water, and the rest. And this would be just the beginning.[13] Diseases whose etiology was first misconceived would have to be denied: no one has ever suffered from malaria, epilepsy, smallpox, or the like. The earth would have to be doubly denied—first because it was conceived as the center of the solar system, then because it was conceived as composed of atoms. The universe would suffer a like fate because of multiple errors concerning its size, age, and composition. We may feel sure that such inferences are mistaken, but why are they? What has gone wrong?

Language has been idealized, unrealistically. Here, again, Wittgenstein's remark is apposite: "In philosophy we often *compare* the use of words with games and calculi which have fixed rules, but cannot say that someone who is using language *must* be playing such a game."[14] If most of our terms are theory-laden and any of our theories might turn out to be false, language must accommodate this possibility. And it does. In familiar discourse, we go right on talking about planets, regardless of our cosmology. We go right on speaking of chairs, regardless of our views about subatomic particles. We go right on speaking about seeing objects, regardless of our theories of perception. We keep the term and change our analysis.[15] We only deny the seeing when nothing of that general sort occurs—as we deny witches because nothing of that general sort exists. But we are never related to our brains in any such general way as we are related to chairs, tables, or the sun that we see; so we do not say that we see our own brains. And we are right not to. Generalized, Russell's approach, rigidly defining terms by popular beliefs, would destroy language.

How, though, should we understand such phrases as "that general sort" and "any such general way"? Where should we draw the line? How extensive or serious must the error be before denial replaces accommodation—for instance, before we stop calling this or that person a witch and deny witches altogether, or stop saying someone sees an object and deny seeing altogether? Subsequent chapters will address these queries more fully, but first I should note the relevance of the preceding discussion for contemporary variants of Russell's thinking.

"Folk Theory" and Its Language

"Common sense," write Michael Devitt and Kim Sterelny, "is best seen as a mix of *folk theories* or, if talk of theories seems too pretentious here, *folk opinions.*"[16] At various levels of sophistication, "We are all full of intuitions, quick unreflective judgments about the world. The most basic of these identify instances and non-instances of some kind with which we are familiar: the folk will say, 'This is a cat but that is not'; the zoologist will say, 'This is an echidna but that is not'; the paleontologist will say, 'This is a pig's jawbone but that is not.'"[17] We should trust people's intuitions, the authors add, only to the degree that they are expert in the area in question. Doubtless, then, "This is a cat," at the lowest, commonsense level, merits least confidence. For, "Folk theories differ from scientific ones in being immature: they are less precise, systematic, and explicit; they lack a methodology for development. More seriously, they differ in being believed uncritically."[18]

Our discussion of Russell reveals possible problems with such talk, and its dangers. Russell's error was to identify sensation statements with one theory of sensation—a theory not held by the majority of those who presently make such statements, including Russell. Some speakers are naive realists, some are mediate realists, while others are idealists of one stripe or another. Yet they all speak of seeing trees, feeling the wind, hearing it howl through the branches, and so forth. And they are right to do so; for such everyday utterances are noncommittal, indicating no preference for one theory rather than another. "'Naive language,'" wrote Wittgenstein, "that is to say our naive, normal way of expressing ourselves, does not contain any theory of seeing—does not show you a *theory* but only a concept of seeing."[19]

The like holds for "This is a cat." Presented a bona fide specimen, a Platonist would agree (Platonically). So would an Aristotelian (distinguishing matter and form, substance and accidents). So would a Cartesian (splitting the cat into primary and secondary qualities). So would a Berkeleyan idealist (lumping the primary qualities with the secondary as divinely orchestrated appearances). So would a Kantian (distinguishing the cat phenomena from the thing in itself). So would a phenomenalist (dropping the thing in itself). So would chemists, physicists, and biologists (analyzing the cat in ways never dreamed of by earlier cat theorists). Which, then, is the theory expressed by saying "This is a cat?" No one of the above. The bond uniting those who make this "folk" judgment is a certain use of words. "They agree in the *language* they use," said Wittgenstein of such everyday utterances. "That is not agreement in opinions but in form of life."[20] When "folk theory" is challenged (e.g., concerning cats), such is often the implicit target, not clearly identified as such: the language used, the form of life.

In an important sense, often overlooked by critics of commonsense beliefs, language is neutral—neutral, yet also theory-laden. This paradoxical-sounding combination causes difficulties. How can language be neutral, it may be wondered, and how can it therefore be accepted as a reliable guide to predication, if it is theory-laden? Well, think again of "witch." When people believed in witches, the word was loaded with that theory. They believed that the women they called witches possessed supernatural powers. Yet even at that time they could employ the same term, in the same sense, to either affirm or deny the existence of witches: the mere word committed them neither way. It was, and is, theoretically neutral. Again, think of a term like "table." Though loaded with various scientific and philosophical theories, past and present, the word does not commit speakers to any one of them. They can deny matter, atoms, secondary qualities, things-in-themselves, or what have you and still say with the rest of us, "The table is set" or "The tables were arranged in a circle." And they should. "Table" is the right word for the objects in question.

Note, now, the general relevance of this discussion for the Issue of Language's Authority. In many ways, for many reasons, word meanings get conflated with theories or opinions.[21] Therewith, the presumption in favor of familiar meanings is reversed. It is evident that as a medium of communication, a language known to all is preferable to one known only to the speaker. It is equally evident that popular assumptions or theories are more likely to be mistaken than those of experts. Hence, once meanings are confused with theories, and everyday meanings with everyday opinions, the skepticism that the opinions often merit is transferred to the meanings. Appeals to respect established meanings sound obscurantist and ultraconservative. "If we philosophers want to get beyond the cake of 'common sense' and make any fresh discoveries or win any new perspectives," one critic characteristically declares, "this cult of 'ordinary language' will never do."[22] Established word uses (here lumped with "common sense") can and should be ignored. Tractarian practice can and should continue.

12

Malcolm and the "Ordinary-Language" Debate

THE PRECEDING TWO chapters cast some initial light on the murky twentieth-century debate about the authority of "ordinary language" in philosophy. However, more must be said about that controversy, for in the
history of Western thought it came closest to addressing the larger issue
that here interests us: the authority of language of whatever kind (familiar or exotic, natural or artificial) in discourse of whatever kind (philosophical, scientific, social, or other). Unfortunately, dispute swirled about
this unperceived center without focusing on it; the broader, more fundamental question of language's authority did not get stated or thrashed out
even at that most propitious moment. This failure largely accounts for the
impression of futility that lingers over the scene of battle half a century
later and for contemporary reluctance to revisit the issues there so badly
handled. To spot what went wrong, we can start with a much-discussed
piece, "Moore and Ordinary Language," by Norman Malcolm, Wittgenstein's friend and disciple.

Malcolm on Moore

Malcolm opens his account with a sample list of twelve philosophical
propositions, all of which had been or were then maintained by various
philosophers, and all of which Moore would deny in much the same fashion. "I think," Malcolm writes, "that showing the point and the justification of Moore's method of attacking this type of philosophical statement
will throw great light on the nature of philosophy, and also explain
Moore's importance in the history of philosophy."[1] To take the best-
known illustration, a philosopher claims, for example, that there are no
material things. Moore holds up his hands in refutation: here are two

hands, and they are material things. At first glance, this response to the skeptic appears no more impressive than Samuel Johnson's kicking a stone and exclaiming, "Thus I refute him!" However, Moore's appeals to common sense, Malcolm suggested, amounted to appeals to ordinary language and, as such, were justified. So, too, for the Russellian claim "All that one ever sees when one looks at a thing is part of one's own brain." To this Moore would typically reply: "This desk which both of us now see is most certainly not part of my brain, and, in fact, I have never seen a part of my own brain."[2] This answer is true, said Malcolm. Furthermore, it is "a *good* refutation, a refutation that shows the falsity of the statement in question."[3] It does this through an appeal to ordinary language. "The essence of Moore's technique of refuting philosophical statements consists in pointing out that these statements *go against ordinary language.*"[4]

In what sense do they "go against" ordinary language? At first Malcolm's exposition takes a surprising tack. The trouble with Russell's statements, he suggests, is not that they violate or deviate from ordinary language; rather, they make mistaken claims about ordinary language. Since Russell and Moore agree about the facts of the case, it appears "that they disagree, not about any empirical facts, but about what *language* shall be used to describe those facts. Russell was saying that it is really *a more correct way of speaking* to say that you see a part of your brain, than to say that you see the postman."[5] Thus:

> The philosophical statement, "All that one ever sees when one looks at a thing is part of one's brain" may be interpreted as meaning, "Whenever one looks at a thing it is really more correct language to say that one sees a part of one's brain, than to say that one sees the thing in question." And Moore's reply, "This desk which both of us see is not a part of my brain," may be interpreted as meaning, "It is correct language to say that what we are doing now is seeing a desk, and it is not correct language to say that what we are doing now is seeing parts of our brains."[6]

Malcolm thought that when the dispute is seen in this light, it is perfectly clear that Moore is right and Russell is wrong.[7]

This is unpersuasive.[8] In defense of any statement one has made, one may cite word usage as well as nonverbal facts (as Russell did, for example, in reply to Nagel); but this does not show that the statement was about words. As Roderick Chisholm noted, "From the fact that people use language differently . . . it does not follow that they disagree about language."[9] Disagreement *in* language should not be mistaken for disagreement *about* language. More basically, Malcolm's analysis in terms of "correct language" perpetuates the confusion to be clarified. If "language" means, for instance, the English language—a system of communication, then language is neither correct nor incorrect. It may be more or less suitable for its purposes, but it is not right or wrong. If, on the contrary, "language" means discourse—things we say, then language is correct or incorrect. For what we say is true or false. So the question remains: what makes Moore's saying true and Russell's false? In reply, Malcolm shifts to a second sense of "go against ordinary language": "Any philosophical statement which *violates* ordinary language is false."[10]

Malcolm might have backed this claim in the way already suggested. He might have distinguished between language as instrument and language as act—between individual terms and their customary uses on the one hand and complete statements on the other; and he might then have specified the former as the "ordinary language" with which philosophical assertions should conform whenever philosophers have not indicated other, special senses for their terms. However, this Malcolm did not do. The "ordinary expressions" whose customary use he defended were now individual words or phrases, now whole sentences, without distinction. Thus, at one point, in quick succession he identified the phrase "to the left of," the clause "it is certain that," and the sentence "There's a ghost" as "ordinary expressions." Since no living person may have ever heard or spoken the latter words ("There's a ghost"), he explained:

> By an "ordinary expression" I mean an expression which has an ordinary use, i.e., which is ordinarily used to describe a certain sort of situation. By this I do not mean that the expression need be one which is frequently used. It need only be an expression which *would* be used to describe situations of a certain sort, if situations of that sort were to exist, or were believed to exist. To be an ordinary expression it must have a commonly accepted *use*; it need not be the case that it is ever *used*. All of the above statements, which various philosophers have thought were self-contradictory, are ordinary expressions in this sense.[11]

Here Malcolm again takes the fatal turn to "statements," thereby invalidating his case and provoking legitimate objections. Suppose, as Malcolm suggests, that we either do or would all employ some sentence to "describe a certain sort of situation": what would make the description correct? Does it suffice that everyone agrees? Is common sense infallible? To answer these common objections, Malcolm would need to distinguish, say, between the word "ghost" and the utterances in which it might occur, and make a case for using the word in its familiar sense whenever no unfamiliar sense has been stipulated in its place. When you affirm or deny the existence of ghosts, he might enjoin, use the word "ghost" in its familiar sense. Mean by "ghost" what others mean by "ghost," then affirm or deny the existence of ghosts in that common sense of the term. Whether or not you agree with the common verdict, respect the language you are speaking. Unfortunately for his case and for the whole debate, Malcolm kept pointing in the opposite direction, away from individual words and toward whole sentences or statements. "On my view then," he later summarized, "Moore's so-called defence of Common Sense, in so far as it is an interesting and tenable philosophical position, has nothing to do either with common sense, properly speaking, nor common belief, but is merely the assertion, in regard to various *sentences*, that *those sentences* have a correct use in ordinary language."[12] The words that I have here italicized Malcolm wrote without emphasis, or recognition of their significance.

Chisholm's Critique

Citing ordinary sentences or statements rather than ordinary word meanings, Malcolm did not succeed in his general critique of paradoxical assertions such as those he listed. Specifically, he did not successfully critique Russell's paradoxical claims about sensation or come to grips with Russell's defense (not yet published when Malcolm wrote). However, even had he done so, in the way the last chapter suggested, Chisholm would not have been satisfied. "When, finally," he wrote,

> we *have* learned that a philosopher is using words incorrectly, what follows? Suppose the epistemologist does use the word "certain" incorrectly; he uses it, not as it is ordinarily used, but, say, to refer to a type of cognition which it would be logically impossible for any man to attain. Clearly, when we have pointed this out, we have not *refuted* him. To be sure, now that we *understand* him, we are no longer shocked by his statement that "certain," in his sense, does not apply to beliefs about the furniture. In all probability his statement which formerly seemed paradoxical now seems trivial and uninteresting. But we have not refuted him, since we have not shown that what he is saying is *false*. Indeed we now see, what we had not seen before, that what he is saying is *true*, since, presumably, our beliefs about the furniture *do not* have what he calls "certainty."[13]

Rather, I suggest, what he means is true; what his words say is not. But I shall not argue the point.[14] The views expressed are what matter, it may be urged, not the words that express them; and, as Chisholm notes, the views are not refuted by appeals to familiar forms of speech. They are perfectly correct. However, as Chisholm acknowledges, "When we show that the epistemologist's statement is trivial, we may not refute him, but possibly we will *silence* him."[15] He will no longer utter common platitudes in paradoxical, misleading terminology. In the circumstances, this is the appropriate—and important—result. It answers this study's interest in what we should and should not say. It recognizes the authority of language.

Chisholm's conflation of what a speaker means and what the words mean, together with his insistence on the truth of the former, veils both the nature and the seriousness of the "correctness" of which he speaks. Russell, a master of the English language, would deny that he was "using words incorrectly." So would other thinkers who have used words as Russell did. Thus the ordinary-language philosophers were raising no idle issue; they just failed to clarify the nature of their legitimate complaint. So Russellian practice continues and objections are brushed aside. Thanks to the ordinary-language controversy, many suppose, we now know better than to take such criticism seriously. Chisholm dealt with it long ago, as did others—for instance, Herman Tennessen.

Tennessen on Austin

In a paper titled "Permissible and Impermissible Locutions," Tennessen wrote: "When the late John Austin was in Norway, October, 1959, he is reported to have made the following statements: 'That there are rules prohibiting something from being said, does not say more than that we never say so and so.' And: 'We say there is a rule against saying X, when X is never said.'"[16] In these and similar sayings Tennessen detects "the underlying assumption that *natural language* is in a way, at least *'in its ordinary employment,' perfect and unimpeachable, consistent and complete in itself—incorrigible*, so to speak."[17]

Against Austin's reported formulae, Tennessen objects: "Ample material from several empirio-semantic investigations point to some rather obvious fallacies in any attempt to reject a locution (as nonsensical, logically odd or otherwise impermissible) on grounds of its linguistic non-occurrence—*without taking into consideration the most likely reason for its scarcity*."[18] People may refrain from saying something because they all consider it a false hypothesis (e.g., "The Earth is flat"). Or certain sentences may not be uttered "because they are unanimously interpreted to express platitudes or otherwise idle and uncalled for, obviously, undoubtedly true or advisable propositions. Thus if, in a perfectly normal situation a normal person is yawning a normal yawn, it is clear that we should neither say: 'That person is *not* yawning now,' *nor* should we (ever or ordinarily) say: 'That person is yawning.'"[19]

As quoted, Austin's claims do invite criticism. Had he adverted to Tennessen's counterexamples, he might have distinguished, more carefully than reported, between those cases and the kind he had in mind. To illustrate the latter, let us imagine a little exchange. Russell says, "I see my brain." Austin replies, "People never say that." How might Russell respond? Not: "That's because it is so obvious." Nor: "That's because it is so obviously false." Nagel considered it obviously false, but Russell did not. And if most people would agree with Nagel, doubtless the reason extends beyond this single saying. "I see my brain" represents a whole class of excluded sayings: "He looked down and saw his brain," "She opened the window and gazed upon her brain," "Sunsets are my favorite time to see my brain." It is generally true that people are not said to see their own brains when their skulls are intact and their gaze is directed elsewhere, but are said to see objects toward which their gaze is directed. Such is the use of "see" in the English language. The exclusion of "That person is yawning" is not similarly explained, by the contrary use of "yawn" in the English language, but rather by the obviousness of the particular yawn in question and of the term's applicability to it.

This response again points away from whole utterances and toward individual meanings or word uses as arbiters of predication. However, it does no more than gesture in this general direction, and neither, on the whole, do the accounts offered by "ordinary-language" philosophers in the last century. Thus there was much truth in C. W. K. Mundle's complaint: "Philosophers sometimes make dogmatic and false statements that something is said, or cannot or may not be said, without apparently being willing to endorse any general rules about language from which these statements would follow. This is what I call 'legislative linguistics.'"[20] He explained: "'Legislative linguistics' is to mean the practice of making false assertions about what we do say, or do not or cannot or may not say, in the interests of some philosophical theory or thesis, but without formulating or being willing to endorse any general rule(s) or principle(s) about language from which these assertions would follow."[21]

John Austin came closest to answering this challenge when he proposed an account, now to be examined, of what makes statements true. Had his analysis been more adequate and translatable into a general norm of predication, it might have furnished the kind of general rule or principle that Mundle failed to find in ordinary-language philosophy.

13

Austin, Statements,
and Their Truth

A T THE END of the previous chapter I suggested, counterfactually, that Austin's analysis of truth, if adequate and translatable into a norm of predication, might have furnished the sort of general rule that Mundle requested. Passing from the analysis to the norm, Austin might have spelled out the role of language in determining what we should say. For reasons that will appear, Austin's analysis was not, in fact, completely adequate, and would not have yielded a completely satisfactory norm of predication, had he explicitly proposed it as a norm. Even if revised, it is doubtful that the analysis could have yielded a comprehensive, exceptionless norm, covering all assertions. Comprehensive, exceptionless, substantive norms of any kind are difficult to come by. Nonetheless, if refined, Austin's attempt might furnish the best general guidance available. Truth may not always be an overriding consideration and lying may not always be wrong. However, in philosophy, at least, and in intellectual endeavors generally, truth appears such a dominant consideration that any account that illumines truth may thereby illumine the issue on which this study is centered—that of language's authority.

Austin on Truth

In his opening contribution to a 1950 symposium on truth, Austin proposed to address the question "What is truth?" by focusing on the uses of the word "true." In his view, these are various. "We say (or are said to say) that beliefs are true, that descriptions or accounts are true, that propositions or assertions or statements are true, and that words or sentences are true: and this is to mention only a selection of the more obvious candidates."[1] The primary ascription, Austin argued, is not to mere sentences, whose truth value may vary from utterance to utterance, or to beliefs or abstract propositions, but to statements, in the sense of individual utterances or speech acts. "A statement is made and its making is a historic event, the utterance by a certain speaker or writer of certain words (a sentence) to an audience with reference to a historic situation, event or what not."[2] For such utterances to do their job, there must be a stock of symbols of some kind (the "words"), something other than the symbols (the "world") that the symbols are used to communicate about, and two sets of conventions relating the symbols to the world: *descriptive* conventions correlating the words with the *types* of situation, thing, event, and so on, to be found in the world, and *demonstrative* conventions correlating the words with the *historic* situations, and so on, to be found in the world. Applying this distinction to the query "When is a statement true?" Austin replies: "A statement is said to be true when the historic state of affairs to which it is correlated by the demonstrative conventions (the one to which it 'refers') is of a type with which the sentence used in making it is correlated by the descriptive conventions."[3] In the presence, say, of a feline stretched on a mat, I say, "The cat is on the mat," and thereby pick out a historic situation of a kind conventionally characterized in those terms. Not that this cat exactly resembles the things previously called "cats" or the mat exactly resembles the things previously called "mats" or the position of this cat on this mat exactly resembles the positions of the things previously said to be "on" other things; but the historic situation picked out by the utterance "is sufficiently like those standard states of affairs" with which the sentence used in making the utterance is correlated by the descriptive conventions.[4] What degree of likeness counts as sufficient, Austin does not specify. He just sketches and defends this general account of what makes statements true.

From this much, Austin's general reply to the Issue of Language's Authority is clear. Neither the cat on the mat, by itself, nor the English language's descriptive and demonstrative conventions, by themselves, determine the truth of the utterance "The cat is on the mat." The reality and the language do the job together, in the manner described. And the like holds for any assertion. Thus, in Austin's view language figures as a determinant—indeed as the chief determinant, together with the reality described—of utterances' truth. The amendments that I shall consider to Austin's formulation will not alter this verdict. Neither will they affect what, in the following list, appear important virtues of his account:

1. Austin's broad acceptance, in accordance with common usage, of beliefs, propositions, sentences, and utterances as true (or false) seems commendable. He does not assert, for example, that "When we ascribe truth (or falsity) to beliefs and statements we do not ascribe it to believings or statings, but rather to *what is believed* and *what is stated*"[5] (that

is, to the abstract propositional content of the beliefs and statements). Argumentation in favor of such a reductive, essentialistic thesis would have to ignore the complex, fluctuating facts of linguistic usage, in the manner of the *Tractatus*.[6] The preferable alternative, it seems, is to note how, and in what sense, beliefs, propositions, sentences, and utterances, respectively, may be called true; how the truth of each relates to that of the others; and where, if anywhere amid all this multiplicity, conceptual primacy lies—as Austin does.

2. Focusing on utterances rather than on abstract propositions or be-liefs (which belong to no language), Austin's analysis indicates the kind of linguistic basis on which we do make our truth assessments when, for in-stance, we respond, "That's true," or, "Truer words were never spoken."[7] The fact that beliefs and propositions are linguistically expressed, in some specific language, veils their inadequacy as guides to predication, much as Plato's naming his Forms with Greek terms veiled their nonlinguistic na-ture and consequent inability to indicate what they or anything else should be called. To assess the truth of the utterance, "These sticks are equal in length," the Form Equality is no help, and neither is the proposition thus expressed. The English sentence "These sticks are equal in length" is at least linguistic and contains expressions of a specific language, with demonstrative, descriptive, and other conventions; but of course the sen-tence's mere words (not uttered, on any occasion, in any context) do not suffice by themselves to establish their truth or falsehood. Thus, for a more adequate account of when and why we apply the word "true," Austin looked in the right direction—to sentences as used, to utterances.

3. Focusing on utterances rather than bare words, and on their rela-tionship to language and the world, Austin's analysis counteracts the ten-dency we have so frequently observed to overlook language and its relevance for truth. Even Donald Davidson, close student of language though he was, could write: "If we ask, for example, what makes the sen-tence 'The moon is a quarter of a million miles away' true, the only answer we come up with is that it is the fact that the moon is a quarter of a million miles away."[8] Austin would suggest that an account of what makes the sen-tence true would have to say something about the sentence—about its use in an utterance (actual or assumed), the language spoken, its words, and its conventions. The moon by itself gets us no farther than Plato's sticks.

4. Since the features Austin cites are all well-known (e.g., the use of "mat" to name mats and of "cat" to name cats) and do guide our appli-cation of "true," his analysis faces no problem of self-reference. He may plausibly claim that his own statements about true utterances pass the same test as those about mats and cats. They accurately describe, in the manner prescribed, "historical states of affairs" of kinds commonly char-acterized as "true."

5. Since Austin does not confuse the truth of an utterance with our knowing its truth, his account extends truth beyond verification or even the possibility of verification. For instance, it may be true to say that Charlemagne's favorite color was magenta even if there is no evidence warranting the assertion nor any prospect of such evidence turning up.[9] Unbeknownst to us, the assertion may satisfy both of Austin's criteria: the demonstrative and the descriptive.

6. The symbols which Austin cites are not whole sentences, as in Malcolm, but individual words or other devices (e.g., signal flags) employed in making statements.[10] This opens the possibility, not developed by Austin, that assertions made by the whole populace may still be wrong. All, for example, may say that the earth is flat, yet the reality referred to may not be of the kind conventionally called "flat."[11]

7. Austin's analysis indicates a possible escape from the kind of circle mentioned earlier: defining a true statement as one expressing a true belief, then a true belief as one expressed by a true statement; or, defining a true proposition as one stated by a true utterance, then a true utterance as one stating a true proposition. For reasons developed more fully elsewhere than in chapter 4 and in these present remarks,[12] I believe that Austin was right in his choice of exit, via utterances, and no doubt Austin chose the one he did because he found it more enlightening. Beliefs, propositions, and utterances are not true for independent reasons, and the truth of utterances throws more light on that of beliefs and propositions than vice versa.

8. Specifically, Austin's focus on words and linguistic conventions resolves problems of reference and resemblance that prove insurmountable for mentalistic conceptions of truth. Chapter 1 questioned the possibility of nonverbally thinking the sense of any sentence in that chapter, or in philosophical writings generally, and chapter 4 added the everyday statement "This summer I vacationed in Switzerland." No nonverbal mental representation can pinpoint the referent of the name "Switzerland," but the name can, thanks to the demonstrative conventions of the language. So, too, no mental portrayal can depict the event described (the person's summer vacation in Switzerland), save in the spotty way book illustrations do; but the words can: thanks to the descriptive conventions of the language, they can accurately convey the time, person, place, and activity.[13]

9. The resulting "correspondence" holds, not between beliefs or propositions and the world but between use and usage, world and world: between the thing called a "cat" and other things called "cats," between the thing called a "mat" and other things called "mats," between the country referred to as "Switzerland" and the country previously referred to by that name, and so forth. The correspondence is now stronger and less problematic than in those rival accounts.[14]

10. This Austinian analysis makes sense, dialectically, of the common conviction that true statements "correspond with reality." The thesis that puts the correspondence in the mind's mirroring of reality is mistaken. So is the antithesis that, noting this error, denies all correspondence. The synthesis that retains the truth in both thesis and antithesis recognizes correspondence but locates it in language, this comprehensive form of life (speakers, hearers, speech acts, surrounding world), not in the mind.

11. From such an account, with its strong, world-world correspondence (cats with cats, mats with mats, etc.), we can sense the importance of truth and why people have valued it so highly. Correspondence matters. So does conformity with conventions, for there could be no successful linguistic communication without them. If you inadvertently tell a person the ice is thick, meaning it is thin, your hearer's subsequent fate may strikingly attest the importance of "mere conventions."[15]

12. Given these merits, Austin's analysis might also serve as a norm of predication: as a rule, when making statements we should employ words in the way described. If valid, such a general norm, dictating how words should be used in every area and type of discourse, would have greater significance than the analysis of the way the single word "true" is in fact employed. However, some of the objections urged against Austin's analysis would also tell against a norm derived from it.

Strawson's Critique

In the 1950 symposium, Peter Strawson was Austin's first respondent. Many at the time considered Strawson's criticisms decisive. While his objections do have some force, the one he urged with strongest emphasis does not. "Certainly," he wrote, "we use the word 'true' when the semantic conditions described by Austin are fulfilled; but we do not, in using the word, *state* that they are fulfilled."[16] It is "absurd" to suppose that we "assert" any such thing.[17] It is "*patently* false" to suggest that in calling a statement true we "talk about" the meanings of the words or "say" that they have been correctly used.[18] Austin might agree. For he posed and answered his question in the way Strawson approved. He asked "When is a statement true?" and answered with the formula quoted, which begins with the words "A statement is said to be true when . . ." Similarly, to the question "When is it raining," one might reply, "It is said to be raining when drops of water are falling from clouds." And though a person who says "It's raining" does not assert that these truth-conditions are satisfied, or "talk about" the water, drops, and clouds, surely these items belong in any account of what the utterance means. So, too, may the configuration Austin describes belong in an analysis of "That's true."[19]

A second objection of Strawson's has more validity. The term "true," he contends, serves to *assert*, not to *describe*. Granted, we may respond "That's true" after hearing an utterance, and we may therefore suppose that "true" describes the utterance. However, consider such a statement as, "It is true that the general health of the community has improved (that *p*), but this is due only to the advance in medical science." On the use of "true" in the first part of this specimen statement, Strawson comments:

> It is not necessary that anyone should have said that *p*, in order for this to be a perfectly proper observation. In making it, I am not talking *about* an actual or possible speech-episode. I am myself asserting that *p*, in a certain way, with a certain purpose. I am anticipatorily conceding, in order to neutralize, a possible objection. I forestall someone's making the statement that *p* by making it myself, with additions. It is of prime importance to distinguish the fact that the use of "true" always glances backwards or forwards to the actual or envisaged making of a statement by someone, from the theory that it is used to characterize such (actual or possible) episodes.[20]

Strawson, then, denies that the adjective "true" is descriptive and views it as assertive. When I call "*p*" true, he argues, I am asserting that *p*; I am not describing the assertion. Indeed, I am not describing anything.

In defense of his descriptive analysis, Austin had cited different verbal specimens—"His closing words were very true" and "The third sentence on page 5 of his speech is quite false"—which more readily lend themselves to his interpretation.[21] Thus, some evidence points one way, some the other. There is no need, however, to declare this debate a draw. It appears that "true," like many another concept, is bipolar, and that Austin had hold of one pole and Strawson had hold of the other. For comparison, consider the "performative" utterances that Austin made famous. "I forbid you" does not describe an act of forbidding, whereas "He forbade me" does. Similarly, "It is true that *p*" does not describe any utterance, whereas "He spoke true words" does.[22] Continuing the comparison, we can see that, as the nondescriptive occurrences of "forbid" do not preclude a description of forbidding, so the nondescriptive occurrences of "true" do not preclude a description of truth. For both terms have a descriptive as well as a nondescriptive use. Austin may have been one-sided in the evidence he considered, but that does not invalidate his account in the way Strawson alleged.[23]

A third objection is more telling. It may seem relatively plausible, Strawson suggests, to say that the statement (made by me to you) that the cat is on the mat is true is to say that the three-dimensional state of affairs with which the episode of my making the statement is correlated by the demonstrative conventions is of a type with which the sentence I use is correlated by the descriptive conventions. Other species of fact, however, have long been known to present more difficulty: the fact that the cat is not on the mat, for example, or the fact that there are white cats, or that cats persecute mice, or that if you give my cat an egg it will smash it and eat the contents.[24]

Consider, for example, the simplest of these cases, those involving negation. "With what type of state-of-affairs (chunk of reality) is the sentence 'The cat is not on the mat' correlated by conventions of description? With a mat *simpliciter*? With a dog on a mat? With a cat up a tree?"[25] What is more, though a negative utterance such as "The cat is not on the mat" at least employs demonstrative conventions, not all statements do. "Existential statements don't, nor do statements of (even relatively) unrestricted generality."[26] (Think of "Cats exist" or "All cats, actual or hypothetical, are animals.")

Geoffrey Warnock extends Strawson's list of countercases. Austin's formula speaks of "the historic state of affairs" with which a statement is correlated, yet there are "analytic statements, or theorems in logic, or in mathematics; these of course are not asserted on empirical grounds, and there is no question here of our needing to know which 'states of affairs in the world' would be relevant to their truth or falsity, since none would be so relevant; but surely we do often apply to them the predicate 'true.'"[27] Austin's account appears too narrow by far.[28]

On Austin's behalf, it might be pointed out that he said a statement is true "when" his formula is satisfied, not "only when" it is. Strictly speaking, therefore, he stated a sufficient but not a necessary condition of statements' truth. There are indications, however, that he understood his question "When is a statement true?" more broadly. For he drew no distinction between "when" and "only when," and acknowledged no statements for which his account does not hold. In any case, the implication seems clear: if we desire a general norm of predication, covering all kinds of statements (historical, logical, mathematical, hypothetical, existential, etc.), Austin's analysis of "true" cannot provide it. Not as it stands.

14

A Lead Overlooked

From Meaning to Truth

Fʀᴏᴍ ᴛʜᴇ ᴘᴇʀsᴘᴇᴄᴛɪᴠᴇ of this study, the "ordinary language" dispute of the last century is the story of two missed opportunities. First, as already noted, the Issue of Language's Authority rose close to the surface but was never stated or debated. Discussion did not focus on the question: What authority should *language*—ordinary or extraordinary, standard or stipulated—exercise as a determinant of utterances' truth or assertability? Second, Austin's analysis of utterances' truth, which responded to this unasked query, met initial objections and was not carried further. This was a pity, for his account had numerous merits, and came close to satisfying Mundle's plea for a guiding norm; and ideas were then circulating that could have served to remedy the principal defect of Austin's formulation—namely, its incomplete coverage.

Most people would agree that the truth of utterances of any kind depends to a considerable measure on the meanings of the expressions—words, names, numerals, and so on—that they contain. If, then, we could clarify the nature of these "meanings," the way to a less restrictive account of truth than Austin's might become apparent. And from such an account of what makes utterances true, a norm might derive of the kind Mundle found wanting, to guide our use of words. Since, therefore, Wittgenstein famously addressed the question of word meanings, let us look again, from this new perspective, at what he said on the subject.

Wittgenstein on Word Meanings

We have already noted Wittgenstein's suggestion that, on many occasions, when we speak of a word's meaning we are speaking of its "use in the language." For his therapeutic purposes, he felt no need to spell out this suggestion. He did not need to indicate occasions on which the word "meaning" has some other sense (for example, when we speak of a word's meaning in a specific utterance and not in the language as a whole); nor did he need to define precisely what he meant by the "use" of a word in the language. It is clear, however, that the occasions and contexts Wittgenstein had in mind are of prime philosophical significance and have relevance, specifically, for assessing the truth of utterances. And the kind of "use" he had in mind but left undefined reveals traits that are pertinent for such assessment. In his view, such word use is:

Versatile: To the query "how many kinds of sentence are there?" Wittgenstein responded: "There are *countless* kinds: countless different kinds of use of what we call 'symbols,' 'words,' 'sentences.'"[1] Utterances have this diversity, and individual words and symbols have corresponding versatility. To cite Wittgenstein's illustrations, a given word can be used in issuing orders, asking, thanking, cursing, greeting, praying—as also in describing an object, giving its measurements, reporting an event, explaining an event, and other varieties of utterance characterized as true or false.

Specific: A given word shares these varied uses—reporting, explaining, describing, and so forth—with countless other expressions. What distinguishes its "use in the language" from theirs is the specific part it plays in these varied utterances. If someone says, "The weather is fine this morning," each component expression—"the," "weather," "is," "fine," "this," and "morning"—makes its own distinctive contribution to the total utterance.

Varied: In such an utterance, each word's contribution is not only distinctive but also very different—that of "the" from that of "morning," that of "fine" from that of "this," that of "is" from that of "weather," and so forth. Thus, as a single, uniform account cannot be given of the use of hammers, nails, vises, bevels, and cranes, so a single account cannot be given of the use of "if," "maybe," "sugar," "percentage," and "amen." The uses of even a single word may vary greatly. (Think of "in": "in a room," "in love," "in a hurry," "in debt," "in tune," "in time," "in good health," etc.)

Comprehensive: The "uses" of expressions—those on which meaning and truth depend—consist of much more than phonetics or grammar. The use of "I," for example, can no more be explained without mentioning the speaker, or the use of "see" without mentioning eyes and light, or the use of "rain" without mentioning clouds and drops of water, than the use of a hammer can be explained without mentioning people, hands, nails, boards, movements, and the like. As Wittgenstein famously put it, "Only in the stream of thought and life do words have meaning."[2]

Flexible: "How should we explain to someone what a game is?" asked Wittgenstein. "I imagine," he replied, "that we should describe *games* to him, and we might add: 'This *and similar things* are called "games."' And do we know any more about it ourselves? Is it only other people whom we cannot tell exactly what a game is?—But this is not ignorance. We do not know the boundaries because none have been drawn."[3] Here as often, "the extension of the concept is *not* closed by a frontier."[4] Still, not everything counts as a game.

Limited: A word can be stretched, but only so far. How far? Until it bumps into another word. "Red" is surrounded by "orange," "pink," "yellow," and "purple." "Rain" is surrounded by "sleet," "snow," "hail," and "mist." "Chair" is surrounded by "stool," "couch," "sofa," "table," and "desk." "In" is surrounded by "on," "under," "above," and "outside." "Now" is surrounded by "then," "tomorrow," "yesterday," and "hereafter." Each word in a language is bordered by competing terms, each occupying its own position on the conceptual map, each doing its own job. This is how the language needs to be, for effective communication. Some parts of the map (e.g., color terms in English, camel terms in desert lands) are tightly packed with competing expressions, some less densely, and in some directions the terrain is relatively unoccupied. Here, with little competition, terms may freely stretch in the manner Wittgenstein illustrated: "We extend our concept of number as in spinning a thread we twist fibre on fibre."[5] "Red" or "rain" would be more closely circumscribed, but as mathematics ventures out into new areas, we extend the word "number" from cardinal numbers to the integers, rational numbers, and real numbers, and finally to the complex and hypercomplex, without encountering any rival expression in these previously uncharted spaces.

Truth Reformulated

From these Wittgensteinian reflections there emerges a possible substitute for Austin's truth formula. Without mentioning descriptive and demonstrative conventions (though embracing them), the new formula says more broadly:

> A statement is true if, and only if, its use of terms resembles more closely the established uses of terms (whether standard or stipulated) than would the substitution of any rival, incompatible expression.[6]

This revision retains the virtues of Austin's formulation but remedies its chief defect, its narrowness. Strawson's and Warnock's countercases now occasion no difficulty. "The cat is not on the mat" satisfies this test, and so does "No part is greater than the whole" or "Three plus five equals eight."

The formula also resolves the problem Austin left dangling when he explained: "for a statement to be true one state of affairs must be *like* certain others, which is a natural relation, but also *sufficiently* like to merit the same 'description,' which is no longer a purely natural relation."[7] In many respects raccoons resemble cats and carpets resemble mats; so what makes it true to say that a cat is on the mat but false to say a *raccoon* is on the mat or that a cat is on the *carpet*? How close must the resemblance be? Austin offered no indication. However, these simple examples suggest a possible reply: the required similarity is relative to the rest of language. Each of these things—cats, raccoons, mats, carpets—has its own name. And the names may be stretched, indeed may be stretched considerably, but not if they trespass on the territory occupied by competing expressions. Thus, the requisite degree of similarity cannot be stated absolutely, but only relatively to the rest of the language; and the proposed formulation, which does precisely this, may therefore be labeled the "Principle of Relative Similarity."

The principle's formulation is still rough. For instance, it accepts but does not explicate the notion of greater or less similarity between things,[8] or the notion that some expressions (e.g., "cat" and "raccoon") are incompatible whereas others (e.g., "cat" and "animal") are not. Nonetheless, the principle looks roughly right. On the one hand, for the cat on the mat it rules out "A *raccoon* is on the mat," "The cat is on a *carpet*," or "The cat is *under* the mat." "Cat," "mat," and "on" successfully compete with "raccoon," "carpet," and "under." Less obviously, so more interestingly, the Principle of Relative Similarity also rules out Russell's assertion that we see our brains; his denials that we see, hear, feel, taste, or smell objects; and all their many philosophical kin (see chapter 11). On the other hand, the principle rightly does not exclude, for example, atoms being split or computers playing "chess." The computer is not a human being; it sits before no board, moves no pieces. Yet, as a description of its activity, "chess" comes closer than "checkers," "poker," or any other rival expression. So we do say, truly, "Deep Blue beat Kasparov in chess."

Still, do these new definitional borders coincide with those the word "true" traces when it is applied to statements? Consider this case. I draw a figure on the blackboard. I am inclined to call it a "wavy circle" or a "circle with wavy borders," for it is the figure one could generate by drawing two concentric circles then joining them by a wavy line. This wavy figure resembles a circle more than it resembles a triangle, octagon, square, or ellipse. "Circle" comes closest. So is it true to say simply, as the Principle of Relative Similarity would suggest, that I drew a circle on the board? Not at all clearly. Thus, in its defense, proponents of the principle might invoke their "intuition" that the statement does qualify as true, while opponents might cite their contrary "intuitions." We would then be back in the no-man's-land explored by chapter 9. Since the principle's verdict in this instance is clearly favorable and the truth verdict is not, the principle's border does not clearly coincide with that of "true."

What, though, of a norm based on the Principle of Relative Similarity, prescribing or approving the use of words in keeping with the principle's specifications? Though it may not be clearly true to say I drew a circle on the board, is "circle" a word I should or may use in describing the figure I drew? Well, not tout court. "Rough circle" would be better, and "wavy circle" would be better still. The norm picks the right general term ("circle," rather than "square," "ellipse," or "octagon") but it does not go far enough. Though approved by the norm, "circle" by itself might be misleading, and would raise objections. People might disagree about whether I had drawn a circle just as they might disagree about whether the statement was true. Here, then, the verdict on both the Principle of Relative Similarity and its derivative norm (call it the Norm of Linguistic Correspondence) is the same: both the analysis and the norm are too rough to be more than roughly right.

So, should they be refined, or should they be abandoned, or should they be left as they stand, to serve as useful guideposts? These are the chief options—the typical options—that surface at this point.

Three Forks in the Road

Chapter 9, using the example "know," suggested the limits of analytic refinement. Some cases are clear instances of the class in question (e.g., knowledge); some are not but elicit divergent "intuitions." In these latter cases, similarity suggests a positive verdict, dissimilarity suggests a negative verdict, and neither verdict has the backing of the word's application to standard, familiar cases. So it is here. Similarity suggests a favorable verdict on "I drew a circle," while dissimilarity suggests an unfavorable verdict; neither verdict can be educed from existing usage. So, emulating the endless efforts to sharpen the analysis of "know," we might exercise similar ingenuity with regard to "true." However, it is not clear how a modified version of the Principle of Relative Similarity or the corresponding Norm of Linguistic Correspondence could accommodate even this present example, much less all conceivable countercases.

"I drew a circle" would be misleading; "I drew a wavy circle" would not. "Circle" would signal the sameness, "wavy" would signal the difference, and communication would succeed. Similarly (to anticipate the next chapter), it would be misleading to call D_2O simply "water," but not to call it "heavy water." Again, "water" signals the similarity, "heavy" signals the difference. Such extensions, assisted by appropriate modifiers, are familiar, handy, and perfectly legitimate. So a norm of predication might validly endorse them. How, though, could the Norm of Linguistic Correspondence be reworded to accommodate them? How might "appropriate" modifiers be more definitely characterized? Even if we hit on an answer, it would not suffice. For consider again talk of computers playing chess. Here the noun "chess" signals the sameness, while "computers" signals the difference; so the extension works perfectly well. Yet in "Computers play chess," "computers" does not *modify* "chess." Perhaps, then, for more comprehensive coverage, we might stipulate the same basic condition as in the Principle of Relative Similarity (that is, greater similarity compared to rival expressions) but add a general proviso about *somehow* signaling both similarity and difference—when necessary. However, when is that? When does context do what modifiers or subject terms do? When are no such indications necessary?

Other problems could be cited,[9] but I need not insist. The first option, further refinement, does not look promising. What, then, of the second option, rejection? Among philosophers, especially of an analytic bent, one senses this common attitude: If a principle or theory fails at any point, it is false and should be amended; if it cannot be amended, it should be rejected. All or nothing.[10] One can understand this attitude, especially with regard to a concept such as "true." If we seek to determine the truth of an assertion, it is no help to be told, for example, "On most occasions an assertion can be judged by the Principle of Relative Similarity." On what occasions, and is this occasion one of them? If the occasions on which the test applies can be discriminated from those on which it doesn't apply, why not include the discriminating conditions in the formula? If such conditions cannot be discerned or indicated, what good is the formula?

In analytic philosophical circles, theoretical objections might weigh more heavily than pragmatic. If employed as a universal premise, a merely approximative principle like that of Relative Similarity can cause problems for valid inference. And an ill-defined, irregular conception cannot figure in the sort of interlocking scheme often aspired to. For example, with regard to our present focus, on meaning and truth, we read:

> By treating one or a few conceptual connections as basic, we might well hope to exhibit the rest as their consequences. The ideal would be to produce an analysis of the concept of meaning that would manifestly be a solution to the whole set of "equations" into which this concept enters. All of the important internal relations between meaning and other notions (denotation, truth, evidence, explanation, communication, etc.) would flow from this analysis.[11]

The aim of such systematization is to reveal, or perhaps to introduce, some order into the real or apparent chaos of conceptual connections—not to capture the complexities of existing usage by means of ever-more-refined formulations, still less to rest content with imprecise generalizations.

Such ambitions have their problems. What, precisely, one may wonder, is the nature and the point of such a systematizing enterprise? If someone proposed to trim the shifting, irregular clouds in the sky to make them fit together more neatly, we would wish to hear more about the purpose of the exercise. If we were told that the result would reveal more clearly the underlying configuration of the clouds, we would feel more acutely the need for clarification. Leaving until chapter 20 a less figurative statement of such misgivings, let us turn now to the third option for the Principle of Relative Similarity and its corresponding norm: rather than refine them or discard them, should we perhaps accept them as they stand, to serve as useful guideposts?

"It is virtually never possible," notes Michael Scriven, "to express the full meaning of a term in common use (or deeply embedded in a technical domain of discourse) by means of an explicit definition, though such definitions may provide a useful shorthand, with specific, limited purposes."[12] The Principle of Relative Similarity might serve, specifically and limitedly, as a reliable rule of thumb (not a rigid, exceptionless rule) for predication. So understood, it would be comparable, I suggest, to a directive such as "Tell the truth." Exceptional cases arise for which this general rule may not hold and which might have to be judged individually on their merits, but they do not negate the rule's general validity and utility. People should generally tell the truth. Similarly, exceptional cases arise for which the Principle of Relative Similarity and its corresponding norm may not hold and which may have to be judged individually on their merits, but they do not negate the general validity and utility of the analysis and the norm. If people should generally tell the truth, and if the Principle of Relative Similarity is roughly right about truth, then they should generally speak as the principle indicates: their use of terms should resemble more closely the established use of terms than would the substitution of any rival, incompatible expression.[13]

Such a verdict, if valid for all predication, in whatever context, would hold a fortiori in philosophy and other disciplines. In their lectures, conversations, and writings on freedom, foreknowledge, causation, the mind-body problem, and the like, philosophers have slight occasion to mention "wavy circles," indulge in rhetorical exaggeration, or speak in other ways that raise difficulties for the exceptionless validity of the norm of Linguistic Correspondence. Relatively rare in general discourse, such possible exceptions to the Norm are still rarer in philosophical, scientific, or other learned discussion. And when they do arise, they pose little problem: regardless of where the border for "true" or its corresponding norm may fall, we may call the figure a wavy circle or utter the exaggeration, as appropriate. The Norm of Linguistic Correspondence is relevant for more numerous, serious, problematic cases of kinds met and to be met throughout the present study. So might a defense of the third option go.

Doubtless such a defense will strike some as weak and wanting in rigor. In response I might answer as Wittgenstein did, who was all too familiar with the demand for ever-greater precision:

> But isn't it an inexact explanation?—Yes; why shouldn't we call it "inexact"? Only let us understand what "inexact" means. For it does not mean "unusable." And let us consider what we call an "exact" explanation in contrast with this one. Perhaps something like drawing a chalk line round an area? Here it strikes us at once that the line has breadth. So a colour-edge would be more exact. But has this exactness still got a function here: isn't the engine idling?[14]

A Carnapian explication might look more impressive, but what purpose would be served by circumscribing the concept "true" with pinpoint precision on all sides, and how could it be done? How, for a start, might a sharp line be drawn between the figures we readily call circles and the questionable wavy variety, so as to prescribe precisely what figures may truly be described as circular? And what would be the point of such precision? How, more generally, might a single defining formula for "true" ward off vagueness in all directions, not only with regard to all the expressions in the dictionary ("circle," "game," "water," "rule," "number," "chess," "in," etc.) but also, for instance, with regard to the class of utterances covered by the formula (statements, reports, descriptions, explanations, etc.)? And what possible utility could all this nitpicking have? Persistence in this direction would, I fear, invite Wittgenstein's comment: "They are always scuttling around on the surface of questions & do not generally see the really essential thing. When, however, the real task is accomplished, many of those superficial games become obsolete or have to be completely reinterpreted."[15] Endless refining of language does not assure sharper perception of reality, especially when, as in much analytic theorizing, the two things—language and reality—are not clearly distinguished.

I have developed and defended the Principle of Relative Similarity and its norm more fully elsewhere.[16] To that extent they belong, if only peripherally, to the story here being recounted. However, this personal contribution fits within a larger picture. Clearly, the truth of statements depends somehow, to some extent, on the language used and not solely

on the reality described. Clearly, that truth and that relationship determine to some extent how we should formulate our statements. We may
not entirely ignore the instrument we are using. Just as evidently, however, there is no agreement in the philosophical community on the truth-
making or statement-guiding role of language. Indeed, at present there is
widespread disinterest in clarifying language's role. Various reasons
could be suggested for this lack of interest, including some already noted.
However, whatever the explanation, the present chapter's formulations
call attention to this gaping hole in our philosophical understanding, and
implicitly ask: If this is not a satisfactory account of language's relation to
truth and assertability, what is? The question of language's authority is
too fundamental to be ignored.

As it stands, the Norm of Linguistic Correspondence is flexible. It al-
lows, indeed recommends, that we call atoms "atoms" after we have discovered that they can be split, Earth "Earth" after we have discovered that
it is spherical or is not the center of the planetary system, and so forth.
However, some linguistic philosophers, whose views we shall now examine, would probably consider such a norm too loose and would therefore
answer the question of language's authority somewhat differently.

15

Kripke, Putnam, and Rigid Designation

IN THE 1970S, Saul Kripke and Hilary Putnam advanced a doctrine of "rigid designation" whose relevance for the Issue of Language's Authority can be suggested by Putnam's "Twin-Earth" fantasy. Let us imagine, wrote Putnam, that somewhere a planet exists which exactly duplicates ours, except that the liquid there called "water," which in all superficial respects resembles what we call "water," does not consist of H_2O but rather of XYZ (an abbreviated formula for something very long and complicated). Now, doubtless the Norm of Linguistic Correspondence formulated in the previous chapter would endorse our calling this Twin-Earth stuff "water," or at least "Twin-Earth water," for "water" comes closer than any rival expression. We have no competing term for any stuff with that XYZ composition, and the density, fluidity, transparency, freezing point, boiling point, and so forth of this stuff are those of water and not of vinegar, wine, milk, kerosene, or any other earthly substance. We do in fact extend the term "water" to D_2O (heavy water), which behaviorally resembles ordinary water less than does this Twin-Earth liquid, and we might similarly refer to this substance as "Twin-Earth water." What label would be handier? In Putnam's view, however, we would not and should not call the Twin-Earth stuff "water."[1] For "once we have discovered that water (in the actual world) is H_2O, *nothing counts as a possible world in which water isn't H_2O*" (Putnam's italics).[2] Thus water is necessarily H_2O; H_2O constitutes its essence. The word "water" rigidly designates H_2O regardless of what superficial properties the H_2O may or may not have in some philosophically conceivable world.[3]

This claim has a familiar ring. Putnam's intuition tells him that the Twin-Earth stuff is not water and others' intuitions disagree,[4] much as in chapter 9 intuitions clashed concerning Mr. Truetemp and whether he

"knows" the temperature that he states with such accuracy. Yet there is a
difference here. Typically, when philosophers adduce their intuitions in
support of conflicting theories, they do not trace the intuitions to established word uses but simply disregard the authority of language. Not so
in this instance. True, for Putnam "What the essential nature is is not a
matter of language analysis but of scientific theory construction."[5] But
that is because the term "water" rigidly designates whatever science reveals water to be (that is, whatever it rightly believes it to be). This, for
Putnam as for Kripke, is how the word functions, as do countless other
equally rigid terms, in English and in other tongues. To some extent, then
(limits will appear), the Kripke-Putnam doctrine of rigid designation does
not challenge the authority of language but rather a more Wittgensteinian conception of how language functions and what respect for its authority entails. Whereas traditional essentialism tended to ignore
language, this variety does not.

Though confined to fewer philosophers, the Kripke-Putnam version
has been influential and merits attention here, for two reasons. One is the
doctrine's breadth. In Putnam's opinion, essentialistic rigidity similar to
that of "water" characterizes not only other natural-kind terms such as
"gold," "lemon," "tiger," and "acid,"[6] but also "the great majority of all
nouns," for instance "the names of artifacts—words like 'pencil,' 'chair,'
'bottle,' etc.," and "other parts of speech as well."[7] In each instance, the
extension of the term is fixed by the "important physical properties"[8] or
"hidden structure"[9] revealed, or still to be revealed, by science. For
Kripke, a similar account holds "for various species names, whether they
are count nouns, such as 'cat,' 'tiger,' 'chunk of gold,' or mass terms such
as 'gold,' 'water,' 'iron pyrites.' It also applies to certain terms for natural
phenomena, such as 'heat,' 'light,' 'sound,' 'lightning,' and, presumably,
suitably elaborated, to corresponding adjectives—'hot,' 'loud,' 'red.'"[10]
Others have extended the doctrine's scope still more broadly. "I also believe," writes James Carney, "that it can be plausibly argued that 'art' is a
rigid designator and that even aesthetic terms such as 'unified,' 'graceful,'
and 'balanced' are also rigid designators."[11] Putnam has gone so far as to
assert that "most terms are rigid."[12]

A second reason for examining such a doctrine is that it suggests and
supports a style of philosophizing far more widespread than the doctrine.
Many other philosophers still draw sharp, restrictive borders, as Kripke
and Putnam do. Many others adduce hidden necessities or essences, but
without any hint how their theories relate to or receive support from the
language they speak or the meanings of the terms they employ. Kripke
and Putnam offer a possible rationale for such insouciance. If rigid designation applies as widely as they claim, then perhaps for knowledge,
meaning, reference, identity, truth, or what have you, as for water, cop-

per, fire, lions, bottles, chairs, and the rest, one may legitimately adopt Putnam's attitude: "What the essential nature is is not a matter of language analysis but of scientific theory construction." Absolved from Wittgensteinian scruples, philosophy, too, can be scientific.

In Kripke and Putnam, it is difficult to discern any argument demonstrating their position,[13] but negative and positive considerations that they adduce could suggest one. Negatively, the doctrine might receive support from the alleged flaws of alternative accounts. Thus of a term such as "gold" Putnam writes: "If we put philosophical prejudices aside, then I believe that we know perfectly well that no operational definition does provide a necessary and sufficient condition for the application of any such word. We may give an 'operational definition,' or a cluster of properties, or whatever, but the intention is never to 'make the name *synonymous* with the description.' Rather 'we use the name *rigidly*' to refer to whatever things share the *nature* that things satisfying the description normally possess."[14] From this it would appear that, without considering or discussing a wide variety of analogous cases, actual or possible, to which the name might be extended, we speakers of the language (not known for the rigid regularity of our linguistic practice) somehow agree in ruling out any such extensions, even before we know what nature the things thus named actually possess. This would need to be shown—and not simply by critiquing this or that alternative theory.

Positive support for the doctrine might seem to derive from the verdicts Kripke and Putnam give on test cases. "The general methodology that Putnam adopts," writes John Dupré, "is to consider counterfactual situations in which we encounter an item that is in some interesting respect novel, and then to decide (intuit?) whether we would apply a particular term to it."[15] For example, envisaging Twin-Earth XYZ, we determine that it is not water and would not be called water by anyone who knew its composition. How, though, is this verdict reached? It does not follow from the doctrine of rigid designation; rather, the doctrine follows from this and similar verdicts. The verdicts, however, like this one, appear to hang in midair, unsupported.

Given this initial impression, we might incline to pass on to theories more deserving of serious consideration. However, people believe many things for which they present little or no argumentation but for which there is, nonetheless, considerable evidence. Is it so here?

How Rigid?

Before seeking any ground, origin, or explanation for the doctrine of rigid designation, it is necessary to grasp the doctrine more clearly. If, for example, we knew exactly how far the doctrine extends—what expressions count as rigid designators and which do not—that might tip us off to the doctrine's underlying rationale or possible justification. However, neither Kripke nor Putnam indicates just where the borderline runs. In particular, they offer no hint whether the terms of greatest philosophical interest qualify as rigid designators. If, as Putnam suggests, terms for artifacts (e.g., "table" and "chair") designate rigidly, what, for instance, of terms for linguistic artifacts—"name," "word," "language," "sign," "symbol," "definition," "meaning," "sense," and so forth? What, too, of terms for thoughts, images, feelings, desires, intentions, memories, hopes, and other "natural kinds" of the mind?

Questions also arise concerning the nature and degree of the terms' alleged rigidity. Consider, for example, Kripke's account of names. "By a name here," he explains in "Naming and Necessity," "I will mean a proper name, i.e. the name of a person, a city, a country, etc."[16] Such names, he says, "are always rigid designators."[17] That is, in any possible world, including the existing one, they designate the same object.[18] Such is the "intuitive thesis" he sets out to expound and defend.[19] Understood one way, this thesis hardly needs defending, but is as noncommittal as Tarski's account of truth. If, for example, Richard Nixon is defined by a disjunctive cluster of characteristic traits (e.g., a, b, c, d, and e), then whatever individual, if any, in a given world possesses enough of these traits (e.g., a, b, and c, or c, d, and e) will be Nixon. As stipulated, the name "Richard Nixon" will always designate the same person. Clearly, this is not Kripke's understanding of his thesis. "Those," he writes, "who have argued that to make sense of the notion of rigid designator, we must antecedently make sense of 'criteria of transworld identity' have precisely reversed the cart and the horse; it is *because* we can refer (rigidly) to Nixon, and stipulate that we are speaking of what might have happened to *him* (under certain circumstances), that 'transworld identifications' are unproblematic in such cases."[20] Well, then, what might have happened to *him*—Nixon? In Kripke's view, he might not have been president,[21] might have had a different personality,[22] might have done very few of the things commonly attributed to him[23]; but might he have been born without arms, or with two heads? Might he have been born a month earlier, or a year later, or have died in infancy? Kripke has a way of italicizing a proper name or pronoun, as though to emphasize thereby that it leaves no doubt who is in question. And indeed it does not; we do know who is meant. But knowing who is meant offers no clue as to how much of Aristotle, Moses, Nixon, or Pavarotti—how large, varied, or definite a set of present, past, and future intrinsic or extrinsic properties—the designator carries with it into counterfactual, otherworld discourse.

In Kripke's account, the rigidity of natural-kind terms such as "gold" and "tiger" turns out to be equally indefinite. In parallel with Putnam's Twin-Earth scenario, he imagines an animal that has all the external appearances of a tiger yet has an entirely different internal structure.[24] Such an animal, he holds, would not be a tiger. To this extent, at least, the term "tiger" is rigid. Yet for Kripke, not only might a tiger have none of the familiar external features of a tiger and still count as a tiger,[25] but he leaves open how much internal difference suffices to disqualify an animal as a tiger.[26] Might it, for instance, have two hearts, or four stomachs, or lungs front and back rather than side by side? Aside from the single veto ("completely different" internal structure), our imaginings are allowed free play, unrestrained by any natural necessities. So far as we are told, the strangest beasts—legless, chirping, living in the sea—might count as tigers provided they had enough of the right organs (heart, lungs, liver, etc.).

Putnam gives a more rigid account of "water." Not only does he rule out the Twin-Earth stuff with an entirely different internal structure, XYZ, but he excludes many substances with a structure more similar to that of standard water. As Eddy Zemach has noted, "heavy water is commonly regarded as a kind of water. The same holds for aggregates of T_2O, HDO, HTO, and DTO molecules (the number of varieties is eighteen, since in each case the oxygen can be either O^{16}, or O^{17}, or O^{18}). All these, we say, are different kinds of water."[27] Yet Putnam excludes them all. "Nothing counts as a possible world in which water isn't H_2O." In other directions, however, greater indefiniteness opens. The stuff in the Cuyahoga River that caught fire was still "water"; so we wonder: how much admixture of other elements does the "rigid designator" "water" permit? Or how much admixture of silt before the water becomes mud?

Further indefiniteness appears if we turn from the necessity of Putnam's essence to its sufficiency. Let us imagine (with disregard equal to Putnam's for physical possibilities) a Twin-Earth substance that is as solid, black, heavy, and flammable as coal—which, in fact, has all the observable characteristics of coal, save that its chemical composition is H_2O. Would Putnam call this stuff water? Would he claim that the term "water," as employed in the English language, so requires? If not, just where would he draw the line—and why?

Why?

These illustrations reveal such variations of definiteness and indefiniteness from example to example, that it is difficult to conceive any single argument that might back all of Kripke's and Putnam's verdicts, or any single explanation that might account for them all. However, one possible source holds special interest, not only for the doctrine of rigid designation but for the Issue of Language's Authority in general.

Kripke drops a clue when he writes: "It seems more plausible that there should be some weighting, that some properties are more important than others. A theory really has to specify how this weighting goes."[28] The term "gold" illustrates this new consideration (not yet addressed in this chapter or the previous, where the Principle of Relative Similarity and the Norm of Linguistic Correspondence spoke only of "closer resemblance," without any mention of weighting). "There might be a substance," Kripke suggests, "which has all the identifying marks we commonly attributed to identify the substance of gold in the first place, but which is not the same kind of thing, which is not the same substance. We would say of such a thing that though it has all the appearances we initially used to identify gold, it is not gold. Such a thing is, for example, as we well know, iron pyrites or fool's gold. This is not another kind of gold. It's a completely different thing which to the uninitiated person looks just like the substance which we discovered and called gold."[29] Well, not a completely different thing; it looks the same. But, for whatever reason, it doesn't have nearly the same value as gold. So there is no mystery why the cutoff occurs where it does and the name "gold" is not extended without warning to the relatively worthless stuff. The dissimilar chemical composition counts far more weightily (for someone mining gold, selling gold, buying rings, etc.) than does the similar appearance.

This, however, is not the whole story, as can be sensed from an example such as "water." The Twin-Earth claimant to the name "water" serves just as well as our water for washing, nutrition, and the rest; but, being an idle fiction, it doesn't have the scientific cachet of real-Earth H_2O. Even primitive people know the appearances of water, gold, tigers, and the rest, but only science knows their inner structure, or knows it in-depth. And in a scientific culture, scientific discoveries carry greater weight than nonscientific observations or imaginings. Hence, let appearances vary as they may: gold is what science says it is, water is what science says it is, tigers are what science says they are, and so on. Here is the strong thread running through Kripke's and Putnam's accounts of natural-kind terms. Their weighting is scientific.

Thus Putnam writes: "The reason we *don't* use 'cat' as synonymous with a description is surely that we know enough about cats to know that they do have a hidden structure, and it is good scientific methodology to use the name to refer rigidly to the things that possess that hidden structure, and not to whatever happens to satisfy some description."[30] Similar weighting appears in Kripke's remark that "scientific investigation generally discovers characteristics of gold which are far better than the original set,"[31] and that "statements representing scientific discoveries about what this stuff *is* are not contingent truths but necessary truths in the strictest possible sense."[32] No rival considerations carry equal weight. Thus, Kripke observes, the fact that we identify light in a certain way may seem a crucial, indeed necessary, characteristic of light, but this is an illusion; only its intrinsic constitution rigidly defines light.[33]

Scientifically minded as most of us are, we may agree about "light," "water," and "gold" and, requiring nothing more by way of argument, we may accept the limits Kripke and Putnam claim for these terms. (As one commentator has remarked, "In a culture in which the natural sciences are highly developed and enjoy great respect, and in which philosophers have sometimes regarded themselves as mere under-labourers to natural science, the claim that essences are a matter of *scientific* discovery may indeed seem to require barely any defence."[34]) But what about "Nixon," say, and other less scientifically loaded expressions such as philosophers have defined with similar rigidity?

Intuitions

Consider a typical passage from Kripke:

> can we imagine a situation in which it would have happened that this very woman [the Queen of England] came out of Mr. and Mrs. Truman? They might have had a child resembling her in many properties. Perhaps in some possible world Mr. and Mrs. Truman even had a child who actually became the Queen of England and was even passed off as the child of other parents. This still would not be a situation in which *this very woman* whom we call Elizabeth the Second was the child of Mr. and Mrs. Truman, or so it seems to me.[35]

Kripke's "so it seems to me" resembles the "intuitions" critiqued in chapter 9. It signals the familiar combination so crucial to much philosophical theorizing: lack of firm backing in any standard or stipulated use of the terms employed (fairly obvious in this instance), and lack of concern about such backing. The truth or acceptability of claims such as Kripke's does not discernibly depend on the meanings of the statements' constituent expressions. His doctrine of rigid designation may be about word meanings, and may therefore give the impression of heeding the authority of language, but it is not based on word meanings.

In response to such misgivings and in defense of his procedure, Kripke writes: "Of course, some philosophers think that something's having intuitive content is very inconclusive evidence in favor of it. I think it is very heavy evidence in favor of anything, myself. I really don't know in a way what more conclusive evidence one can have about anything, ultimately speaking."[36] From this closing remark, we may surmise that for Kripke

"Seven plus two equals nine," say, or "My toe hurts" would have "intuitive content." However, we do not know the truth of the first statement through direct inspection of the numerals; we have to know arithmetic. Similarly, we do not know the truth of the second statement simply by having a painful toe; we have to know a different, nonmathematical set of signs ("my," "toe," "hurt") and the language to which they belong. Normally, we do not speak of "intuition" in such instances as these but reserve the term for cases where the backing for our statements is less evident and strong. These are of two very different, indeed opposed, kinds. There are cases where what we surmise, if true, would clearly exemplify the terms employed. For example, we may not have firm evidence that a person is reluctant to accept an invitation (in an ordinary, unproblematic sense of the term "reluctant"), but, given certain clues, we "intuit" the person's reluctance. Other cases, commoner in philosophical discussion, reverse the source of uncertainty. The nonlinguistic facts look clear enough (often they are simply stipulated, as in Kripke's and Putnam's suppositions); but it is not clear whether these facts exemplify the expressions in question—whether, for instance, the language Kripke speaks backs his denial that anyone who had different parents would be "the same person." He offers no evidence to suggest that it does. "Intuition" saves him the trouble.[37]

What verdict might the Principle of Relative Similarity or the Norm of Linguistic Correspondence render in such a case? At first glance, it might appear that, with just a difference of parents, the verdict "same person" would conform more closely to the established use of expressions in the language than would the substitution of any rival, incompatible expression (e.g., "different person"). However, Kripke does not specify what the change of parents would bring with it. Would the person in question be born and raised, perhaps very differently, in a different place, family, and social milieu? With different genetic makeup, would she have a different appearance and personality? As so often in philosophers' fantasies, the particulars of the case are here left too indefinite to permit serious application of a norm such as that of Linguistic Correspondence.

Suppose, though, that we model this case on Putnam's Twin-Earth scenario and, ignoring probabilities or scientific laws, simply stipulate that everything else remains the same save the person's parents. What verdict would the Principle of Relative Similarity and the Norm of Linguistic Correspondence then indicate? Although this question about this single case lacks interest, the methodological issue it raises does not. Should we assess the similarities and dissimilarities numerically—one dissimilarity versus countless similarities—and conclude that the woman born of the Trumans would be the same person? Or would that one dissimilarity perhaps carry more weight than all the similarities combined?

Logical atomism's separation rule over actual interconnectedness of events.

It is easy to see why it might appear to do so, and also why the appearance should be questioned. In the ordinary course of events, that one dissimilarity would entail countless others, but here, by hypothesis, it is stripped of such significance. So, too, for Putnam's Twin-Earth sample. As he himself noted, hidden structure looks important because of its connection with surface features (specific gravity, fluidity, freezing point, taste, characteristic feel, etc.).[38] But his Twin-Earth fiction cuts this connection; despite its entirely different microstructure, the stuff on that other planet has just the same appearance as our water. Anyone who noted this further difference, and not just the one Putnam focused on, might not attach the customary importance to hidden structure. For some strange reason, the strong structural dissimilarity between H_2O and XYZ would have even fewer consequences than that between H_2O (ordinary water) and D_2O (heavy water).

Details such as these—commercial weighting (for "gold"), scientific weighting (for water), otherworld weighting (for the Twin-Earth lookalike), etc.[39]—land us in a predicament similar to that in chapter 14. There, modifiers looked important (e.g., "*wavy* circle"), but there seemed little prospect that the Principle of Relative Similarity or the Norm of Linguistic Correspondence could be refined to state precisely what kinds of modifiers would be required on what occasions in order to warrant the extension of what kinds of expressions. Here, weighting looks important, but there seems equally little prospect that the Principle of Relative Similarity or the Norm of Linguistic Correspondence could be refined to state precisely how much weight should be accorded to this or that aspect of this or that sort of expression in these or those circumstances. With respect both to modifiers and to weighting, individual cases look surer than any all-embracing, abstract formula. For effective communication, "wavy circle" may aptly express what needs to be said, and so may "Twin-Earth water." That much seems clear. Whether either predication satisfies the Norm of Linguistic Correspondence looks less evident. Thus the norm may provide a handy rule of thumb and may point in the right direction, but it permits no ready verdict in many problematic cases.

Implications

All this indefiniteness has important implications. In the absence of any general account of modifiers, weighting, and their role in legitimating predication, philosophers who draw sharp lines in the manner of Putnam and Kripke are likely only to prompt needless controversy. "It seems to me" is not a convincing argument when, in the absence of linguistic backing, it may and often does seem otherwise to other people. Besides, what does it matter, for example, whether Queen Elizabeth would count as the same person if she had different parents? What need is there to decide such far-fetched conundrums either way?

It may be thought, and often is, that a verdict in such a particular instance can tell us something of fundamental importance—in this case about personal identity, and indeed about identity in general. "It seems to me," opines Kripke (in the same revealing fashion as above), "that anything coming from a different origin would not be this object."[40] Viewed as a fact about the world, this surmise looks significant: the mind, through its intuitive power, glimpses reality's hidden structure. However, Kripke's question is not scientific, but conceptual. And the concepts in question are those of everyday language, for he has not stipulated any alternative senses for his terms ("same," "same person," and the rest). These everyday concepts, like most, have indefinite borders. This is not a puzzling fact. It is what one might expect of the general population, employing adaptable expressions for various purposes in varying contexts. Once, however, these verbal spectacles are worn and not examined— once attention is directed, for example, to Elizabeth II and what she might have been or done and not to the terms employed in discussing her possibilities—deep mystery descends and metaphysical interest quickens. Could this very woman have had different parents? Can anything have a different origin and still be the same thing? Similarly, could any stuff be XYZ and still be water? Can any natural kinds have a different inner structure or composition and still be the same kinds? Here, it seems, are deep issues for philosophical investigation, on a par with those of the natural sciences. "*Philosophy*," declared Russell, with emphasis, "*is the science of the possible.*"[41]

In a scientific age, perhaps no question is more crucial for philosophy than this one: Can philosophy be scientific, as Russell desired, and still remain philosophy, or must it simply merge with science? Perhaps, too, no question highlights the Issue of Language's Authority more prominently than this one. For it is in philosophy far more than in science that the authority of language is challenged, precisely by the attempt to be scientific. If I here speak of a challenge to the authority of language, in general, and not to that of "ordinary" or "everyday" language, it is for the familiar reasons exemplified in the present discussion. To be truly scientific, Kripke and Putnam might have stipulated that, for theoretical reasons of precision, simplicity, fruitfulness, or what have you, they would draw the line here for personal identity, there for natural kinds, and so forth. But they did not. They simply used existing concepts to state their intuitions, that went beyond the concepts.

Let us bring this fact—this familiar, representative fact—into sharp focus. Kripke says that it "seems to him" that Queen Elizabeth could not have had other parents. The impossibility here in question is not biological but of some other variety. Kripke might call it "metaphysical" (his favored term),[42] but he would less likely call it "linguistic." For then he would have to cite linguistic evidence for his verdict, and of course there is none. No one has ever had other parents. No occasion has ever arisen for the English-speaking populace to call such a person the "same" or not the "same." No inference can be drawn from familiar paradigms of personal sameness (e.g., Elizabeth II at ten and Elizabeth II at twenty) to this far-fetched, imaginary case. So Kripke is on his own, and the best he can do is "it seems to me." As a "metaphysical" intuition, this looks respectable; one cannot be sure about such deep, difficult matters. However, such un-sureness as this is irremediable. As Plato sensed already in the *Cratylus*, no reality—neither Queen Elizabeth nor water nor tigers nor anything else—can furnish any *answer*, by itself. It cannot tell us what to say: "same" or not "same," "water" or not "water," "tiger" or not "tiger." Perhaps language might somehow fill the gap and codetermine what to say—not, however, in any way that Kripke and Putnam reveal.

As I noted at the start, these thinkers, unlike many, do advert to language and its functioning. "When I say that a designator is rigid," Kripke remarks, "and designates the same thing in all possible worlds, I mean that, as used in *our* language, it stands for that thing, when *we* talk about counterfactual situations."[43] Why, then, did Kripke not consult "our language"? Why did he resort to intuitions and "seems-to-me" arguments rather than report how we do speak about counterfactual situations? Clearly, because "our language" can furnish no answers to the questions he asked. It can furnish no answers if "our language" is that of philosophers, for their answers diverge. It can furnish no answers if "our language" is that of the hoi polloi, for they have never envisaged or discussed unrecognizable tigers, people born of other parents, Twin-Earth liquids, and the like.

This is one reason why such cases interest philosophers. To be sure, the stuff in our streams is water. To be sure, the creatures in Bengal are tigers. To be sure, the adult Elizabeth II is the same person as the infant Elizabeth II. Everyone knows these things. They pose no problems worthy of philosophical scrutiny. But how about the Twin-Earth stuff, the creature with different innards, the woman born of other parents? Here, it seems, are more interesting questions, demanding special, philosophical expertise for their solution. Thus, venturing beyond familiar cases and commonsense verdicts, philosophers enter the depths of which Wittgenstein spoke and which he knew so well from personal experience:

> there seemed to pertain to logic a peculiar depth—a universal significance. Logic lay, it seemed, at the bottom of all the sciences.— For logical investigation explores the nature of all things. It seeks

to see to the bottom of things and is not meant to concern itself whether what actually happens is this or that.—It takes its rise, not from an interest in the facts of nature, nor from a need to grasp causal connexions: but from an urge to understand the basis, or essence, of everything empirical.[44]

When Wittgenstein removed and examined his linguistic spectacles, he abandoned such dreams. Other thinkers, however, who still harbor them, would favor a different metaphor: with his emphasis on returning expressions to the language-game that is their home, Wittgenstein constructed a linguistic prison from which these critics would liberate themselves. For a less restrictive perspective, more favorable to theoretical aspirations, they may turn, for example, to Willard Van Orman Quine.

16

Quine, Linguistic Truths, and Holistic Theory

M OST PHILOSOPHERS HAVE believed in necessary truths; Kripke and Putnam just multiplied them more than many would. Quine, at the other extreme, contested such distinctions as that between contingent and necessary, a posteriori and a priori, or synthetic and analytic statements. In itself, Quine's influential critique has interest for the Issue of Language's Authority, since it appears to challenge the widely held view that language alone determines the truth of some statements, whereas it only codetermines the truth of others. Perhaps more important, the thinking revealed in this particular critique of Quine's may call into question the whole approach here taken thus far to the Issue of Language's Authority.

Our attention has focused, fairly narrowly, on individual expressions and utterances. Should you say, we asked, that you see the chair or that you see your brain? Should you say that Flew's young man, unpressured, "freely" marries the woman of his choice? Should you say that Mr. Truetemp "knows" the temperatures he states so accurately, that Putnam's Twin-Earth stuff is water, that you drew a (wavy) circle on the board, and so forth? Discussion of these utterances has conformed with the principle that Tarski stated: "the concept of truth essentially depends, as regards both extension and content, upon the language to which it is applied. We can only meaningfully say of an expression that it is true or not if we treat this expression as a part of a concrete language."[1] In Quine, this principle undergoes a shift: "truth, as Tarski appreciated, is meaningfully predicated, rightly or wrongly, only within the *theory* that is operative at the time."[2] My added emphasis highlights a significant difference: whereas for Tarski language is an essential codeterminant of truth, for Quine theory appears to take its place. And for Quine theory is holistic. Thus he explains:

The idea of defining a symbol in use was, as remarked, an advance over the impossible term-by-term empiricism of Locke and Hume. The statement, rather than the term, came with Bentham to be recognized as the unit accountable to an empiricist critique. But what I am now urging is that even in taking the statement as unit we have drawn our grid too finely. The unit of empirical significance is the whole of science.[3]

However it is understood, this, certainly, is a broader, more comprehensive perspective than we have adopted thus far. So have we perhaps been myopic in our fixation on this or that particular statement? To understand the implications of Quine's holism for the Issue of Language's Authority and discern whether it does demand a broader focus, we can start with the reasoning that led to the remarks just quoted, in one of Quine's best-known and most influential pieces, "Two Dogmas of Empiricism." The first of the two dogmas in question is the analytic-synthetic distinction favored by empiricists and many others.[4]

Quine's Critique

For Quine, Kant's formulation of this distinction—in terms of the inclusion or noninclusion of the predicate in the subject term of a statement—is flawed. "But Kant's intent," Quine suggests, "evident more from the use he makes of the notion of analyticity than from his definition of it, can be restated thus: a statement is analytic when it is true by virtue of meanings and independently of fact."[5] For example, the meanings of its English terms, it is thought, assure the truth of the statement "No bachelor is married" in any possible world; regardless of whether the world contained any bachelors and what else might be true of them, no bachelors there would be married. What, though, asks Quine, are these "meanings" that make such statements true? They are not the objects denoted by the names or words that have the meanings; they are not for instance, the human beings denoted by the term "bachelor." What, then, are they? Without canvassing other replies (for instance Wittgenstein's, in terms of word use[6]), Quine concludes: "Meanings themselves, as obscure intermediary entities, may well be abandoned."[7] Thus, rather than explain the analyticity of "No bachelor is married" through the synonymy of "bachelor" and "unmarried man," and that in turn through the sameness of their meanings, perhaps we may just explain the analyticity directly through the synonymy and drop the meanings as superfluous. But what, in that case, is synonymy?

"A natural suggestion," Quine replies, "deserving close examination, is that the synonymy of two linguistic forms consists simply in their interchangeability in all contexts without change of truth value—interchangeability, in Leibniz's phrase, *salva veritate*."[8] Such interchangeability, he notes, may be difficult to discover. Even for the familiar pairing "bachelor" and "unmarried man," there are problems; "unmarried man" cannot, for instance, be substituted for "bachelor" in "bachelor of arts" or "bachelor's button." More serious, the interchangeability required for synonymy is not merely accidental. For "bachelor" and "unmarried man" to be synonymous, it cannot just happen to be the case that no bachelor is married. But to explain the difference between such extensional, de facto agreement and the kind required, we have need of such notions as synonymy or sameness of meaning, and these are the notions we are seeking to elucidate.

An explanation of analyticity in terms of verification proves no more satisfactory. Here the second "dogma" of Quine's title—empiricist reductionism—becomes pertinent. According to radical reductionism, Quine explains, "Every meaningful statement is held to be translatable into a statement (true or false) about immediate experience."[9] In subtler forms of reductionism, "The notion lingers that to each statement, or each synthetic statement, there is associated a unique range of possible sensory events such that the occurrence of any of them would add to the likelihood of truth of the statement, and there is associated also another unique range of possible sensory events whose occurrence would detract from that likelihood."[10] This second, reductionist dogma connects with the first, analytic-synthetic dogma as follows: "as long as it is taken to be significant in general to speak of the confirmation and infirmation of a statement, it seems significant to speak also of a limiting kind of statement which is vacuously confirmed, *ipso facto*, come what may; and such a statement is analytic."[11] Against this conclusion and its premise Quine objects that verification cannot proceed statement by statement: "Taken collectively, science has its double dependence upon language and experience; but this duality is not significantly traceable into the statements of science taken one by one."[12] Thus the analytic-synthetic distinction breaks down, for within science as a whole,

> [a]ny statement can be held true come what may, if we make drastic enough adjustments elsewhere in the system. Even a statement very close to the periphery can be held true in the face of recalcitrant experience by pleading hallucination or by amending certain statements of the kind called logical laws. Conversely, by the same token, no statement is immune to revision. Revision even of the logical law of the excluded middle has been proposed as a means of simplifying quantum mechanics; and what difference is there in principle between such a shift and the shift whereby Kepler superseded Ptolemy, or Einstein Newton, or Darwin Aristotle?[13]

This holistic perspective does not challenge the authority of language. Science as a whole retains its "double dependence upon language and

experience," and so do individual statements. "In general," Quine
acknowledges, "the truth of statements does obviously depend both upon
language and upon extralinguistic fact."[14] The question is, how does this
double dependence work—atomically or holistically? Preceding chapters
have taken a word-by-word, statement-by-statement approach to truth and
assertability, and it appears that Quine might judge that approach to be
deficient. Would he, though, and if he did, would he be right? Initial light
can be cast on both questions by considering whether he was right about
the analytic-synthetic distinction. That question (which, as noted, has its
own interest for the Issue of Language's Authority) was a principal focus of
the discussion evoked by Quine's "Two Dogmas."

Grice and Strawson's Response

Paul Grice and Peter Strawson distinguished two parts in Quine's critique.
In one, analyticity and related notions are criticized on the ground that they
have not been adequately explained. In the other, a positive theory of truth
is outlined, supposedly incompatible with views to which believers in the
analytic-synthetic distinction either must be, or are likely to be, committed.[15] With regard to the first part, concerning analyticity, the authors concede that it is difficult to state necessary and sufficient conditions for the
application of this and related notions without using the same notions and
thus going round in definitional circles. However, the same holds for other
conceptual clusters, including terms Quine continued to countenance—for
example, "the group which includes the propositional connectives and the
words 'true' and 'false,' 'statement,' 'fact,' 'denial,' 'assertion.'"[16] With regard to these, too, "The fact, if it is a fact, that the expressions cannot be
explained in precisely the way which Quine seems to require, does not
mean that they cannot be explained at all."[17] Thus, we can use examples to
bring out important differences even if the differences cannot be rigorously
formulated. For instance, to convey the difference between logical impossibility and natural or causal impossibility, we might take as our examples
the logical impossibility of a child of three being an adult, and the natural
impossibility of a child of three understanding Russell's Theory of Types.
Conversely, we might use the example to illustrate the difference between
logical necessity (a child's not being an adult) and logical contingency (a
child's not understanding Russell's theory).[18]

The Quine of "Two Dogmas" would contest this distinction.[19] Even
"A child is not an adult" might be given up; no statement is immune to
revision. Grice and Strawson can accept this claim, provided full weight
is given to the distinction, which Quine ignores,

> between that kind of giving up which consists in merely admit-
> ting falsity, and that kind of giving up which involves changing

or dropping a concept or set of concepts. Any form of words at one time held to express something true may, no doubt, at another time, come to be held to express something false. But it is not only philosophers who would distinguish between the case where this happens as the result of a change of opinion solely as to matters of fact, and the case where this happens at least partly as a result of a shift in the sense of the words.[20]

To illustrate, in the first sort of case the three-year-old child is produced and expounds Russell's theory correctly, answers questions on it, criticizes it, and so on, and we are forced to acknowledge that the claim was literally true: in the same sense that others understand Russell's Theory of Types, this child understands the theory. In the second kind of case, "understanding" a theory may, for instance, be so defined that understanding the description of the theory (e.g., understanding that Russell's Theory of Types is a theory held by Russell concerning types of expression) counts as understanding the theory, and therewith a child who possesses none of the preceding extraordinary abilities might nonetheless be recognized as understanding Russell's Theory of Types. Quine may eschew talk of "meanings" or "senses," but there is no denying the difference—the important difference—between these contrasting kinds of cases.[21]

Returning, then, to "No bachelor is married," we might apply Grice and Strawson's distinction and say that this statement cannot be falsified without a shift in the meaning or sense of some word, for instance "bachelor." The meaning is no longer the same. To this, Quine might respond by urging his principal objection (not noted in "Two Dogmas") against "meanings" or "senses," namely, "their want of satisfactory individuation."[22] We have some idea when bodies are different or the same, but meanings are much more nebulous. Does "tool" have the same meaning as "instrument," or "instrument" as "implement"? Does "instrument" have the same meaning in "musical instrument" as in "instrument of God's wrath"? Who is to say? We might remark that Quine's favored terms do not fare much better, unless specially tailored to his purposes. What counts as the same "object," "entity," "word," "term," "expression," "sentence," "statement," "referent," "form," "science," or "conceptual framework"? However, in these instances as in the others, fuzzy borders are still borders. There is no doubt that "sycamore" is not the same word as "coda" and does not have the same meaning, sense, or use in the language. So, too, for "bachelor": if "bachelors" can be married or can be women, the word has changed its sense.

I agree, then, with Tyler Burge: "The idea that there is something cognitively suspect about the notion of meaning—an idea that has been made common by Quine's doubts during the last forty years—seems to me difficult to support. There are many such notions in ordinary life that do not enter into general laws of the sort found in the natural sciences. It would be absurd to suggest that all such notions are cognitively disreputable."[23] If, then, we may speak of senses and their sameness or difference, perhaps we should counter Quine's claim that no statements are immune to revision. Some statements *are* immune to revision, provided the senses of their terms are not changed. However, it is time to note a distinction Quine neglected in "Two Dogmas." He used the word "statement," he later explained, to refer to declarative sentences;[24] and, whether declarative or other, "A sentence is not an event of utterance, but a universal: a repeatable sound pattern, or repeatedly approximable norm."[25] In Quine's view, as in Austin's, "What are best seen as primarily true or false are not sentences but events of utterance."[26] That is, I suggest, they are the kind of speech acts ordinarily called "statements" or "assertions." To cite Quine's example, "If a man utters the words 'It is raining' in the rain, or the words 'I am hungry' while hungry, his verbal performance counts as true"[27]—and also as a true statement. Thus, in a familiar sense of the term, a statement is something more than a "repeatable sound pattern." A person who has made a statement has not simply proffered a set of words; if the sense of the words differs so does the statement. So perhaps we should conclude, tout court, without proviso, that some *statements*, in the sense of assertoric utterances, are immune to revision. They cannot be false. The senses of their terms assure their truth. Use the English language to say "No bachelor is married" (not merely utter the words), and you cannot be wrong.

In apparent opposition to this verdict, Putnam has written: "As long as being an unmarried (or never-been-married) male adult person is the only known and generally employed criterion for being a bachelor, then the word 'bachelor' will continue to function (in purely referential contexts) as virtually an abbreviation of the longer phrase 'male adult person who has never been married.'"[28] However, this situation "may change *as a result of empirical discovery*, with no stipulative redefinition of these words, and no unmotivated linguistic drift, being involved." That is, the use of "bachelor" might alter in the same general way as the use of "atom" did when atoms were split. How this particular shift, to married bachelors, might occur, I have no idea and neither, I imagine, does Putnam. So what does this far-fetched hypothesis have to do with the present claim, in the language as it stands, that no bachelor is married?

Putnam might reply as follows.[29] Once we thought all swans were white. Then we made an empirical discovery of black birds so similar that, without any stipulative redefinition of the term "swan," we called them, too, swans, by natural analogy. The term's intension was open to this extension. Similarly, Putnam might suggest, the term "bachelor" is open to his suggested extension. As we found black swans, so we might find married bachelors. And as "All swans are white" was thereby falsified, so too would "All bachelors are unmarried" be falsified. No doubt it would, in this hypothesis. But how might we discover married bachelors? What would they look like? Like the married men we presently *don't* call bachelors? No, if they were men and were married, no natural analogy would bridge the gap. For married men to count as bachelors, we would have to redefine the term "bachelor." I therefore repeat: use the existing term to deny that any bachelors are married and you cannot be wrong. Language by itself can guarantee truth.[30]

In "Carnap and Logical Truth," Quine granted as much. "There can be no doubt," he first noted, "that sheer verbal usage is in general a major determinant of truth. Even so factual a sentence as 'Brutus killed Caesar' owes its truth not only to the killing but equally to our using the component words as we do."[31] Language and the reality codetermine its truth. A logically true sentence, on the contrary, "is a sentence which, *given* the language, automatically becomes true, whereas 'Brutus killed Caesar,' given the language, becomes true only contingently on the alleged killing."[32] Quine's italics ("*given* the language") place the emphasis where I would, but for a different reason. I would call attention to the authority accorded language, which is here complete. Quine underscores the contingency of the language and hence of the "logical," "analytic," "necessary" truths established in and by the language.[33] There is no "de re" necessity, he would insist, discernible in things themselves independently of us, our language, and our logic.

William Kneale marks the same distinction in a way that highlights its significance for the Issue of Language's Authority:

> A statement is truistic in a given language, if, and only if (*a*) it consists of symbols for which restrictive rules exist in that language, and (*b*) all statements inconsistent with it are forbidden by the rules of that language. It is not surprising that such a statement should be said to be necessarily true, for there is indeed no alternative to its truth. Knowledge of the rules enables us to certify this, apart from all reference to experience.[34]

One may wonder where these restrictive rules, these prohibitions, are to be found. English-speakers do not, in fact, call women or married men "bachelors," but where is it written: "Thou shalt not call women or married men (or children or chimpanzees or umbrellas) 'bachelors'"? These and innumerable other prohibitions lie implicit in the legitimate expectation that people's word use will be idiomatic: the authority of language should be respected.[35]

In Between

At the start I spoke of two challenges that would focus this chapter. The first challenge, now answered, was to the view that language alone determines the truth of some statements. It does—if the statements in question are utterances. (In some book we may read, for example: "Bachelors are not married and neither are widowers, but this study treats them differently.") However, some who accept this verdict nonetheless question its significance. For one thing, clearly analytic utterances seldom occur outside of philosophical contexts. In the context of linguistic instruction, like-sounding sentences (e.g., "Bachelors are unmarried men") may state contingent linguistic facts (e.g., about the use of "bachelor") rather than necessary facts about things (e.g., bachelors). Or, given the contextual fluctuation of word and sentence meanings, the utterances' status may be uncertain. Thus, "Over and beyond the clear-cut rules of language, on the one side," writes Putnam, "and the clear-cut descriptive statements, on the other, are just an enormous number of statements which are not happily classified as either analytic or synthetic."[36] Kai Nielsen agrees, emphatically: "The whole demarcation thing is hopeless and pointless, for there are multitudes of sentences in all sorts of domains that are not untendentiously classifiable as one or the other."[37] Consider, Nielsen suggests,

> the following more or less randomly selected list, "True Christians believe in the trinity," "Nothing can be both red and green all over," "Moral judgments are impartial," "Beliefs to be justified require evidence," "There is a past," "Kinetic energy is equal to one half the product of mass and velocity squared," "All physical laws must be Lorentz-invariant," "A straight line is the path of a light ray," "The world did not come into existence five minutes ago replete with false memory traces," "There are atoms," "Light rays travel in a curved space," "No well adult needs ten hours sleep a day," "Every substance has some solvent," "No one ever really knows the thoughts of another," "Dreams have no logic," "Without social solidarity social life is fragmented," "Alienation is inescapable," "Language acquisition is an innate capacity," "A society without classes is impossible," "Jealousy is a natural feeling."[38]

None of these statements, Nielsen maintains, goes clearly into either slot—the a priori or the a posteriori, the analytic or the synthetic.

One might agree, and still stress the importance of the analytic-synthetic distinction. Indeed, Nielsen's evidence might be used to indicate the distinction's significance. If the distinction were important but consistently easy to spot, it would have less significance. The distinction would just articulate an evident difference and therefore would have little useful application. If, however, as Nielsen's sampling suggests, the difference between verbal and empirical truth is often much more difficult to detect than in the paradigm examples that establish its existence, the distinction may have frequent, important application. Whether it does is a question of evident interest for the Issue of Language's Authority. In how many instances does language by itself determine truth or assertability, in how many instances does it not, and in how many instances, perhaps, is it indeterminate whether it does or does not? According to Nielsen, a multitude of sentences "are not untendentiously classifiable" either way. If he is right, how is truth or assertability determined in that large in-between zone? What authority does or should language exercise there, and how?

For closer insight, let us return to an earlier example: "Atoms are indivisible." According to Nielsen, for the Greek cosmologists this statement was virtually analytic, whereas for modern physicists it is a plainly false empirical statement.[39] I would note, however, that since neither a common language nor shared theory links these two worlds, the Greek and the modern, it is not clear what common statement Nielsen has in mind. Of more interest, therefore, is the status of such an utterance in more recent times, within a single language and culture, made before and after atom splitting. Had the earlier utterance been considered analytic, no one would have tried to split any atoms; or, when the particles so labeled were split, they would no longer have been recognized as atoms. However, the actual transition from indivisible to divisible atoms suggests greater linguistic flexibility; atoms were not indivisible by definition. Considerations cited earlier, in chapters 11 and 14, tend to confirm this verdict. For the most part, neither scientists nor people generally apply terms essentialistically. If we change our beliefs about the earth, we still call it "the earth." If we change our beliefs about sight, we still call it "sight." If we change our beliefs about atoms, we still call them "atoms." Of the expressions available, "earth," "sight," and "atoms" come closest.[40]

This example, "Atoms are indivisible," illustrates the power of the Principle of Relative Similarity, or the like, to clarify the status of many utterances. This one, for instance, is not analytic. Yet the principle, as we have seen, leaves much indefiniteness, as would any plausible variant. Moreover, the lack of consensus concerning the principle and, more generally, concerning the whole Issue of Language's Authority affects linguistic practice in ways that further blur the indefinite borders between true and false, analytic and synthetic. So yes, a vast twilight zone does stretch between clearly analytic utterances and clearly synthetic ones. However, this indefiniteness, again, does not detract from the interest of the analytic-synthetic distinction. If anything, it heightens the distinction's interest. Rightly understood, the analytic-synthetic split looks sound, and backs the authority of language to determine on its own the truth of many utterances. But the distinction is tricky to apply, and merits special attention for that reason.

Nothing said so far suggests any reason to question the statement-by-statement, utterance-by-utterance approach of previous chapters. The Principle of Relative Similarity, or a variant, can be applied to determine the truth of utterances and to determine whether their truth is analytic or synthetic. Sometimes the principle will give a verdict one way or the other, sometimes it will not. But even the lack of a clear answer will itself be an answer: the utterance has insufficient backing, from language alone or from language together with the reality described, to guarantee the utterance's truth. In each instance, such a judgment is in a sense holistic, since the principle is itself holistic, calling for comparison between rival expressions available in the language. However, this semantic holism differs from Quine's theoretical variety, which remains to be considered. Quine does not say simply to pick the closest expression of those available; he says to consult a whole interrelated system of propositions—central, peripheral, and in between—and see where adjustments should be made. This preceding chapters have not done or recommended and perhaps should have. Such is the second challenge now to be addressed.

Crafting Language versus Using Language

Here, too, Quine's words "*given* the language" are pertinent. Consider his example. Determining whether Brutus stabbed Caesar and Caesar died as a result may demand holistic reflection on historical sources, character, motivation, related events, and so forth. But if the fact is agreed on, then the choice of the verb to describe what he did requires no such holistic considerations. If Brutus stabbed Caesar and Caesar died as a result, then, given the English language as it currently stands, it is true to say "Brutus killed Caesar." Language should be accorded this authority, as codeterminant of truth and assertability, as in previous discussions. If, however, the language is not given but is under consideration, language can exercise no such authority. In that different setting, very different considerations come into play.

This distinction is important for the present chapter and the present study. For the question on which the study centers—what words to use in assertions and why—may arise in the context either of language use or of language creation (or, all too often, in a context where these alternatives are confusingly conflated). By way of comparison, consider the similar distinction that arises for the question: what tools should we choose and why? In a tool-using context, this query might be answered by selecting a hammer rather than a mallet from the toolkit. In a tool-buying context, it might be answered by buying both a hammer and a mallet, or just one or the other, or neither. In these different settings, very different considerations apply. Picking the tool from the shelf, I adopt a focused perspective and consider simply whether I intend to drive a nail or a wedge with it. Buying the tool, I adopt a broader, holistic perspective: I consider alternative brands, how much the tool costs, whether I already own a tool of that kind, how frequently I am likely to drive nails or wedges, what other things I might buy with the money, and so forth. No such considerations arise when I simply pick a mallet rather than a hammer to drive a wedge rather than a nail.

So it is for words. Very different considerations apply when picking them from the existing toolkit and when fashioning the kit. To illustrate the difference, consider the contrast between Russellian predication (chapter 11) and Carnapian explication (chapter 6). Speaking the English language, Russell asserts that we see our brains, not tables, trees, or fountains, and cites facts of English usage in his defense. Holding that the beliefs typically expressed by the verb "see" are mistaken, he does not propose a change in our system of communication but rather in what we say with it and what beliefs he thinks we thus communicate. Carnapian explication reverses this focus. Leaving our beliefs as they are, Carnap views explication as perfecting our system of communication, our conceptual toolkit, for theoretical advantages (exactness, fruitfulness, simplicity). The innovation aimed at is not a true statement or theory, as for Russell, but an improved concept, more suited to scientific purposes.

Clearly, the question of language's authority looks very different in these different settings. Carnapian explication "deviates deliberately from the meaning of descriptions in the ordinary language," and it does not look to any other language, natural or formal, for guidance. In this context, the only shred of authority that any language retains is Carnap's stipulation that the new concept somewhat resemble the old. Of the remaining requirements, Carnap stresses increased precision, but he does not assign weights to go by when the requirements conflict, as they may. Hence, in the context of explication, no single rival emerges to compete with language. Indeed, no rival whatever emerges as a determinant of truth or assertability, for, as Carnap noted, in explication there is no question of truth or assertability. The concepts fashioned may be used to make true statements, but they are not themselves statements and are neither true nor false. From this contrast, it appears how important it may be, for the Issue of Language's Authority, to distinguish between choosing words *in* speech and choosing words *for* speech—that is, between using the verbal toolkit and creating it.

Thus, to sum up, nothing in Quine's holism precludes our proceeding as we have. For the context of our discussions has consistently been, not definition or explication, but communication. (Russell denied that we see physical objects, Flew asserted that the young man weds freely, some claimed that Mr. Truetemp knows the temperature, others denied it, etc.). Furthermore, in that context, there was agreement about the pertinent nonlinguistic facts (the physics and physiology of vision, the absence of social coercion, Mr. Truetemp's abilities, etc.). So attention could and did focus on how those facts should be described in the language employed. Neither side suggested that the language be revised. Neither side engaged in any form of Carnapian explication, nor needed to. But had they done so, a different, more holistic sort of discussion would have resulted concerning "what to say." Alternative forms of speech would have had to be assessed for their overall merits.

Concerning such assessment, Quine advised:

> Our standard for appraising basic changes of conceptual scheme must be, not a realistic standard of correspondence to reality, but a pragmatic standard. Concepts are language, and the purpose of concepts and of language is efficacy in communication and in prediction. Such is the ultimate duty of language, science, and philosophy, and it is in relation to that duty that a conceptual scheme has finally to be appraised.[41]

Thus, for Quine the ultimate obligation of language, science, and philosophy is not to truth; for, in his view, "to call a statement true is just to reaffirm it."[42] So why affirm it in the first place? Quine gave a pragmatic answer, as will Richard Rorty and Stephen Stich in chapter 18. First, though, a further aspect of Quine's thought can open an important dimension of the Issue of Language's Authority.

17

Quine, Indeterminacy, and the Opacity of Language

IMPLICIT IN QUINE'S thought, as some have read it, lies a further, fundamental challenge to the authority of language. So far, various rivals for linguistic authority—Platonic Forms, Thomistic concepts, Tractarian projections, Carnapian theories, Tarskian "satisfaction," metaphysical "intuitions"—have proved inadequate guides to predication. However, can language do better? The Principle of Relative Similarity, revising Austin's analysis, suggests that it can; but the moment has come to take a closer look at the "established word uses" which that principle cites as arbiters of predication. Critics have contested the availability of such guidance, and Quine's doctrine of "indeterminacy," now to be considered, could suggest that in this direction, too, the search for a valid claimant to linguistic authority reaches a dead end. Such might well be the implication of the doctrine if, as William Alston states, "Quine's argument leads to the conclusion that no one means anything determinate either by any of his terms or by any of his non-observation sentences."[1]

Indeterminacy of Translation

"No single doctrine of Quine's," writes Roger Gibson, "has vexed his readers more than the doctrine of indeterminacy of translation. There is little agreement among Quine's critics and commentators concerning what the correct formulation of the indeterminacy thesis is, what the thesis asserts, how the thesis is related to other of Quine's doctrines and commitments, and whether the thesis is true or false."[2] I shall not undertake to clarify all these questions, but, relating this chapter to the previous one, I shall just suggest the doctrine's relevance for the Issue of Language's Authority.

In this connection, recall Quine's words in "Two Dogmas of Empiricism": "Any statement can be held true come what may, if we make drastic enough adjustments elsewhere in the system. Even a statement very close to the periphery can be held true in the face of recalcitrant experience by pleading hallucination or by amending certain statements of the kind called logical laws." Indeed, as Quine later noted in *Word and Object*, "Any of various systematic changes can accommodate the recalcitrant datum."[3] Given this flexibility, we can imagine different people employing the same terms in reaction to identical sensible stimuli but within very different systems of signs. And in that case, if all we had to go by were those verbal reactions and those stimuli, we could not tell what the signs meant in the mouths of those different people.

Quine's paradigm scenario exemplifies this situation. A linguist in the field, who knows nothing of a tribe's language, is observing their verbal behavior. "A rabbit scurries by, the native says 'Gavagai,' and the linguist notes down the sentence 'Rabbit' (or 'Lo, a rabbit') as tentative translation, subject to testing in further cases."[4] Perforce, this testing takes an active form: having somehow acquired a sense of native assent and dissent, the linguist asks "Gavagai?" in various stimulatory situations and notes each time whether the native assents, dissents, or neither assents nor dissents. So doing, he discovers that native reactions for "Gavagai" match his for "rabbit," and his hypothesis appears confirmed: in the native language, "gavagai" means "rabbit." And yet, Quine observes, if this is all the linguist has to go by, "gavagai" might just as readily designate undetached rabbit parts, or temporal segments of rabbits, as whole rabbits. Or the word might designate the fusion of all rabbits ("that single though discontinuous portion of the spatiotemporal world that consists of rabbits") rather than discrete, individual animals. Or perhaps "gavagai" functions "as a singular term naming a recurring universal, rabbithood." The sound might even serve as a verb ("rabbiteth," like "raineth") rather than as a noun. In each supposition, the verbal reactions to the sensible stimuli would be the same.[5]

Quine had emphasized the difference between questions of meaning and questions of reference, judging the latter notably less foggy and mysterious than the former. (If, for instance, an animal pokes its head up and someone says, "There's a rabbit," the object indicated is clearer than the meaning of the word "rabbit.") However, here in gavagai land Quine finds both meaning and reference engulfed in the same indefiniteness:

> Certainly likeness of meaning is a dim notion, repeatedly challenged. Of two predicates which are alike in extension, it has never been clear when to say that they are alike in meaning and when not; . . . Reference, extension, has been the firm thing;

meaning, intension, the infirm. The indeterminacy of translation now confronting us, however, cuts across extension and intension alike. The terms "rabbit," "undetached rabbit part," and "rabbit stage" differ not only in meaning; they are true of different things. Reference itself proves behaviorally inscrutable.[6]

If the linguist knew the native language but not this specific word, "gavagai," he might resolve his uncertainty by asking appropriate questions ("Is 'gavagai' a name?" "What things does it name?" "How do you number them?" etc.) However, even for a speaker of the same tongue similar problems might recur, as Quine explains:

> On deeper reflection, radical translation begins at home. . . . [W]e can systematically reconstrue our neighbor's apparent references to rabbits as really references to rabbit stages, and his apparent references to formulas as really references to Gödel numbers and vice versa. We can reconcile all this with our neighbor's verbal behavior, by cunningly readjusting our translations of his various connecting predicates so as to compensate for the switch of ontology. In short, we can reproduce the inscrutability of reference at home.[7]

And if both reference and meaning are inscrutable, we may now wonder, what guidance can our language provide? How can we make our use of words agree with their "established uses"?

We have already met something similar. Some people are naive realists, others are not, but all agree (with Russell the occasional exception that proves the rule) in saying that they see sunsets, hear bells, smell bacon frying, and the rest (as Russell also did when he took a holiday from philosophy). Their differing theories of sensation do not affect their application of sensation expressions. This is as it should be, chapter 11 suggested, for it makes communicative sense for our use of words to conform more closely with established word uses than would the substitution of any rival expressions. And so it does: whatever our naive, scientific, or philosophical conceptions of sight may be, we say we see cats, cliffs, and trolley cars and not our brains. (Figuratively speaking, we all say "Gavagai" when rabbits run by, regardless of our conceptions of gavagais.)

Quine himself is untroubled by his far-fetched surmises; for, "if two speakers match in all dispositions to verbal behavior there is no sense in imagining semantic differences between them."[8] It makes no better sense, Quine's comparisons suggest, than imagining that semantic differences might result from inner variations in our color perceptions, with one person's blue being another person's yellow, and so forth.[9] We naturally include the inner experience in the meaning of each color term, but that is because we assume relative interpersonal uniformity in our experience of colors. Were there no such uniformity, despite our verbal agreement, we might treat the inner datum as Wittgenstein suggested: "one can 'divide through' by the thing in the box; it cancels out, whatever it is."[10] That is, it cancels out semantically; it forms no part of the language-game. We can ignore it in our choice and application of terms as completely as we do, in Quine's further example, "the circumstance that different neural hookups can account for identical verbal behavior."[11]

Here I am slanting Quine's discussion toward the Issue of Language's Authority. His own interest was different. In his view, the main lesson to be derived from thinking about radical translation of exotic languages "concerns the empirical slack in our own beliefs."[12] Quite varied beliefs can accommodate the same experiences. My concern, in parallel wording, has been possible *semantic* slack in our *expressions*. For, given too much slack, "established word uses" might offer little guidance. As it is, Quine's remarks, acknowledging some semantic determinateness amid all the indeterminateness, suggest no reason to downgrade language's authority. More serious misgivings may arise from a point that Quine, with his different focus, did not single out for attention. Given all the linguistic diversity, fluctuation, and indefiniteness his doctrine of indeterminacy highlights, how available is the guidance of language? "Keep to the channel," the Mississippi River pilot may advise, but how can that be done, with the river so shifting and its waters so muddy?

The Opacity of Language

Most of us, including most philosophers, are not linguists, observing, pen in hand, how people employ the expressions of our own or any other language. We may be masters of our mother tongue, but, as earlier chapters have suggested, practical mastery does not imply reflective awareness. Wittgenstein was right: "Man possesses the ability to construct languages capable of expressing every sense, without having any idea how each word has meaning or what its meaning is—just as people speak without knowing how the individual sounds are produced."[13] Although this assessment may sound extreme, even philosophers who have scrutinized language have given divergent accounts of even the most basic, familiar expressions. Consider an example already noted. For some the term "true" applies properly or primarily to sentences, for others to utterances, for others to beliefs, for others to abstract thoughts or propositions. For some the term has one descriptive content, for others another, and for others the content varies according to the bearer. Again, for some the word "true" describes, for others it merely signals assent, for still others it does both. Disagreement is nearly total, concerning this common expression.

It might seem, therefore, that obedience to the authority of language would require continual assistance from professional linguists—more than they might be willing or able to furnish and more than philosophers or others might think reasonable to request. Thus, in his inquiry "On the Verification of Statements about Ordinary Language," Benson Mates dismissed "the comfortable suggestion that the average adult has already amassed such a tremendous amount of empirical information about the use of his native language, that he can depend upon his own intuition or memory and need not undertake a laborious questioning of other people, even when he is dealing with the tricky terms which are central in philosophical problems."[14] The facts, Mates maintained, contradict this convenient hypothesis. "It has been found that even relatively careful authors are often not reliable reporters of their *own* linguistic behavior, let alone that of others."[15] In response, Stanley Cavell conceded that philosophers' linguistic claims do sometimes clash; yet native speakers of a language "do not, in *general*, need evidence for what is said in the language; they are the source of such evidence. It is from them that the descriptive linguist takes the corpus of utterances on the basis of which he will construct a grammar of that language."[16] Granted, Mates might reply; but they are the *unreflective* source of those utterances, much more attentive to the topics they discuss than to the medium in which they discuss them.[17] However, I see no point in prolonging this debate. For I suggest that, not surprisingly, linguistic details of a kind that linguists alone might reliably supply are seldom such as philosophers, let alone less speculative speakers, genuinely need.

Examples in previous chapters illustrate this judgment. Recall a few. Moore, in chapter 1, had no need of instruction about the use of "good"; had he been interested in the word's everyday use, he could readily have ascertained, as he later did, that it had a variety of standard applications and not the single one he envisioned. Likewise, Aquinas did not need to be told that people commonly spoke of some laws as just and others as unjust; his disagreement had a different, nonlinguistic source. Again, no lack of linguistic data explained Tarski's negative verdict on the everyday concept "true"; the most accurate data, treated the same way, would have yielded the same semantic paradoxes. The like holds for Flew: nothing a linguist might have told him would have altered his judgment about the "freedom" of an uncoerced marriage. Again, warring "intuitions," for instance concerning knowledge, do not result from linguistic ignorance but from disregard of language and its authority. So, too, Russell's denial that we see physical objects revealed no ignorance of our customary ways of speaking, but disagreement with our verdicts, in view of the naive realism Russell assumed to be widespread in the population. None of these thinkers had need of professional assistance from linguists.

In fuller illustration, recall chapter 9's observations about knowledge. Those who, like Williams, seek to define precisely the nature of knowledge do not appeal to linguistic usage. Doubtless they realize that usage would not reveal any borders as precise and uniform as they desire. Perhaps, too, they sense that if they did discover precise linguistic borders and based their definition on them, the definition would have no metaphysical, non-linguistic interest of the kind that motivates their search. They do not wish to know how people happen to employ the term "knowledge" or its kin; they want to know the nature of knowledge. On the other side of the debate, critics who, like Ayer, recognize the indefiniteness of the concept "knowledge" and renounce attempts at precise definition, are equally un-interested in hard-to-come-by facts of usage. Who cares what percentage of those interrogated would respond favorably and what percentage unfavorably to some far-fetched imaginary case (e.g., Mr. Truetemp's uncanny weather predictions)? If, however, as noted in chapter 6, someone like Carnap starts speaking about knowledge that might be false, it may be necessary to cite some less recondite facts of usage. Thus, this and the preceding paragraph's examples suggest a general dichotomy: if linguistic data are needed in philosophy, to guide predication, they are available; if they are not available, they are not needed.

To test this generalization, consider a specimen that Zeno Vendler cites:

> Ryle had claimed that the philosophically important word *voluntarily* is used only in connection with actions that seem to have been someone's fault. Austin denied this by pointing out that one can make a gift voluntarily. Then Cavell strikes a middle course by suggesting that at least there must be "something fishy" about the performance thus characterized. Finally Fodor and Katz reject this, referring to the possibility of joining the army voluntarily, in which case nothing fishy need be involved. Now who is right?[18]

According to Vendler, linguistic science cannot answer this question. Yet perhaps the expression "voluntarily" (and not just the psychological facts so labeled) is philosophically important, as he holds. So perhaps there are exceptions to the rule just proposed. Perhaps the linguistic data needed to guide predication are not always available. It would not be surprising if there were at least some exceptions to such a broad generalization. However if, as in Ryle's case, memory fails or is not thoroughly searched, others can cite the missed facts of usage, as Austin, Fodor, and Katz did in this instance without calling on professional assistance. The pertinent linguistic data were accessible.

In further illustration of the correlation between need and availability, consider again the concept "true," used at the start of this section to suggest the opacity of language. Aquinas, who placed truth primarily in mental judgments, did not suffer from a lack of pertinent linguistic data; he simply did not take linguistic data as his guide (when, for instance, he denied that the things people call bad laws are really laws). Wittgenstein, targeting the essentialism that underlay the traditional conception of truth, did attend to the use of words (e.g. "language," "game"), but the reminders he offered were available to all. Similarly, in their debate about truth, Austin knew the verbal samples that Strawson stressed and Strawson knew the samples that Austin emphasized, but each tried to give a single account covering both kinds of utterances— the descriptive-sounding ones ("No truer words were ever spoken") and the nondescriptive ("It is true that her motives were sincere"). And so for the rest: difference by difference, doctrine by doctrine, the disagreements previously cited with regard to truth reveal no need of linguistic data inaccessible to the disputants.

Here, then, we encounter no new dead end. What blocks effective implementation of language's authority, I suggest, is not the opacity of language but neglect or rejection of its authority (as in Moore, Plato, Aquinas, the early Wittgenstein, Carnap, and Tarski) or misunderstanding of its authority (illustrated here, in my view, by Flew, Russell, Malcolm, Kripke, and Putnam). Many such thinkers, especially the former, sit so loosely to linguistic restraints that I am reminded of Wittgenstein's aphorism: "The philosopher is not a citizen of any community of ideas. That is what makes him into a philosopher."[19] The two thinkers now to be considered make a similar impression. Like the reaction assessed in the present chapter, they exemplify a massive post-Wittgensteinian shift back away from concern about the authority of language, and are of interest for that reason.

18

Rorty, Stich, and
Pragmatic Assertability

"I CAN COMPLAIN, justly or else unjustly," writes Gilbert Ryle, "that what you said was tactless, irrelevant, repetitious, false, inaccurate, insubordinate, trite, fallacious, ill-timed, blasphemous, malicious, vapid, uninformative, over-informative, prejudiced, pedantic, obscure, prudish, provocative, self-contradictory, tautologous, circular or nonsensical and so on indefinitely."[1] Utterances may succeed or fail in many ways. How illusory it may therefore appear, amid so many competing considerations, to focus on truth alone, as we have largely done till now, and propose, "This is how we should consistently speak." Remarks of Winston Barnes offer parameters for a response:

> Truth is not the only virtue that speech can have. First, there are the rhetorical virtues of eloquence, suggestiveness, persuasiveness. Secondly, there are the linguistic virtues corresponding to the vices of ambiguity, confusion, vagueness, looseness, etc., which we sum up under the term clarity. Thirdly, there are the cognitive virtues of truth, consistency, coherence, probability, plausibility, insight, profundity. It is well if a philosopher has the rhetorical virtues in due measure, but he may be a great philosopher without them. Better still if he has the linguistic virtues, but some great philosophers have in fact not possessed them; and, as I have shown . . . , to make these linguistic virtues flourish where they are lacking, is not the essential task even of the analytical philosopher. It is the cognitive virtues with which the philosopher is concerned.[2]

Chief among these has been truth. In the still dominant view, not only is truth the primary cognitive value, and not only is it the primary value in philosophy; it is the foremost value in all areas of cognitive discourse. When conflict arises with some other value, truth usually has greater weight. But conflict seldom arises with the values Barnes enumerates. Truth does not conflict with the other cognitive values—consistency, coherence, probability, plausibility, insight, profundity. Neither does it conflict with the virtues of clarity. It may clash with those of eloquence, especially persuasiveness; but that depends on whether one wishes to persuade others of the truth, and doubtless one generally should. Thus, speaking from within the general perspective here evoked, Grice has singled out a "supermaxim" to guide the choice of words: "Try to make your contribution one that is true."[3] It may be, he suggests, that other maxims come into operation only on the assumption that this maxim is satisfied. And within the realm of informative discourse—of philosophy, science, history, and the like—doubtless he would endorse the primacy of truth still more unreservedly. There, many have supposed, where no SS or Mafiosi seek their victims and no patients need reassurance about their condition, truth and warranted assertability coincide. If it isn't true, you shouldn't say it; if it is true, or you think it is, you may or should say it.

Chapter 14 raised peripheral doubts on this score. If I say that I drew a "wavy circle" on the board, my choice of words may be perfectly appropriate. Those hearing my statement will get a good idea of what sort of figure I drew and will probably have no need of a fuller description for the purposes of our exchange. Pragmatically, the utterance looks fine. It is not clear, though, whether my statement, however apt, is true. Reflecting on this contrast, we might wonder: why worry about the statement's truth? Doesn't effective communication suffice—effective communication of what I did and what the figure looked like? And doesn't the like hold generally? As a rule, no doubt true utterances are warranted and warranted assertions are true, but perhaps not always even in philosophical discourse. So a split begins to open between the two tests I have so far associated without worrying which one to prefer—truth or warranted assertability.

If it opens no wider, truth may still be the chief determinant of assertability; and language may be a chief determinant of truth. However, some recent thinkers have seen things differently. Turning from "objective truth" as the goal of inquiry, they have taken a more pragmatic view of assertability, and within this pragmatic perspective, the authority of language, as here understood, has received slight recognition. Let us trace this development in the thought of Richard Rorty, then of Stephen Stich, and see where authority does come to reside.

Rorty

William James, Rorty's pragmatic predecessor, noted limited ways in which mental contents might correspond with reality, but none general enough to constitute truth. (Your idea of the clock on the wall may truly picture its dial, James acknowledged, but what of its works or their elasticity?) Searching discourse rather than the mind, Rorty reaches a similar conclusion:

> To say that the parts of properly analyzed true sentences are arranged in a way isomorphic to the parts of the world paired with them sounds plausible if one thinks of a sentence like "Jupiter has moons." It sounds slightly less plausible for "The Earth goes round the sun," less still for "There is no such thing as natural motion," and not plausible at all for "The universe is infinite."[4]

Thus, for Rorty, in agreement with "the pragmatists," the great fallacy of the tradition "is to think that the metaphors of vision, correspondence, mapping, picturing and representation which apply to small routine assertions will apply to large and debatable ones."[5] The question, therefore, "is precisely whether 'the true' is more than what William James defined it as: 'the name of whatever proves itself to be good in the way of belief, and good, too, for definite, assignable reasons.'"[6] With regard to those reasons, for assertions as well as for beliefs, Rorty adds:

> [Pragmatists] see certain acts as good ones to perform, under the circumstances, but doubt that there is anything general and useful to say about what makes them all good. The assertion of a given sentence—or the adoption of a disposition to assert the sentence, the conscious acquisition of a belief—is a justifiable, praiseworthy act in certain circumstances. But, *a fortiori*, it is not likely that there is something general and useful to be said about what makes all such actions good—about the common feature of all the sentences which one should acquire a disposition to assert.[7]

Neither here nor elsewhere does Rorty envisage the type of correspondence account examined in chapter 14, which obviates the difficulties of isomorphic matching. There is no problem, for instance (to cite his examples), in supposing that the things called moons resemble other things called moons or that the relation between them and Jupiter resembles the relation indicated on other occasions by the verb "has" or that this resemblance has something to do with the truth of the utterance "Jupiter has moons." Similarly, there is no implausibility in supposing that agreement between its use of terms and the terms' established uses in the language helps to account for the truth of an utterance such as "The universe is infinite." The trick is to give an accurate account, not only in this instance but more generally, of such linguistic correspondence and its relevance for truth. Rorty comes no closer than James to providing such an account, for Rorty, too, does not look in this direction. Correspondence as picturing is the only kind he envisages.

What, then, for Rorty, determines what we should say? How does an assertion qualify as "good"? He suggests that when we wish to praise or blame assertions such as those just cited, about Jupiter, natural motion, and the universe, "we show how the decision to assert them fits into a whole complex of decisions about what terminology to use, what books to read, what projects to engage in, what life to live."[8] Here, the authority of language is nowhere in sight; for, though Rorty mentions terminology, he says nothing about how it should be chosen. Indeed, his list furnishes no effective guidance as to what we should say. He cites various considerations but says nothing about their respective roles, rankings, or interrelations. Pragmatically, we are left entirely in the lurch.

The type of approach exemplified by the Principle of Relative Similarity does better in this regard. Indeed, the pragmatic advantages of such linguistic correspondence are so evident that this may help explain Rorty's silence about them and about this study's central issue. As Wittgenstein remarked, "The aspects of things that are most important for us are hidden because of their simplicity and familiarity. (One is unable to notice something—because it is always before one's eyes.)"[9] Various passages in Rorty's writings give this impression, specifically with respect to truth, for instance one in *Contingency, Irony, and Solidarity*. There Rorty again decries the notion of "objective truth": "Truth cannot be out there—cannot exist independently of the human mind—because sentences cannot so exist, or be out there. The world is out there, but descriptions of the world are not. Only descriptions of the world can be true or false."[10] The world may decide between the truth of "Black wins" and "Red wins" or between "The butler did it" and "The doctor did it," but the world does not split itself up, on its own initiative, into corresponding chunks called "facts." Language does the splitting. And "When the notion of 'description of the world' is moved from the level of criterion-governed sentences within the language games to language games as wholes, games which we do not choose between by reference to criteria, the idea that the world decides which descriptions are true can no longer be given a clear sense."[11] Implicit in this account is a notion of objective truth too familiar and commonsensical to arrest Rorty's attention.[12] The world, he acknowledges, can determine the truth of an utterance such as "The butler did it"; it can do so, he also notes in passing, within a given language-game. Thus, somehow the world and the language codetermine the utterance's truth. Just how they do so, Rorty does not pause to consider, nor how practically advantageous it is for them to do so, nor how much weight such truth should therefore be accorded in determining what we should say. The window momentarily blinks open, then quickly closes, and the Issue of Language's Authority passes by unnoticed and unheeded.

This oversight centrally affects Rorty's thought, as can be sensed from Bjørn Ramberg's recent summation:

> For thirty years or more, Rorty has worked to break the grip on analytic philosophy of two problem-defining assumptions. The first is the Kantian idea that knowledge, or thinking generally, must be understood in terms of some relation between what the world offers up to the thinker, on one side, and on the other the active subjective capacities by which the thinker structures for cognitive use what the world thus provides. The second is the Platonic conviction that there must be some particular form of description of things, which, by virtue of its ability to accurately map, reflect, or otherwise latch on to just those kinds through which the world presents itself to would-be knowers, is the form in which any literally true—or cognitively significant, or ontologically ingenuous—statement must be couched. Together, these comprise what Rorty calls representationalism.[13]

The "active subjective capacities" on which we have seen Rorty focus are linguistic, and the "particular form of description" we have seen him critique is isomorphic mapping. We have not seen him contemplate or clearly envisage an alternative form of cognitive structuring and linguistic correspondence such as that considered in chapter 14. Yet there can be no doubt that somehow and to some extent language determines the truth or assertability of assertoric utterances. Just how and to what extent it does so Rorty has not examined. He has not squarely addressed the Issue of Language's Authority. For someone with his concerns, this seems a notable omission.

Given a recent dialectical development in his thought, Rorty may now be more receptive to this neglected perspective. The long-standing thesis position conceived truth as isomorphic correspondence. Rejecting this conception, Rorty rejected truth as correspondence; there was no such thing as "getting things right." Now he recognizes that this antithetical reaction was excessive. "Ramberg has persuaded me," he reports, "to abandon two doctrines which I have been preaching for years: that the notion of 'getting things right' must be abandoned, and that 'true of' and 'refers to' are not word-world relations."[14] So the question previously ignored now demands consideration: if the traditional correspondence account was mistaken, what account is correct? How do we "get things right," linguistically? A satisfactory synthesis combining the truth in both the traditional account and Rorty's reaction—correspondence on the one hand and pragmatic advantages on the other—requires attention to the Issue of Language's Authority.

Stich

Truth, Stich argues in *The Fragmentation of Reason*, has been a false divinity; for, contrary to traditional assumptions, it possesses neither intrinsic nor instrumental value. Stich's critique focuses on true beliefs, but the implications for language's authority look clear. The truth of utterances may not depend on the truth of beliefs, but if true beliefs have no value, then true assertions derive no instrumental value from their causal connection with true beliefs, and language derives no authority from its assurance of assertions' truth. In that case, what authority, if any, does it retain? Stich's reply resembles Rorty's, but reflects different considerations.

Stich relies heavily on a distinction between truth as presently conceived, which he labels simply "truth" and which he takes as his target, and truth as it may one day be conceived. Perhaps the currently favored account—"including Tarski's theory of truth, the Putnam-Kripke causal theory of reference, and functionalism in the philosophy of mind"[15]—is an accurate rendering, so far as it goes. However, "what must be shown is that true beliefs are superior to the indefinitely many alternative categories of belief (TRUE*, TRUE**, and the rest) that are built on alternative accounts of REFERENCE and TRUTH CONDITIONS—accounts that are not sanctioned by commonsense intuition."[16] Given all this competition, to cling to our contemporary category "true," as though it enshrined an intrinsic, eternal value, would be "conservative, limiting, and idiosyncratic."[17]

In place of the traditional standard of truth, Stich proposes a pragmatic criterion. "Though it's hard to see why anyone but an epistemic chauvinist would be much concerned about rationality or truth, we can count on people caring about the pragmatic evaluation of their cognitive processes because that evaluation is tied to goals that they themselves take to be intrinsically valuable."[18] Stich notes and addresses some prima facie objections to this consequentialist approach, but he does not recognize or deal with the quandary in which he appears to place his readers. They may suppose at the start, and may innocently continue to assume, that Stich intends his various assertions to be true, and they may assess them accordingly; for he issues no explicit caution to the contrary. However, to judge from his theory, at no point should we presume that Stich is interested in truth. What, then, does interest him? Should readers take the trouble to divine his guiding goals and judge his claims accordingly? Or should they, instead, assess his assertions by their own interests and goals? If so, may an interest in truth figure among them? In short, what is the name of the game? It would be much simpler just to judge the truth or falsehood of the claims—as Stich himself appears to have done.[19]

Yet Stich does not implicitly contradict himself. He does not aim to get things right about the matters he treats while disclaiming any interest in doing so. For he does not equate truth with getting things right. What he challenges is truth as presently conceived in analytic philosophy, for instance in Tarski's explication of truth, whose limitations chapter 7 noted. Other conceptions might be better. What Stich does not envision is their being better because they get things right. Chapters 13 and 14 suggest and develop this possibility in a way that Stich, too, does not envision or assess. Neither he nor Rorty envisages linguistic correspondence as a possible key to truth and its value.

The pragmatic relevance of such a conception, already noted, can be further suggested by reference to Stich's own linguistic activity. Suppose Stich knew in advance the identity of all those who would one day read his book or learn its contents indirectly; and suppose he had intimate knowledge of the values and desires of all these people, in pertinent detail; and suppose he had some notion of how what he said would further or hinder the pursuit of their values and desires: how would he write his book? How could he accommodate his varied audience? The best he could do, if he had their interests at heart, would be to tell them the truth as he saw it. Truth is common currency. Like money, it helps us do whatever we desire.

"It is widely believed," Stich might respond, "that the instrumental value of true belief is obvious—that having true beliefs is clearly good for lots of things. However, it is my contention that this doctrine is anything but obvious."[20] It becomes more evident, I suggest, if we assess the truth of beliefs by the truth of the utterances that express them and the truth of the utterances by linguistic correspondence, in the manner chapter 14 proposed. To return to an earlier illustration, suppose your neighbor Mrs. Smith tells you the ice is thick. You believe her and go skating. If she has spoken truly—if, for example, her use of "thick" agrees with its customary use—the ice holds, and you enjoy yourself. If she has spoken falsely—if her use of "thick" does not agree with normal usage—you do not succeed in skating nor do you enjoy yourself. You may not even survive. In such a simple paradigm, the need for linguistic correspondence is fairly evident. Thick ice will hold you, thin ice will not. "Thick" is used for the first condition, "thin" for the second. And you are familiar with this usage. So Mrs. Smith should speak accordingly. She should say the ice is thick when it is thick and say it is thin when it is thin.[21] For then, if you believe her, your beliefs will also be true, and you will have a better chance of surviving.

But suppose she wants you to die? In that case, won't falsehood serve her purposes better and in that sense have more instrumental value? Yes, in that sense. But when I suggest that she should tell the truth, I have a less subjective sense in mind. I assume that it is usually not good to cause the death of an innocent person interested in the possibility of skating. More generally, I suppose that, on the whole, truth-telling is more conducive to human welfare than lying. Though my illustrative example is jejune, the same sort of advantages that recommend correspondence in "The ice is thick" recommend it in weather predictions, estimates of tensile strength, budget reports, doctors' diagnoses, market analyses, hypotheses concerning the greenhouse effect, and so forth. Correspondence pays.

In a much fuller account of why truth matters, both instrumentally and intrinsically, than I shall here attempt, Michael Lynch observes: "Cynicism about truth is not just the result of confusion and misunderstanding. It is also the result of the prevalence of certain philosophical theories about what truth is."[22] The reaction of Rorty and Stich to inadequate past and present theories of truth exemplifies Lynch's assessment. Both, I suggest, might discover more pragmatic interest in truth if they conceived it more linguistically.

And not just pragmatic interest. Lynch argues persuasively that truth has more than purely instrumental value and therefore makes strong claims on us. "Something is *normative*," he writes, "if it is worthy of aiming at, or caring about. But something is *deeply normative*, or a value properly so-called, when it is worthy of caring about for its own sake."[23] Such, he maintains, is truth. If so, and if linguistic correspondence is constitutive of truth, perhaps language's role in establishing such correspondence should be recognized as deeply normative. However, Lynch does not distinguish between the truth of utterances and that of beliefs; and it might be suggested that verbal truth has value only instrumentally, in relation to mental truth, which alone has intrinsic value. "There are times in all of our lives," writes Lynch, "when we simply want to know for no other reason than the knowing itself."[24] Notice: the knowing, not the saying or the hearing. However, our knowing, it seems, is no less linguistic than our thinking; and chapter 1 suggested how pervasively linguistic that is. True, as we can have nonlinguistic thoughts, so we can have nonlinguistic knowledge. But, as it is difficult to entertain any written or spoken thought nonlinguistically (try "Thompson was acquitted," I suggested, or "Stocks climbed higher today"), so it is difficult to conceive the corresponding knowledge being had nonlinguistically. I leave the reader to ponder the interesting question how much of the knowledge that appears most desirable—knowledge of our individual selves, humankind, the universe, the riddle of existence—we might acquire or possess if deprived of any linguistic medium.

19

Habermas, Communicative Speech, and Validity

W HAT CLAIMS, I asked at the start, can be made on language's behalf? The chief answer I spotted in linguistic philosophy was "authority." For the "assertoric" utterances in terms of which I have defined the Issue of Language's Authority and which are of most interest in philosophy, this means that language, together with the reality described, may determine such utterances' truth or assertability. So far, I have not troubled to define precisely what class of utterances this suggestion covers; for language's authority, I shall now suggest, extends beyond any one type of utterance. In prescribing, interrogating, promising, forbidding, encouraging, warning, and many other varieties of speech act no less than in describing, explaining, predicting, reporting, or the like, language does and should play a major role in determining what to say. Locating the Issue of Language's Authority within this larger setting will introduce new perspectives and raise new issues.

In this widening, Jürgen Habermas ("arguably the most important philosopher of the late twentieth century," according to one admirer[1]) can serve as guide. Breaking with the narrow "logos characterization of language" that privileges its representational function, Habermas has undertaken to "generalize the concept of validity beyond the truth of propositions and identify validity conditions no longer only on the semantic level of sentences but on the pragmatic level of utterances."[2] So doing, he has traced a broad theoretical framework within which the Issue of Language's Authority can be viewed.

Communicative Utterances

In *The Theory of Communicative Action*, Habermas describes communicative action very generally as "the interaction of at least two subjects capable of speech and action who establish interpersonal relations (whether by verbal or by extraverbal means)."[3] <u>Focusing on the verbal</u> <u>means, he distinguishes between "communicative" speech acts, oriented</u> <u>to mutual understanding, and "strategic" speech acts, oriented to some</u> <u>other end.</u> To illustrate the difference: a person may say "A storm is coming" simply to communicate information, or may intend the statement to warn a hearer, make her hurry, or get her to take precautions. In Austin's terms, which Habermas adopts, the informing is an "illocutionary" speech act, with an "illocutionary" effect, whereas the warning, say, is a "perlocutionary" speech act, with a "perlocutionary" effect. Habermas develops this distinction sufficiently for present purposes when he writes:

> The illocutionary aim a speaker pursues with an utterance follows from the very meaning of what is said; speech acts are, in this sense, self-identifying. By means of an illocutionary act a speaker lets a hearer know that he wants what he says to be understood as a greeting, command, warning, explanation, and so forth. His communicative intent does not go beyond wanting the hearer to understand the manifest content of the speech act. By contrast, the perlocutionary aim of a speaker, like the ends pursued with goal-directed actions generally, does not follow from the manifest content of the speech act; this aim can be identified only through the agent's intention. For example, a hearer who understands a request directed to him can just as little know thereby what *else* the speaker has in view in uttering it as an observer who sees an acquaintance hurrying along the street can know why he is in a hurry. The addressee could at best infer the speaker's perlocutionary aims from the context.[4]

In *The Theory of Communicative Action*, Habermas stresses the possible conflict between illocutionary and perlocutionary aims. Thus, whereas "A storm is coming" might accurately inform one's hearers, "A *huge* storm is coming," though less accurate, might more effectively achieve the aim of warning them, frightening them, or getting them to take precautions. Often, however, there is no conflict, but perlocutionary effectiveness requires illocutionary accuracy. For instance, to prepare one's hearers for appropriate action, to explain one's own preparations, or to demonstrate one's competence, one should indicate the weather accurately. In any case, different standards apply to the two kinds of speech acts. Questions of "validity," in Habermas's broad sense of the term, arise with regard to illocutionary speech acts (predictions, reports, queries, commands, explanations, promises, etc.) but not with regard to perlocutionary speech acts (intended to frighten, confuse, encourage, assist, alienate, ingratiate, etc.). Our attention will therefore center on the former.

Generalizing the concept of validity beyond propositional truth, Habermas makes it embrace all forms of "rational acceptability."[5] Basically, he suggests, all communicative utterances, aimed at understanding, can be assessed by the three criteria of truth, rightness, and sincerity.[6] However, in any given speech act, one or the other of these aspects—truth, rightness, or sincerity—is more prominent; or, as Habermas puts it:

> the illocutionary role . . . determines the aspect of validity under which the speaker wants his utterance to be understood *first and foremost*. When he makes a statement, asserts, narrates, explains, represents, predicts, discusses something, or the like, he is looking for an agreement with the hearer based on the recognition of a truth claim. When the speaker utters a first-person experiential sentence, discloses, reveals, confesses, manifests something, or the like, agreement can come about only on the basis of the recognition of a claim to truthfulness or sincerity. When the speaker gives an order or makes a promise, appoints or warns somebody, baptizes or weds someone, buys something, or the like, agreement depends on whether those involved admit the action as right.[7]

Truth, sincerity, rightness—let us consider the role of language in establishing each type of claim.

Language's Extended Authority

Many have agreed with the idea, proposed in chapter 1, that reality and language codetermine the truth of statements. Habermas extends language's authority beyond truth and statements to other aspects and types of speech acts. "The illocutionary 'aims' of reaching understanding," he writes, quite generally, "cannot be defined without reference to the linguistic means of reaching understanding: the medium of language and the telos of reaching understanding inherent within it constitute one another reciprocally."[8] Thus, if you wish to inform, promise, command, apologize, welcome, introduce, greet, or interrogate, you need to use the right words—the words suggested by the language you are speaking. Truth, rightness, and sincerity require it.

Consider promises, under each of these three headings. *Truth:* Although only certain theorists call them true or false, promises may reveal true or false assumptions. If, for instance, I say, "I promise to repay you," but owe you nothing, I reveal a false assumption, and my utterance fails a crucial test. Its failure derives partly from my lack of indebtedness and partly from my use of the word "repay"—both together. *Rightness:* In illustration of this aspect, Habermas writes: "communications are sometimes 'inappropriate,' reports 'out of place,' confessions 'awkward,' disclosures 'offensive.'"[9] Suppose, then, that a friend says, "Don't trouble about that loan," and I reply, "I promise to repay you." This response could call the sincerity of the friend's remark in question. "I want to repay you" or "I'd like to repay you" would not. The choice of words, with the meanings they have in the language, makes a difference. *Sincerity:* I can sincerely say "I promise to pay you tomorrow" but I cannot sincerely say "I promise to pay you yesterday"—not if I know the meanings of the words I am speaking. It is doubtful whether such an utterance would even qualify as a promise. And the difficulty, both for the sincerity and for the promising, would arise not solely from the impossibility of acting in the past but also from the word "yesterday," which points to the past.

I could amplify these indications for promises, then run through other speech acts—questions, commands, greetings, avowals, and so forth—in the same way, noting the role of language in determining their truth, rightness, and sincerity. And as Habermas extends the term "validity" to cover all these aspects, so I might extend the term "authority" to cover all these ways in which language codetermines what we should say. If, as most would agree, we should speak truthfully, rightly, and sincerely, then we should pay proper heed to language, the medium employed.[10]

An alternative approach complements this one. Rather than examine Habermas's three aspects of validity for their relation to language, we might do the like for the three basic types of utterance that he distinguishes: assertoric, regulative, and expressive. Each of these may succeed or fail in its function: an assertion in its informative function, a promise or command in its regulative function, an avowal in its expressive function. And in each instance, patently, success or failure depends in part on language.

Again, consider promises. If a person promises another to repay a debt, yet owes the other nothing, a natural way to assess the utterance's invalidity is to say that it fails to do what a promise is meant to do: it establishes no obligation on the speaker's part and no expectation on the hearer's part. Why it does not can be traced, as above, to the fact that the speaker owes the hearer nothing, but the relevance of that fact is determined by the use of the word "repay" and by the meaning it has in the language spoken. The success or failure of such an utterance depends partly on the words used and not solely on the facts of the case. These indications, too, we could amplify for promises, then run through other regulative utterances in the same way, then pass on to still more varied utterances. We could note language's role in the success or failure of utterances that succeed or fail in ordering, greeting, apologizing, expressing sympathy, and so forth. And, again, adopting Habermas's broad term of assessment, we might speak of the utterances' "validity" or "invalidity" and of language's role in determining both.

Shared Authority

We have now taken a quick look around, viewing other kinds of validity besides truth and other kinds of utterance besides factual assertions, and noted what they intimate about the authority of language. In Habermas's terms, what they suggest is a fundamental presupposition of communicative speech: namely, that language be accorded authority, not only for assertions but also for promises, queries, commands, and other types of utterance. However, other factors, too, deserve consideration. Not only have we viewed other kinds of validity besides truth and other kinds of utterance besides factual assertions; we have also noted other determining factors of validity besides language. These, too, have a claim to "authority"; but, unlike various rivals we have considered (Platonic Forms, Thomistic concepts, Tractarian thinking-out, theoretical "intuitions," etc.), they complement language rather than compete with it.

Take context and illocutionary aim. In assertions, these too must be taken into account as well as language; but all three—language, context, and illocutionary aim—work together to determine the appropriate choice of words. The context, for example, may be a third-grade classroom and the teacher's illocutionary aim may be to explain; or the context may be a criminal court and the prosecutor's illocutionary aim may be to demonstrate; or the context may be an evening newscast and the anchor's illocutionary aim may be to inform. In each instance, the context will codetermine what to say, as will the illocutionary aim, and as will the language spoken: all three, without conflict or competition.

Here, too, and not just with respect to language's rivals, a certain preeminence might be claimed for language. Generally speaking, it might be suggested, the truth of assertions is a weightier consideration than their contextual or illocutionary aptness (better true and gauche than apt and false). And language, it might further be argued, is what chiefly codetermines assertions' truth. So of these three—language, context, and illocutionary aim—language, together with the reality described, chiefly determines assertability. However, it really does not matter, practically, whether language is accorded primacy relative to these friendly competitors. Choosing our words, we can consider all three—language, context, and illocutionary aim. On the contrary, it matters a great deal how much authority language is accorded relative to its rivals.

These rivals, notice, compete with language but not with illocutionary aim or context. In illustration, consider the successive confrontations in this study. In no instance, from Plato on, did a rival claimant to authority override context or illocutionary aim. Though little considered, these remained constant and unchallenged determinants of what to say. And the like holds generally in philosophy. Philosophers aim to describe, inform, or explain, and they do so in the context of philosophical discussion, not of historical narration, weather prediction, courtroom debate, or gospel proclamation. These aspects of philosophical discourse are taken for granted— but not the authority of language. Manifestly, not that. The great confrontation, on which we have therefore focused, has been between language and its competitors. The next chapter's survey of the contemporary scene will reveal no new rivals, but it will indicate how strong resistance to language's authority continues to be in philosophy.

20

Past, Present, and Future
An Overview

THE TALE NOW told has at least this much unity: it sketches the story of the Issue of Language's Authority. The sampling of authors and issues, limited but representative, traces this single path through the history of Western thought. Why, then, given this single direction, did the tale not have a more unified, coherent plot? A simple explanation would be that the Issue of Language's Authority was never raised and debated, so did not advance systematically, coherently, via response and counterresponse. But then that fact demands explanation. Why, if the issue is as fundamentally important as here claimed and amply exemplified, has it received so little attention? Thomas McCarthy provides an illuminating clue when he writes:

> In modern Western philosophy cognitive concerns with knowledge, truth, objectivity, and the like, particularly when prompted by exemplary achievements in the formal and physical sciences, have tended to predominate. The results of "theoretical" analyses have typically set the stage for the treatment of "practical" philosophical issues, even when thinkers like Kant defended the primacy of practical reason. What has been too often ignored and always underanalyzed is the pervasive normativity of social life.[1]

I know no better illustration of this closing remark than the Issue of Language's Authority. It is a normative issue of social life, it has far too often been ignored, and it has always been underanalyzed. Indeed the issue, explicitly stated, has not figured in philosophical discussion.

The *Cratylus* came close to stating it. Reality, it appeared, cannot dictate its own verbal description; it cannot, by itself, tell us what we should say. Can linguistic conventions fill the gap, Plato wondered; is that where we should look for guidance? If subsequent answers have taken so many directions—if language has had many rivals and its guidance has been variously interpreted—a principal explanation, it seems, is the one McCarthy's remark suggests: inattention to the "normativity of social life." Consider first some illustrations from our story up to this point.

The Past

In the *Phaedo*, with which our narrative began, human beings do not learn what to say from linguistic intercourse with other human beings. Rather, before it learns any language or is immersed in any linguistic milieu, the disembodied soul somehow receives guidance on what to say from its acquaintance, one-on-one, with Platonic Forms. The Forms, not social conventions or the needs of communication, dictate what words to use. A more striking exemplification of McCarthy's assessment could hardly be imagined. Here, the normativity of social life is indeed ignored and underanalyzed.

In the tradition represented by Aquinas, the intellect is equally isolated from linguistic intercourse and its requirements when, directly acquainted with sensible particulars, it abstracts universal concepts that then provide the same sort of guidance that the *Phaedo* traced to the Forms. Words, in this perspective, are a mere code, a handy convenience for transmitting ideas from mind to mind. Get the ideas right, and the words can largely take care of themselves. And to get the ideas right, you must look to the objects of thought and their essences, not to linguistic practice. The notion that (in Wittgenstein's terminology) "essence" might be determined by "grammar" lies far over the horizon.

Young Wittgenstein, continuing the mentalistic tradition, required that meanings be sharp, regardless of what social life or effective intercourse may require. He was thereby led into a never-never land where speakers, unbeholden to linguistic conventions, privately projected their words, picked out atomic objects, and pictured reality as its logical structure dictated. Proposition, thought, and world stood in line one behind the other, each equivalent to each—and the "normativity of social life" was nowhere in sight. Language as a social phenomenon was ignored.

Carnap, replacing private thinking-out of signs with public explication, invested language with some authority, but not enough effectively to check his theoretical inclinations. When, for example, he declared all ethical and metaphysical utterances to be meaningless, the resulting outcry testified how little he had considered the requirements of effective communication. As he himself later recognized, "This formulation caused much unnecessary opposition."

For Tarski, linguistic discourse—the "social life" of signs—appeared too fraught with incoherence for him to trouble about its normativity. His focus on true sentences rather than their employment in true utterances is symptomatic of his disinclination to examine the actual functioning of words. With his explication of "true," he departed to a formal semantic realm from which no guidance did or could descend for those left behind in the thickets of actual discourse.

Had they attended to the needs of linguistic intercourse, it is questionable whether Kripke and Putnam would have said what they did about rigid designators (their application controlled by scientific essences rather than by natural analogy), and still more doubtful whether Russell would have said what he did about sensation (denying that we see, hear, feel, or smell external objects; claiming that we only see our brains). However, Russell revealingly observed that "In fundamental discussions of language, its social aspect should be ignored, and a man should always be supposed to be speaking to himself—or, what comes to the same thing, to a man whose language is precisely identical with his own."[2] That is, he should ignore the "normativity of social life"!

As for Quine, it was his focus on mere sentences rather than their occurrence as utterances within linguistic intercourse that appeared to eliminate the analytic-synthetic distinction and to demand a more holistic assessment than individual utterances do in fact require, given the language spoken and the meanings of its terms.

With their attention, too, fixed elsewhere—on true sentences or beliefs, mistaken past conceptions of truth, preferable future conceptions, the choice of alternative language-games—rather than on utterances and their successful communicative functioning, Rorty and Stich saw no reason to prize truth as a value or, with it, the authority of language.

These piecemeal indications could be multiplied. However, the pertinence of McCarthy's observation appears more comprehensively in the way already suggested. The Issue of Language's Authority, concerning how we should employ words in linguistic intercourse, is a question—fundamental, pervasive, and persistent—regarding the normativity of social life; and, as already noted, this issue has not been formulated or debated, much less has it been fully analyzed. Had Plato stated the Issue of Language's Authority more squarely and suggested its fundamental significance more urgently than he did in the *Cratylus*, and had subsequent discussion of that issue then focused more fully and consistently on the social requirements of linguistic exchange, a historical account of the discussion might have looked less erratic than the tale just told. Also less needful, today as in the past.

The Present

To the preceding historical listing, I might have added G. E. Moore, met back in the first chapter. To recognize how aptly Moore illustrates McCarthy's saying, recall what he said about "good." He would use that word, he wrote, "in the sense in which I think it is ordinarily used; but at the same time I am not anxious to discuss whether I am right in thinking that it is so used. My business is solely with that object or idea, which I hold, rightly or wrongly, that the word is generally used to stand for." The normativity of linguistic social life was far from Moore's concerns, as it was from those of representative thinkers just cited and as it appears to be from those of many present-day thinkers.

Doubtless some contemporary philosophers unreflectively accept the authority of language and some unreflectively reject it, while others accept or reject it more knowingly. One may surmise that these latter are more numerous nowadays than they were before the linguistic wave briefly crested in the last century. However, it is not possible to estimate even roughly just how many thinkers currently fit, more or less, into each of these categories. The thinkers are too numerous, many are not consistent in their practice, few explicitly address the linguistic issue, and those who do at least advert to the relevance of language often do not reveal at all clearly where they stand in its regard. Basically, their ambiguity resembles Moore's, but now takes new forms—forms that, as in Moore's case, suggest unfinished business. The Issue of Language's Authority still waits to be confronted.

For a sample sounding, we can dip into the vast contemporary analytic literature concerning identity, or sameness, and we can focus specifically on the dispute about the necessity or contingency of this relation. Consider, for example, a lump of clay that begins and ends its existence simultaneously with the statue it constitutes. Are the lump of clay and the statue identical, and, if so, are they necessarily or only contingently identical? Opinions are divided. Partisans of contingent identity point out that the same lump of clay might have survived the statue—might, for example, have been squeezed into another shape before the clay hardened. So the identity of statue and lump is not necessary, but contingent. For opponents, identity, in this instance as in others, is always necessary. In support of this view, Ken Akiba has recently argued as follows:

> [Kripke] gave a simple but conclusive proof that there can be no
> such thing as contingent identity; that identity is necessary. The
> proof goes as follows: Take any objects *a* and *b*. Suppose that they
> are identical. (So they are actually not two objects but one.) Obvi
> ously, any object is necessarily identical to itself. So, in particular,

a is necessarily identical to *a*. But we have Leibniz's Law: if *a* and *b* are identical, then for any property φ, *a* has φ if and only if *b* has φ. Take φ as *being necessarily identical to a. a* has this property, and *b* is identical to *a*; so *b* must also have this property. Therefore, *b* must be necessarily identical to *a*. This shows that if *a* and *b* are identical, then they must be necessarily identical; that it is impossible for potentially two objects to be identical but only contingently so. Contingent identity is impossible.[3]

Thus is the game often played. With language and its complications disregarded, the proof is deemed "conclusive." However, viewed linguistically, such argumentation looks shaky. Clearly, the statue and the lump of clay can give no instructions, on their own, as to how they should be described. They cannot dictate that the word "identity" be restricted to strict identity, with one term of the relationship indiscernible from the other, or decree how strict the indiscernibility must be (whether, for example, it must extend to modal as well as to descriptive properties, as in Akiba's argument). Neither can any Platonic Form of Identity so determine. Neither does English or any other natural language. Neither does any language as employed by philosophers (witness this sample altercation). Thus, Akiba's refutation, floating in a semantic void, looks far from decisive.

However, Akiba's thinking has another side to it. After making his case, he inquires: "what are the friends of temporary or contingent identity doing? They are in fact dealing with relations different from identity. It is partly a terminological issue whether or not those relations are to be called temporary and contingent *identity*. Philosophers nowadays use a better term: (temporary and modal) *coincidence*." Yet, adds Akiba, "Whatever these relations are called, they are not genuine, or strict, identity."[4] Notice the resemblance with Moore's remarks about the nature of the good and its independence of how anybody uses the term "good." Akiba's remarks elicit similar puzzlement. How, if the terminology is optional, does strict, Leibnizian identity qualify as the only genuine variety? How, if the terminology is optional, can Akiba declare apodictically "Contingent identity is impossible"? If coincidence, too, may be called identity, and if Leibniz's Law does not apply as strictly to coincidence, what becomes of Akiba's "conclusive proof"?

On the other side of the debate, Allan Gibbard takes a different approach, as representative of contemporary analytic practice as Akiba's. "This brief for contingent identity," Gibbard writes, "begins with an example. Under certain conditions, I shall argue, a clay statue is identical with the piece of clay of which it is made—or at least it is plausible to claim so. If indeed the statue and the piece of clay are identical, I shall show, then the identity is contingent . . . This claim of contingent identity,

if true, has important ramifications."[5] Such a passage suggests interest in
the truth of the matter and not merely in a preferable terminology. Yet
the case Gibbard makes for his position looks akin to Carnapian explication (cf. chapter 6), which does concern terminology and makes no
truth claims. This impression is strongest when Gibbard cites linguistic
advantages and disadvantages of his stance. It might be objected, he
notes, that with contingent identity "we shall be unable to say many of
the things we need to say, both in scientific talk and in daily life." Indeed,
"Perhaps we can maintain contingent identity only at the cost of tying
our tongues, and that, if it is true, might be a strong reason for rejecting
contingent identity."[6] This sounds Carnapian, and so does Gibbard's re-
joinder: "The remainder of my argument for the plausibility of the system
I am advocating will concern this issue. I shall give devices which I think
will enable us to say anything that we ought seriously to regard as meaningful, and say it in the system I am advocating." And he continues in like
fashion: "Carnap's system, I think, is the best one for handling quantified
modal talk of concrete things." But then he adds (naming his sample
statue "Goliath" and his lump of clay "Lumpl"): "It fits my claim that
Goliath = Lumpl."[7] Is this apparently factual claim a Carnapian linguistic recommendation in disguise? If so, it is well disguised. If not—if neither familiar word meanings nor stipulated substitutes are accorded any
authority—what does establish the truth or assertability of "Goliath =
Lumpl"? Where are we?

Suppose no scientific definition of "fish" had as yet been proposed
and accepted, and someone were to deny that whales, porpoises, and
other fishlike mammals are fish. That would cause needless confusion.
The rational procedure would be to focus on the scientific advantages of
the proposed terminology and leave all "claims" until later. When and if
the new terminology was adopted, the denial that porpoises and whales
are fish would look no more problematic than would the assertion that
mackerel and trout are fish or the assertion that frogs and katydids are
not. At that point, such a "claim" would be pointless; made earlier, it
would obscure the fact that the whole issue was terminological. The same
appears true of Gibbard's claim "Goliath = Lumpl": it does not make
good sense whichever of these two perspectives one envisages (preadop-
tion or postadoption), and there are no others to choose from. For practical purposes, the disjunction is complete.

By now the reader may sense why I suggested similarity between
Moore's approach and the sort of analytic thinking represented here by
Akiba and Gibbard, and why I see McCarthy's remark about the normativity of social practice as pertinent to both. Both in Moore's discussion
of good and in this debate about identity, serious problems arise for effective communication, and they appear to arise for the same reason: dis-

regard of language and its authority, based on the needs of communication. Simply put, when the distinction between message and medium is ignored, there is no telling what is message and what is medium. Readers or
hearers, if attentive to this distinction, do not know how to understand
the claims that are made, so do not know by what evidence or arguments
to assess them. Language has gone on holiday.

So runs a critique, from a linguistic viewpoint, of some characteristic
thinking in the contemporary analytic mode. Now, how might practi-
tioners such as Akiba and Gibbard reply? Would they accept language's
authority and claim that they honor it, or would they reject its authority?
I have received rejoinders of both kinds.

In a response of the first kind, it has been suggested that thinkers
such as Akiba and Gibbard might defend themselves against the charge of
linguistic arbitrariness by saying that they are playing the analytic-philosophy language-game. Thus, they do have linguistic backing: their practice conforms to this well-established use of words. This strikes me as
similar to saying that they are playing the chess-checkers game. There are
rules for chess and rules for checkers, but none for chess-checkers. Likewise, there are rules for linguistic description and rules for linguistic stipulation—rules that make good sense for each of these distinct tasks—but
none for linguistic description-stipulation. (In confirmation, notice how
differently Akiba and Gibbard play the game.) At what point, we are
made to wonder, may an analytic philosopher be required to produce evidence for a "claim," and at what point may he or she reply, "Oh, that's
just my suggested use of words"?

A still more appropriate reply to this proposed defense of analytic
practice would recall chapter 1's distinction between a language (e.g., English) and a language-game (e.g., description or stipulation) that makes
use of the language. In the analytic-philosophy language-game exemplified by Akiba and Gibbard, there is no telling whether claims have the
backing of a language, because there is no telling what language is being
employed—the natural language, such as English, whose words are made
use of, or a substitute terminology introduced in the guise of a preferred
theory. Conceivably, one language or the other might back the authors'
claims, but not both.

An alternative defense of analytic practice raises an objection precisely
at this point. Repeatedly, as just now, I have envisaged only two alternatives: either stick with existing, elastic word meanings or stipulate substitute meanings. Either alternative can be reasonable, but if neither is
accepted—neither existing meanings nor substitute meanings—words will
have no meanings and babel will result. Such, grossly stated, has been my
recurring assumption. Now, the objection questions this dichotomy. Certainly, analytic philosophers have not felt bound by any such either-or

requirement, nor perhaps should they have. In illustration of their freer practice, consider this sample:

> The definition of knowledge I will propose has not yet reached a level of precision that permits it to withstand all such attacks. However, I will begin such a test in this book, bearing in mind that precision is but one virtue of a definition, one that must be balanced against simplicity, elegance, conciseness, theoretical illumination, and practical usefulness.[8]

This sounds doubly familiar. It recalls Bernard Williams's similar remarks on the same topic, acknowledging the imprecision of his formulation and envisaging further requirements "which need to be spelled out with greater precision." It also recalls Carnap's similar list of virtues—precision, fruitfulness, simplicity—for effective explication. However, here, as often, the term "definition" does not indicate unambiguously the nature of the proposed enterprise. It leaves unclear whether the author's aim is (like Williams's) a more accurate account of knowledge or (like Carnap's) an improved terminology. These different aims relate very differently to the question of language's authority (cf. chapter 16 on "Crafting Language versus Using Language"). Straddling this distinction much as Akiba and Gibbard did, the quoted proposal leaves obscure whether, how, and to what extent language should be accorded authority.

In this the quotation is widely representative. It is symptomatic of a shift away from the strong "linguistic turn" of the last century, and it is symptomatic of a major reason behind this shift. Truth as mind-thing correspondence appears unrealistic, and no linguistic alternative is envisioned to replace it; so the whole notion of truth as correspondence is abandoned. Yet, as noted earlier, this dialectic looks incomplete. For the linguistic version of truth as correspondence clearly is realistic. Whether we speak, truly, about computers, numbers, or games, the things we call "computers" resemble the things called computers, the things we call "numbers" resemble the things called numbers, the things we call "games" resemble the things called games, and so forth. The resemblance is closer for the word employed than it would be for any rival expression. And such resemblance is important. This, too, seems obvious, at least in familiar, everyday discourse. Why such correspondence becomes either impossible or undesirable in philosophical discourse, for instance about knowledge, is not evident.

It is also unclear how communication can succeed if language is ignored. A language is a shared form of life. The proposed alternative is not. Speakers do not agree that precision, simplicity, elegance, conciseness, theoretical illumination, and practical usefulness should decide what we call knowledge or anything else (taxes, coffins, clouds, graffiti, etc.). They do not agree on the respective weight each of these disparate virtues should be accorded or which virtues should take precedence in cases of conflict. They do not agree that the language spoken need not be consulted when considering what to say. So the proposed approach, disregarding the claims of language, does not look promising for purposes of communication. When confusion descended on the builders at Babel, the people still spoke recognizable languages. A sample debate such as that concerning knowledge suggests that if analytic tower building became systematic and pervasive, communication might break down more thoroughly. In any case, such linguistic questions and concerns are so foreign to contemporary analytic discourse that McCarthy's assessment clearly applies: "What has been too often ignored and always underanalyzed is the pervasive normativity of social life."

An analytic philosopher with whom I discussed the difficulties sketched in this section suggested that, much as scientists must somehow "muddle through," so must philosophers. This response strikes me as overly pessimistic. In any case, it calls for fuller justification than I have seen attempted. If philosophy is condemned to muddle, perhaps philosophy's days are numbered. If, more specifically, analytic philosophy is condemned to muddle, perhaps its days are numbered.

The Future

Georg Henrik von Wright's assessment near the end of the last century sounds equally plausible a decade later:

> In spite of the many tributaries which have, in the course of the years, emptied their waters into this river, I think it is right and illuminating to call analytic philosophy the mainstream of philosophic thinking in this century. In all its heterogeneity it retains the two features which I already mentioned as typical of its origin: the emphasis on logic and the alignment with science. It is, in short, the philosophy most characteristic of a culture dominated by scientific rationality.[9]

It is the philosophy of young Wittgenstein, Carnap, Tarski, Russell, Kripke, and others cited in earlier chapters. It is the philosophy of Akiba, Gibbard, and like-minded thinkers examined in this chapter. And it is a philosophy in constant conflict with the authority of language. For that authority hampers its scientific aspirations, since it makes it much more difficult to achieve universality and precision comparable to those in logic, mathematics, and the natural sciences.

Looking now to the future we can ask: will von Wright's apercu look equally apt fifty years hence? Will Goliath, Lumpl, and their kin still hold interest for philosophers? Will Mr. Truetemp? Will brains in vats, or

brains transferred, in whole or in part, to other bodies? Will the whole
enterprise of case and far-fetched countercase, theory and countertheory,
argued step by analytic step, employing all the tools of modern logic, but
little concerned about the claims of language? Or will philosophers come
to accept Putnam's appraisal as representative of this whole analytic
genre: "Contemporary analytic metaphysics has no connection with anything but the 'intuitions' of a handful of philosophers"?[10]

The label "analytic" proclaims a virtue, not a vice. But it is a virtue
more evident in Wittgenstein's later, linguistic thinking than in his earlier,
metaphysical period; and it is a virtue, the present account suggests, that
would characterize analytic philosophy more fully if it underwent a comparable shift. Whether such a development occurs may depend in part,
first, on whether the Issue of Language's Authority is finally taken seriously and, second, on whether the issue is addressed, as McCarthy's
remarks suggest, in terms of effective communication.

Major obstacles block consideration of the Issue of Language's Authority. One is the impression that the claims of language have already
been taken care of and need no longer concern us. The claims made for
"ordinary language," it is thought, have long since been dealt with, and
Quine's holistic approach has undercut any independent authority language might exercise. Earlier chapters have corrected both of these
perceptions. At the heart of the ordinary-language debate, chapter 12 detected a larger issue: how much authority should *language*—ordinary or
extraordinary, standard or stipulated—be granted as a determinant of
truth or warranted assertability? As for Quine, chapter 16 noted that he
himself recognized "that sheer verbal usage is in general a major determinant of truth." Thus, the common overall impression is mistaken. The
philosophical community has not yet confronted the Issue of Language's
Authority, and it needs to. However, the contrary impression is so
strong—and so convenient for business as usual—that it effectively
blocks reconsideration of philosophy's status vis-à-vis language.

One can readily grasp why philosophers in the mainstream von
Wright describes would resist reassessment of language's authority. "The
challenge presented by philosophy," writes Bede Rundle, "is to state and
support something that is true but not trivial, something that can be reck-
oned as falling within the province of the subject but is not merely destructive of misconception."[11] Clearly, acceptance of language's authority
makes it much more difficult to meet this challenge. The *Tractatus*'s theses, for example, were not trivial; they fell within the province of the subject (they were not scientific); and they were not merely destructive. They
stated boldly the nature of names, propositions, language. But they
lacked linguistic backing. Contemporary philosophers might invoke "intuitions" in support of such theses, but these, too, would lack linguistic

support. Carnapian explication might tailor the terms in the way desired, but then mere verbal stipulations would replace the Tractarian theses. The explications might look far from trivial if it could be shown that for all purposes, or at least all philosophical or scientific purposes, a given terminology—say, the Tractarian—would be preferable; but how could that be demonstrated? And how, if the explicating terms retained their indefinite meanings, could the explicated term acquire sufficient precision for rigorous theory construction? (Recall the radical indefiniteness that the term "satisfaction" left in Tarski's renowned explication of truth.) These twists and turns suggest how cramped many contemporary analytic philosophers would feel if deprived of their favored solution for Rundle's challenge—namely, the Tractarian tactic of stating theses and theories without backing either from current linguistic usage or from satisfactory explications distinct from the theses or theories.

Doubtless the alternative to linguistic disregard appears uninviting in other ways as well. Typically, in the absence of explicit stipulations of meaning, accepting the authority of language means taking existing usage as one's guide, and most existing usage strikes many as intolerably messy in comparison with the precision and coherence of abstract formal systems. Furthermore, reasoned acceptance of language's authority would likely bring with it the alien perspective that chapter 14 evoked with regard to linguistic norms and that McCarthy indicates more generally:

> By their very nature, general rules *must* understate the complexity of the concrete circumstance to which they apply. They are *supposed* to cover an indefinite range of specific instances, and those instances are not marked out as such in advance of any interpretive work. This is *a fortiori* true of the largely implicit, approximate, ambiguous, and open-ended norms that structure interaction in everyday life. Like any general rules, but even more so, they come without a detailed, exhaustive set of instructions for applying them. Thus they cannot determine, and hence cannot fully explain, specific, concrete actions in specific, concrete situations. Their "application" requires not unthinking conformity but competent practical reasoning to deal with contingencies as they arise and competent for-all-practical-purposes judgements in the light of concrete circumstances. And this of course means that there is always an element of the ad hoc and discretionary about their meaning-in-practice.[12]

A switch to such a perspective from that of contemporary analytic philosophy would be so wrenching that it cannot be expected to occur any time soon. Indeed, in view of powerful historical and cultural influences such as those cited, I would be surprised if it did.

Yet not astonished. The current dissatisfaction of so many philosophers with contemporary analytic philosophy may hint at things to come.[13] And there is much truth in the Hegelian notion that thought proceeds dialectically. In reaction to the linguistic insouciance exemplified by Wittgenstein's *Tractatus*, the linguistic tide rose high in the mid-twentieth century, but not high enough: it did not formulate or confront the Issue of Language's Authority concealed within the debate about "ordinary language." So the tide dropped backward, toward the *Tractatus*'s disregard of language. Yet it did not recede all the way back: the "intuitions" now invoked suggest some awareness of the arbitrariness of Tractarian theorizing. When and if this solution is viewed as inadequate, linguistic interest may return, stronger than before. Philosophers may finally confront the issue on which this study has focused.

With this overview of past, present, and future, I can finally collect a promissory note. By the end of this study, I remarked at the beginning, the thesis may at least appear plausible that the Issue of Language's Authority is *the* central issue of linguistic philosophy, in the sense that it is more important than any other central issue: it exerts a greater influence and has weightier implications not only within linguistic philosophy but beyond. Within are the later Wittgenstein, Flew, Malcolm, Austin, Kripke, Putnam, and the many they represent. Beyond lie Plato, Aquinas, young Wittgenstein, and the heterogeneous multitudes they stand for. And from the preceding accounts of these and other thinkers, one can sense that the issue has exerted vast influence, not by being explicitly and variously answered, but in the sense that the positions adopted in its regard have affected fundamentally the course of Western thought. Successful rivals to language's authority have shaped the thinking of nonlinguistic philosophers from Plato to the present. Different readings of language's authority have shaped the thinking of linguistic philosophers from Wittgenstein to the present. And the effect of these rivals and these readings has been so massive that, without them, the history of Western philosophy might have looked unrecognizably different.

So the suggested thesis has much to say for it. However, I also posted a more modest claim: whether or not, in the end, the Issue of Language's Authority is accorded primacy, it merits fuller, more systematic scrutiny than it has previously received. As James noted in another context, "Any hypothesis that forces such a review upon one has one great merit, even if in the end it prove invalid: it gets us better acquainted with the total subject."[14] The present inquiry offers fuller acquaintance with the Issue of Language's Authority. With language's chief rivals identified and its claims scrutinized, readers may be better equipped to grapple with the issue, perhaps even answer it, and may more clearly sense its significance.

The tale here recounted leaves little doubt that if language, the medium of communication, merits recognition as the principal determinant, together with the reality described, of statements' truth and assertability, then an "interesting general answer"—indeed, a uniquely interesting general answer—can be given to Hacking's query, "Why does language matter to philosophy?" On the same supposition, language matters equally in all areas of inquiry; but it is in philosophy that language's authority has been most strongly contested and it is by philosophy that its authority will, eventually, have to be judged.

NOTES

Preface

1. Wittgenstein, *Philosophical Investigations*, §129.
2. Ibid., §111.

CHAPTER 1. The Issue of Language's Authority

1. Gellner, *Words and Things*, 15.
2. Dummett, *Frege: Philosophy of Language*, 667.
3. Ibid.
4. Ibid.
5. Ibid., 669. Cf. Urban, *Language and Reality*, 15; Ricoeur, "Philosophie et langage," 272–73; Dummett, "Can Analytical Philosophy Be Systematic," 442: "For Frege, as for all subsequent analytical philosophers, the philosophy of language is the foundation of all other philosophy."
6. Gregory Currie cites other examples: "The dependence of theories of meaning on epistemology has been a standard pattern in philosophy. I have already given the example of Frege's theory of meaning. The same could be said of the verificationist theory of meaning, which floundered, not on results in the theory of meaning, but on negative logical and epistemological results. Again, Dummett refers often to the debate between intuitionistic and classical logic, which he regards as a debate within the theory of meaning. But it is very clear—from Brouwer's writings for instance—that intuitionism takes its stand primarily on epistemological arguments" ("Was Frege a Linguistic Philosopher?" 88).
7. Wittgenstein, *Philosophical Investigations*, §43.
8. Cf. Baker and Hacker, *Wittgenstein: Understanding and Meaning*, 684–85; Cook, "Fate," 23; Passmore, "Reflections on 'Logic and Language,'" 157 ("To 'clarify the concept of a planet,' for example, is to engage in astronomy"); and Charles Taylor's critique of the claim that linguistic

philosophy such as that of Gilbert Ryle and John Austin is free from all metaphysical presuppositions ("Phenomenology and Linguistic Analysis: I," 226–29).

9. Herder, *Fragmente*, 347, quoted in Schaff, *Language and Cognition*, 9.

10. Whorf, *Language, Thought, and Reality*, 213.

11. Sapir, *Selected Writings*, 10–11.

12. Schaff, *Language and Cognition*, 8.

13. Cf. Black, "Linguistic Relativity," 233–36 (on Whorf's claim that every language "conceals a METAPHYSICS") and Hallett, "The Theoretical Content of Language," 309–11 (on Whorf's claim that one's language determines one's "picture of the universe").

14. Cf. Whorf, *Language, Thought, and Reality*, 243 ("we therefore read action into every sentence, even into 'I hold it'").

15. Ibid., 213.

16. Putnam, "Language and Philosophy," 14.

17. On the similar direction taken earlier, "in the Hamann-Herder-Humboldt tradition," see Lafont, *The Linguistic Turn in Hermeneutic Philosophy*.

18. Wittgenstein, *Philosophical Investigations*, §329.

19. Wittgenstein, *Philosophical Grammar*, 106.

20. Wittgenstein, *Zettel*, §110. For ample illustration, see, for example, Cohen, *The Dialogue of Reason*, 39–40, and Pinker, *The Language Instinct*, 67–73.

21. Wittgenstein, *Philosophical Investigations*, §330 ("I might also act in such a way while taking various measurements that an onlooker would say I had—without words—thought: If two magnitudes are equal to a third, they are equal to one another"); *Zettel*, §100.

22. Wittgenstein, *Last Writings*, vol. 1, §913; cf. *Zettel*, §173.

23. Dummett, *The Interpretation of Frege's Philosophy*, 39. Cf. Dummett, "Can Analytical Philosophy be Systematic," 458, and "The Relative Priority of Thought and Language."

24. Moore, *Principia Ethica*, 58.

25. Ibid. Compare an intriguingly similar passage in David K. Lewis, *Convention*, 3.

26. Putnam, "Language and Philosophy," 9. Cf. Ayer, *Philosophy and Language*, 7:

> It would seem that Moore himself was inclined to reify meanings: the concepts or propositions which philosophers sought to analyse were given the status of non-natural objects. No doubt it was not possible to apprehend them unless one understood the appropriate words, but this applied equally to many of the objects of the sciences . . . just as the mathematician was not concerned with nu-

merals as such but rather with the numbers which they represented, so the philosopher's command of language was merely a necessary means to the investigation of the objective properties of concepts.

27. Moore, *Principia Ethica*, 3 (preface to the projected second edition).

28. Bunge, *Life Science*, 139.

29. I would add that language also serves to direct people; entertain people; elicit information; convey information about the weather, prices, or the Big Bang; and so forth. The closing phrase in this definition (from *The American Heritage College Dictionary*) reflects a tradition here critiqued in chapter 4.

30. Ibid.

31. Ryle, "Use, Usage and Meaning," 223.

32. Mackie, *Contemporary Linguistic Philosophy*, 17.

33. Imagine this exchange. A: "Knowledge is a process, not an act." B: "Not in the English language it isn't, and neither is it an act." A: "Well, that's how I define the word." B: "In that case, all right—though you should have told me you were using the word in an unfamiliar sense." Though neither A nor B has stated or debated the issue, one can sense that B, at least (and the many he represents), accepts the authority of language, standard or stipulated, to determine an utterance's truth or assertability.

34. Gellner, *Words and Things*, 39.

35. Hacker, "Analytic Philosophy," 15.

36. Moore, *Principia Ethica*, 196.

37. A. J. Ayer writes, "[Moore] himself was always careful to say that the practice of what he called analysis was only one of the functions of philosophy. Moreover he did not conceive of it as an inquiry into language. It was concerned, in his view, not with linguistic expressions, but rather with the concepts, or propositions, or facts, for which they stood" (*Philosophy and Language*, 6). Cf. Moore, "A Reply to My Critics," 665: "To define a concept is the same thing as to give an analysis of it; but to define a word is neither the same thing as to give an analysis of that word, nor the same thing as to give an analysis of any concept."

38. Rorty, *Contingency, Irony, and Solidarity*, 14.

CHAPTER 2. The Question's Centrality

1. Harré, introduction to Waismann, *The Principles of Linguistic Philosophy*, xi.

2. Williams, in Magee, *Men of Ideas*, 138.

3. Cornforth, *Marxism and the Linguistic Philosophy*, 9. Cf. Alice Lazerowitz, "Linguistic Approaches to Philosophical Problems," 150 ("I define a linguistic approach to philosophy as one arising from the view

that what a philosopher does when he produces or tries to refute a philosophical theory is to inform one about language").

4. Mackenzie, *Introduction to Linguistic Philosophy*, ix.

5. Flew, "Philosophy and Language," 21–22. Cf. Hacker, "Analytic Philosophy," 23.

6. Cf. Hacker, *Wittgenstein's Place*, 160–61, on Oxford in the heyday of linguistic philosophy.

7. Flew, "Philosophy and Language," 21.

8. A secondary role for language, less stressed by linguistic philosophers, is that indicated by a much-quoted passage of the Oxford philosopher John Austin:

> our common stock of words embodies all the distinctions men have found worth drawing, and the connexions they have found worth marking, in the lifetimes of many generations: these surely are likely to be more numerous, more sound, since they have stood up to the long test of the survival of the fittest, and more subtle, at least in all ordinary and reasonably practical matters, than any that you or I are likely to think up in our arm-chairs of an afternoon—the most favoured alternative method. ("A Plea for Excuses," 182)

Here, language serves as a clue to reality, not as an arbiter of what to say about reality.

9. Tugendhat, *Traditional and Analytical Philosophy*, 5.

10. Moore, *Philosophical Papers*, 89.

11. Hacking, *Why Does Language Matter?* 157.

12. In wide reading, I have not discovered any thinkers other than myself who fit this description, but I do not wish to exclude their possible existence.

13. Wittgenstein, *Philosophical Investigations*, §104.

CHAPTER 3. Plato's Recourse to Nonlinguistic Forms

1. Plato, *Phaedo*, 73A (Bluck translation, Routledge & Kegan Paul, 1955, as hereafter).

2. Ibid., 75B.

3. Ibid., 75C.

4. Ibid., 75CD.

5. Ibid., 60B, 68C.

6. White, *Plato on Knowledge and Reality*, 73 (referring back to chapter 1, section 3).

7. Susan Levin reveals no realization of this gap when she suggests: "For a more elaborate account of Plato's metaphysical views, and his

resulting linguistic commitments, one must turn to the *Phaedo*" ("What's in a Name?" 111).

8. White, *Plato on Knowledge and Reality*, 131 (paragraph break omitted).

9. Plato, *Cratylus*, 384D.

10. Ibid., 384B.

11. Ibid., 383AB (Fowler translation, Heinemann, 1926, as hereafter).

12. Ibid., 423B.

13. Ibid., 426E.

14. Ibid., 385A.

15. Weingartner, *Unity*, 17–18.

16. Plato, *Cratylus*, 435B. Cf. Weingartner, *Unity*, 25: "Socrates' insistence here on convention should be recognized as a confirmation of the fact that, unless we are prepared to say that Socrates flatly contradicts himself, his opposition to Hermogenes' position is not an attack on any *conventional* conventionalism." In her impressive study of the *Cratylus*, Rachel Barney strikes a balance between Cratylus and Hermogenes when she suggests that the dialogue's conclusion "expresses a resignation to the functioning of actual names by convention, yet insists that this is a grave defect on their part" (*Names and Natures*, 164). Torn between realism and conventionalism, Plato was impaled on the problem the present study addresses.

17. Copleston, *Aquinas*, 182.

18. See, for example, Chisholm, *Theory of Knowledge*, 38.

19. Wittgenstein, *Philosophical Investigations*, §96.

CHAPTER 4. Aquinas and the Primacy of Mental Truth

1. Wittgenstein, *The Blue and Brown Books*, 3.

2. On the Aristotelian views from which Aquinas's derived, see Modrak, *Aristotle's Theory of Language and Meaning*.

3. For example, Aquinas, *Summa theol.* I, q. 16, aa. 2 and 3; q. 17, a. 3; *De ver.*, q. 1, aa. 2–3, 9; *In Perih.*, lib. 1, cap. 3, lect. 3, 9; *In VI Meta.*, lect. 4, 1227–1241; *In IX Meta.*, lect. 11, 1898.

4. Aquinas, *In IX Meta.*, lect. 11, 1896 (translation from Aquinas, *Commentary*, vol. 2, 699–700).

5. Cf. Hoenen, *Reality and Judgment*, 3–7. Patrick Lee explains: "Aquinas often uses the word 'similitude' in this context because while there is identity in form or content, the mode of being of the form in the thing is different from its mode of being in the intellect's act, and 'similitude' means identity in form together with difference in other aspects" ("Aquinas," 58).

6. Aquinas, *In Perih.*, lib. 1, cap. 3.

7. Ibid. Cf. *In VI Meta.*, lect. 4.

8. For example, Aquinas, *In Perih.*, lib. 1, cap. 3; *Summa theol.* I, q. 34, a. 1, c.; *Contra gent.*, lib. 4., cap. 11 and 13; *De ver.*, q. 4, a. 1, c ("the interior word is naturally prior, being the efficient and final cause of the exterior") and q. 9, a. 4, c. Cf. Augustine, *De Trin.* lib. 15, cap. 10–11, 19–20; Albertus Magnus, *Metaph.*, lib. 6, tract. 3, cap. 1 ("truth and falsehood in speech are signs of truth and falsehood in the soul").

9. Hallett, *Language and Truth*, chapters 1 and 2.

10. In this readier hypothesis, a Thomist might still envisage a dialectically laborious process of abstraction. In *De anima*, lib. 3, lect. 11, Aquinas himself does not in fact take this approach to tense.

11. A sampling: *Summa theol.* I, q. 14, a. 9, ob. 2; q. 16, a. 2, c.; q. 17, a. 3, c.; q. 27, a. 2, c.; q. 55, a. 2, ob. 1; q. 76, a. 2, ad 4; q. 85, a. 8, ad 3; q. 88, a. 1, ad 2; I–II, q. 51, a. 1, ad 2; In Sent., I, d. 15, q. 5, a. 3, ad 3; d. 17, q. 1, a. 4, ad 4; III, d. 23, q. 1, a. 2, ob. 5–6 and ad 6; *De ver.* q. 2, a. 5, ad 5 and 8; a. 6, c.; q. 4, a. 4, ad 2; q. 8, a. 11, ad 3; *Contra gent.* lib. 1, cap. 53;. lib. 2, cap. 98 and 99; lib. 4, cap. 11; *In VI Meta.*, lect. 4, 1234–36; *In XII Meta.*, lect. 8, 2541; *De anima*, lib. 1, lect. 4 and 12; lib. 2, lect. 12; *In Ioan.*, cap. 1, lect. 11, 2; cap. 7, lect. 3, 7; *Opusc. de intellectu et intelligibili*; *Opusc. de universalibus*, tract. 2; *In X libros Ethicorum*, lib. 6, lect. 1, 1139, a.10.

12. Cf., for example, Boethius, *In Porphyr.*, lib. 1 (*Patrologia Latina* 64, col. 85BC); Albertus Magnus, *Metaph.*, lib. 1, tract. 1, cap. 7: "Oportet autem, quod universale per se et substantialiter sit multorum illorum similitudo."

13. Panaccio in "Aquinas on Intellectual Representation" cites and rightly resists this recent tendency.

14. O'Callaghan, *Thomistic Realism and the Linguistic Turn.* See, for example, the section on "'Similitude' or 'Likeness' in St. Thomas's Account" (227–32). The "attenuated notion of likeness" that Deborah Modrak suggests in her analysis of Aristotle is not one that Aquinas attributed to the Philosopher or that readily fits Aquinas's own writings or that does much if anything to meet the difficulties here cited. When, she proposes, the *phantasma* is employed in a way that enables it to represent a universal, it resembles the universal "by representing general features manifested by the object of which it is the *phantasma*" (*Aristotle's Theory*, 259). Thus the likeness of any specific triangle, say, is ipso facto a likeness of the triangularity common to all triangles.

15. Moore, *Commonplace Book 1919–1953*, 19.

16. Ibid., 21.

17. Consulting Thomistic thinkers for possible flaws in the present critique, I was told that we do, after all, form mental likenesses. This I grant, but the kind of concrete images we believe are likenesses of sensi-

ble realities (chairs, verandas, daffodils) do more to explain, psychologically, belief in intellectual, essentialistic likenesses than they do to provide
any evidence for their existence.

18. Plato, *Republic* 596a (Cornford translation).
19. Frege, *Translations*, 174.
20. Cf. Frege, ibid., 58 ("To every expression belonging to a complete totality of signs, there should certainly correspond a definite sense;
but natural languages often do not satisfy this condition, and one must be
content if the same word has the same sense in the same context").
21. Aquinas, *Summa theol.* I–II, q. 90, a. 2, and q. 95, a. 2, c.
22. Ibid., I–II, q. 90, a. 4, c.
23. Russell, *The Analysis of Mind*, 273–74.
24. Russell, *Logic and Knowledge*, 319.
25. Moore, *Some Main Problems of Philosophy*, 301.

CHAPTER 5. The *Tractatus*: Precise Thought versus Imprecise Language

1. See Hallett, *Language and Truth*, chap. 1.
2. Frege, "Logic," in *The Frege Reader*, 231.
3. Dummett, *Origins of Analytical Philosophy*, 25. See ibid., 131:

The extrusion of thoughts from the mind initiated by Bolzano
led to what is often termed "platonism," as exemplified by
Frege's mythology of the "third realm": for, if thoughts are not
contents of the mind, they must be located in a compartment of
reality distinct both from the physical world and the inner
world of private experience. This mythology served Frege and
Husserl as a bulwark against the psychologism which they opposed. If, now, our capacity for thought is equated with, or at
least explained in terms of, our ability to use language, no such
bulwark is required: for language is a social phenomenon, in no
way private to the individual, and its use is publicly observable.

4. Wittgenstein, *Notebooks 1914–1916*, 67.
5. Ibid.
6. Ibid., 68.
7. Cf. Wittgenstein, *Tractatus Logico-Philosophicus*, 3.5: "A
propositional sign, applied and thought out, is a thought."
8. Ibid., 3.23.
9. Wittgenstein, *Philosophical Investigations*, §39.
10. Russell, *Logic and Knowledge*, 179. Cf. Whitehead and Russell,
Principia Mathematica, vol. 1, 66: "Whenever the grammatical subject of a
proposition can be supposed not to exist without rendering the proposition

meaningless, it is plain that the grammatical subject is not a proper name, *i.e.* not a name directly representing some object."

11. Wittgenstein, *Tractatus Logico-Philosophicus*, 3.26 and 3.261.
12. Wittgenstein, *Philosophical Investigations*, §60.
13. Wittgenstein, *Tractatus Logico-Philosophicus*, 3.3.
14. Ibid., 4.0311.
15. Ibid., 4.5.
16. Wittgenstein, *Notebooks 1914–1916*, 70 (translation amended).
17. Wittgenstein, *Philosophical Investigations*, 18.
18. Wittgenstein, *Tractatus Logico-Philosophicus*, 4.002.
19. Ibid., 3.323–3.325 (original emphasis).
20. Wittgenstein, *Philosophical Investigations*, §309.
21. Wittgenstein, *Notebooks 1914–1916*, 68.
22. Wittgenstein, *Philosophical Investigations*, §55.
23. Ibid..
24. Ibid., §88.
25. Dummett, *Frege: Philosophy of Language*, 647.
26. Wittgenstein, *Philosophical Investigations*, §60.
27. Wittgenstein, *The Blue and Brown Books*, 5 (paragraph break omitted).

Chapter 6. Carnap's Limited Linguistic Turn

1. Carnap, "Intellectual Autobiography," 25.
2. Carnap, "The Elimination of Metaphysics," 76.
3. Ibid. (Carnap's emphasis).
4. Carnap, "The Old and the New Logic," 143.
5. Carnap, "Replies and Systematic Expositions," 933.
6. Ibid., 936.
7. Carnap, *Meaning and Necessity*, 8. For this reason Willard Van Orman Quine judged the term "explication" unfortunate. In such conceptual restructuring, "We do not expose hidden meanings" (*Word and Object*, 258).
8. Carnap, *Logical Foundations of Probability*, 7 (Carnap's italics).
9. Achinstein, "Rudolf Carnap," 518 (original emphasis).
10. Carnap, *Logical Foundations of Probability*, 6.
11. Carnap, *Philosophy and Logical Syntax*, 78.
12. Carnap, "The Elimination of Metaphysics," 76.
13. Ibid., 79.
14. Carnap, "The Old and the New Logic," 145.
15. Carnap, "The Elimination of Metaphysics," 73.
16. Ibid., 61 (Carnap's emphasis).
17. Carnap, *Philosophy and Logical Syntax*, 36.

18. Carnap, "The Elimination of Metaphysics," 61.

19. On the possibility of proposing the verifiability principle as a Carnapian "explication," see Hanfling, *Logical Positivism*, 139–42.

20. Engelmann, *Letters*, 97 (author's emphasis). This judgment about the *Tractatus* is borne out by Wittgenstein's own words in a letter to another friend (ibid., 143).

21. Wittgenstein, *Tractatus Logico-Philosophicus*, pp. 3–4.

22. Wittgenstein, *The Blue and Brown Books*, 17.

23. Ibid., 18.

24. Ibid.

25. "Perhaps it will help to make clearer my way of thinking about such problems," Carnap observed, "if I point out that most of the members of the Vienna Circle were trained primarily in a field of science or mathematics and that this training had a strong influence on our thinking in philosophy. It was due to this background that, when we contrasted legitimate and illegitimate concepts, questions, or ways of thinking, we usually took as typical examples, on the one hand, formulations in the exact sciences or, on the other hand, certain formulations in traditional metaphysics" ("Intellectual Autobiography," 65).

26. Carnap, "The Old and the New Logic," 143–44. "The apparent variety of the concepts used masks, according to Carnap, an underlying unity; there is, at bottom, only one language of science and in that sense only one science" (Hanfling, *Logical Positivism*, 105).

27. Carnap, "Intellectual Autobiography," 45.

28. Carnap, "The Elimination of Metaphysics," 73.

29. Ibid., 61.

30. Carnap, "The Old and the New Logic," 134.

31. Cf. Hanfling, *Logical Positivism*, 36.

32. Carnap, "The Two Concepts of Probability," 529–30.

33. Ibid., 530.

34. Carnap, "Remarks on Induction and Truth," 599, and "Truth and Confirmation," 120 (his italics).

35. Carnap, "Truth and Confirmation," 120, and "Remarks on Induction and Truth," 598–99.

36. Carnap, "Truth and Confirmation," 120–21, and "Remarks on Induction and Truth," 599 (original emphasis).

37. Carnap, "Truth and Confirmation," 120.

38. Ibid., 125.

39. For indications of a subsequent shift in Carnap's conception of philosophy, resembling more that of John Wisdom and the later Wittgenstein, see Carnap, "Replies and Systematic Expositions," 862; Routley, "The Semantical Metamorphosis of Metaphysics," 188–89.

40. Carnap, "Truth and Confirmation," 124.

CHAPTER 7. Tarski, Truth, and Claims of Linguistic Incoherence

1. Carnap, "Truth and Confirmation," 119.
2. Sorensen, "Vagueness," 96.
3. Carnap, "Intellectual Autobiography," 68.
4. Strawson, "Carnap's Views," 513 (original emphasis).
5. Tarski, "The Semantic Conception of Truth," 53 (paragraph break omitted).
6. Ibid.
7. Ibid., 58.
8. Kirkham, *Theories of Truth*, 271–72.
9. Dummett, *The Seas of Language*, 135.
10. See Bar-Hillel, "Do Natural Languages Contain Paradoxes?" 396; Whiteley, "Let Epimenides Lie!" For variants of this type of response, starting with Chrysippus, see Beth, *The Foundations of Mathematics*, 24–25. For a different route to the same conclusion, see Hallett, *Language and Truth*, 191.
11. Tarski, "The Concept of Truth," 153.
12. Ibid., 267. See also ibid., 165, and "The Establishment of Scientific Semantics," 402. Tarski sounds less sure in "The Semantic Conception of Truth," 60: "We may at best only risk the guess that a language whose structure has been exactly specified and which resembles our everyday language as closely as possible would be inconsistent." Cf. Levison, "Logic, Language, and Consistency"; Bar-Hillel, "Do Natural Languages Contain Paradoxes?" 394.
13. Tarski, "The Semantic Conception of Truth," 53–54 (Tarski's italics).
14. Tarski, "The Establishment of Scientific Semantics," 404.
15. To sense the implications of this first difficulty, confer, for example, Devitt, *Realism and Truth*, 25: "I take it that a minimum requirement for something being a notion of truth is that the 'equivalence thesis' (Dummett, 1978, p. xx) holds for it: each instance of 'Schema T',

$$s \text{ is true if and only if } p,$$

obtained by substituting for 'p' a sentence which is a translation of the sentence referred to by the term 's,' must come out true. This thesis is the basis for Tarski's famous Convention T. If the equivalence thesis does not hold for a notion, there seems no good reason for calling it 'truth.'" On the contrary, I suggest, any account that conformed with Convention T would ipso facto not agree with the standard notion of truth that Tarski thought he was preserving.

16. Field, "Tarski's Theory of Truth," 351.

17. Tarski, "The Concept of Truth," 166.

18. Ibid., 190.

19. Ibid., 189.

20. Tarski, "The Semantic Conception of Truth," 71.

21. For a full discussion of "the vacuity objection" against Tarski's theory, see Kirkham, *Theories of Truth*, 182–93.

22. Cf. Stroll, "Is Everyday Language Inconsistent?"

23. For a varied sampling, see Malcolm, "Moore and Ordinary Language," 358.

24. Wittgenstein, *Philosophical Investigations*, §81 (Wittgenstein's italics).

25. Ibid. (Wittgenstein's italics).

26. Wittgenstein, *Lectures and Conversations*, 2.

27. Wittgenstein, *Philosophical Investigations*, §81.

Chapter 8. Wittgenstein's Acceptance of the Authority of Language

1. Wittgenstein, *Tractatus Logico-Philosophicus*, 3.323.

2. Ibid., 3.324.

3. Ibid., 3.325.

4. Wittgenstein, "Some Remarks on Logical Form," 33.

5. Cf. Wittgenstein, *Philosophical Remarks*, 51.

6. Wittgenstein, *Philosophical Investigations*, §47 (original emphasis). See ibid., §48 ("under other circumstances I should call a monochrome square 'composite,' consisting perhaps of two rectangles, or of the elements colour and shape. But the concept of complexity might also be so extended that a smaller area was said to be 'composed' of a greater area and another one subtracted from it. Compare the 'composition of forces,' the 'division' of a line by a point outside it . . .").

7. Ibid., §91.

8. Ibid., §120 (Wittgenstein's emphasis).

9. Ibid., §261.

10. Wittgenstein, *Tractatus Logico-Philosophicus*, 4.5.

11. Wittgenstein, *The Blue and Brown Books*, 17 (Wittgenstein's italics).

12. Wittgenstein, *Philosophical Investigations*, §65 (Wittgenstein's italics).

13. Wittgenstein, *Notebooks 1914–1916*, 96.

14. Ibid.

15. Wittgenstein, *Philosophical Investigations*, §23 (Wittgenstein's italics).

16. Cf. Frege, *Funktion, Begriff, Bedeutung*, 90: "when we use the same sign for diverse but similar things, we really no longer designate the individual things but what is common to them, the concept."

17. Wittgenstein, *Notebooks 1914–1916*, 39 (original emphasis).

18. Compare Frege, "Logic," in *The Frege Reader*, 236: "What if it is objected that I am attaching to the word 'thought' a sense that it does not ordinarily have, and that other people understand by it an act of thinking, which is obviously private and mental? Well, the important thing is that I remain true to my way of using it; whether this agrees with the ordinary use is of less importance."

19. Wittgenstein, *Philosophical Investigations*, §92 (original emphasis).

20. Ibid. (original emphasis).

21. Ibid., §94.

22. Ibid., §371 (original emphasis).

23. Ibid., §373. Cf. ibid., §381: "How do I know that this color is red?—It would be an answer to say: 'I have learnt English.'"

24. Cf. the parenthetical query in *Investigations* §246: "If we are using the word 'to know' as it is normally used (and how else are we to use it?), then other people very often know when I am in pain." In support of the use here made of *Investigations* §116, and the weight attached to it, see the many references, quotations, and illustrations in Hallett, *A Companion to Wittgenstein's "Philosophical Investigations,"* 203–5, and the historical discussion in Stern, *Wittgenstein on Mind and Language*, 167–75.

25. Wittgenstein, *Philosophical Investigations*, §65.

26. Ibid., §66.

27. Ibid., §67.

28. Ibid., §38. Cf. ibid., §39.

29. Ibid., §242. In view of *Investigations* §2, whose imaginary language ("more primitive than ours") contains only commands, doubtless §242 should be understood of languages like our actual ones, which contain judgments expressed by assertions.

30. Wittgenstein, *Philosophical Investigations*, §40 (original emphasis).

31. Ibid., §43 (original italics).

32. For example, "criteria" and "symptoms" in *The Blue and Brown Books*, 24–25, and "language-game" in *Philosophical Investigations*, §7.

33. For example, *Philosophical Investigations*, §§132, 577.

34. Wittgenstein, *Philosophical Investigations*, §124.

35. Ibid., §132.

36. Ibid., §79. Cf. Russell, *Logic and Knowledge*, 179: "You can, for instance, say: 'There are a number of people in this room at this moment.' That is obviously in some sense undeniable. But when you

come to try and define what this room is, and what it is for a person to be
in a room, and how you are going to distinguish one person from another, and so forth, you find that what you have said is most fearfully
vague and that you really do not know what you meant."

37. Wisdom, "Ludwig Wittgenstein," 47.

38. *Eine philosophische Betrachtung*, in Wittgenstein, *Schriften*, vol.
5, 230.

39. See Hallett, *Companion*, 27–34, for a much fuller account.

40. Wittgenstein, *Philosophical Investigations*, §520.

41. Wittgenstein, *The Blue and Brown Books*, 35.

42. *Eine philosophische Betrachtung*, in Wittgenstein, *Schriften*, vol.
5, 219. For more varied instances of this general type of fallacy, see Hanfling, *Philosophy and Ordinary Language*, 45–46.

43. Man. 302, 14 (the so-called *Diktat für Schlick*).

44. Katz, *The Philosophy of Language*, 69.

45. Ibid., 75–76, 80.

46. Wittgenstein, *Philosophical Investigations*, §111.

47. Moore, *Some Main Problems of Philosophy*, 4.

48. Wittgenstein, *Philosophical Investigations*, §340 (original
emphasis; paragraph break omitted).

CHAPTER 9. Wittgenstein versus Theoretical "Intuitions"

1. Wittgenstein, *Philosophical Investigations*, §128 (Wittgenstein's
italics).

2. Williams, "Knowledge and Reasons," 1.

3. Ibid., 5.

4. Ibid., 7.

5. Ibid.

6. Ayer, "Comments," 15–16.

7. Klein, "Knowledge," 271.

8. Ibid.

9. "The most amazing fact about the current fashion of appealing
to intuitions," writes Jaakko Hintikka, "is the same as the proverbial
dog's walking on two feet: not that it is done particularly well but that it
is done at all. For what is supposed to be the justification of such appeals
to intuition? One searches the literature in vain for a serious attempt to
provide such a justification" ("The Emperor's New Intuitions," 130).
Noting this lack, Herman Cappelen and Douglas Winblad propose various justifications and find them all wanting ("'Reference' Externalized,"
344–47).

10. Cf. Crispin Wright on Michael Dummett and Donald Davidson's "underlying assumption about the nature of linguistic competence,

namely, that it is fruitfully to be compared—at least in its basics—to any open-ended computational ability which—like, say, the ability to do simple arithmetical multiplications—deploys finite information in rule-prescribed ways" ("Theories of Meaning," 270).

11. Wittgenstein, *The Blue and Brown Books*, 143. Cf. Ayer, *Language, Truth and Logic*, 85–86: "A being whose intellect was infinitely powerful would take no interest in logic and mathematics. For he would be able to see at a glance everything that his definitions contained, and, accordingly, could never learn anything from logical inference which he was not fully conscious of already."

12. Wittgenstein, *The Blue and Brown Books*, 143.

13. Wittgenstein, *Philosophical Investigations*, §241 (original emphasis).

14. Ibid., §81 (Wittgenstein's emphasis).

15. Ibid., §69 (Wittgenstein's emphasis).

16. Ibid., §464.

17. Noonan, "Responding to Persons," 302.

18. Cf. Wittgenstein, *Philosophical Investigations*, §486.

19. Harman, "Knowledge, Inference, and 'Explanation,'" 164. For a variant of this general stance, cf. Barnes, Bloor, and Henry, *Scientific Knowledge*, 56: "There is no correct or incorrect way of extending an analogy which can be read off, as it were, from the appearances themselves. People must decide what is correct and what is not. From a sociological perspective this usefully highlights the role of collective judgements, negotiated on the basis of a range of more or less compatible individual perceptual intuitions, in defining what will count as correct classification." Not, notice, as a useful classification that, if adopted, will codetermine the truth of assertions made in the newly stipulated terminology. No, as "correct classification," negotiated (as in the debates we have been considering) on the basis of individual intuitions. With familiar usage left behind and no new usage established, language here plays no evident role in determining this "correctness."

20. Wittgenstein, *The Blue and Brown Books*, 18.

21. It is striking, for example, that a recent close study of Wittgenstein's later thought, when summing up notable "flaws" at the heart of the *Investigations*, more positive aspects of its legacy, and other topics of interest in its pages, makes no mention of the methodological issue here discussed (Soames, *Philosophical Analysis*, vol. 2, 60–61).

CHAPTER 10. Flew and Paradigm-Case Arguments

1. Wittgenstein, *Philosophical Investigations*, §118.

2. Cf. Putnam, *Pragmatism*, 27–28, 31–32.

3. Black, *Language and Philosophy*, 3.

4. Cf. Hanfling, *Philosophy and Ordinary Language*, 41.

5. Hancock, "Ideas of Freedom," 286.

6. Ibid., 289.

7. Ibid., 290.

8. Speake, *A Dictionary of Philosophy*, 243.

9. Flew, "Philosophy and Language," 35.

10. Ibid., 36.

11. For more general treatments, see, for example, Donnellan, "Paradigm-Case Argument"; Malcolm, "Moore and Ordinary Language," 361; Martinich, "Ordinary Language Philosophy," 145; Urmson, "Some Questions concerning Validity"; Warnock, "Ordinary Language Philosophy, School of," 151; and the series of articles in *Analysis* initiated by Watkins's "Farewell to the Paradigm Case Argument."

12. Malcolm, "Moore and Ordinary Language," 361.

13. Ibid. (Malcolm's emphasis).

14. Flew, "Again the Paradigm," 263.

15. Ibid., 271. Cf. Flew, "Divine Omnipotence and Human Freedom," 149–51; Black, "Making Something Happen," 22–23, summarized in Hancock, "Ideas of Freedom," 288; Eveling and Leith, "When to Use the Paradigm-Case Argument."

16. Cf., e.g., Passmore, *Philosophical Reasoning*, 118.

17. Danto, "The Paradigm Case Argument," 122 (original emphasis).

18. Ibid., 123 (original emphasis).

19. Ibid., 121.

20. Taylor, "Phenomenology and Linguistic Analysis," 107.

21. Purtill, "Flew," 479.

22. Wittgenstein, *Philosophical Investigations*, §402. For full illustration of the attitude described, see C. A. Campbell, "Common-Sense Propositions," 228–29.

23. Donnellan, "Paradigm-Case Argument," 41.

24. Flew, "*Apologia pro Philosophia Mea*," 81.

CHAPTER 11. Russell's Critique of "Common Sense"

1. Flew, "The Paradigm Case Argument," 116.

2. Ibid.

3. Russell, *Logic and Knowledge*, 193.

4. Russell, *The Analysis of Matter*, 155.

5. Russell, *The Scientific Outlook*, 78 (paragraph break omitted).

6. For a fuller listing, with references for each item, see Hallett, *Language and Truth*, 114–15.

7. Russell, "The Cult of 'Common Usage,'" 304.

8. Ibid., 303.

9. Ibid., 305.

10. Nagel, "Russell's Philosophy of Science," 336.

11. Russell, "Reply to Criticisms," 704.

12. Russell, *The Analysis of Matter*, 133 (Russell's emphasis).

13. Stephen Stich's comments on recent research into the concepts and principles of "folk physics" raise the specter of Russellian conclusions not only concerning the physical world but also concerning the mental world: "What makes this research particularly intriguing is the finding that many people exploit a folk physics that is mistaken about the physical world, and not just in detail. The tacit theory that apparently guides these people's physical judgments and their actions is closer to medieval impetus theory than it is to Newtonian physics. Findings like this may make the eliminativist's thesis a bit more plausible. If people can rely on a seriously mistaken physical theory to assist them in moving around in the world, surely it is at least possible that they rely on an equally mistaken psychological theory when they describe, explain and predict people's behavior" ("What Is a Theory," 351). Should we then conclude, a la Russell, not only that there are no such physical objects and events as people refer to, but also no beliefs, desires, or intentions such as they cite in explanation or prediction of people's behavior?

14. Wittgenstein, *Philosophical Investigations*, §81 (original emphasis).

15. Cf. Thompson, "When Is Ordinary Language Reformed?" 502: "Suppose that at some time ordinary language reflected the belief mentioned in Aristotle that thunder is a quenching of fire in the clouds. An analyst of ordinary language at this time might conclude that the move from 'That is thunder' to 'That is fire being quenched in the clouds' was analytic in ordinary language. Do we want to say that in this case ordinary language needs reform because one of its discernible rules reflects a false belief? Surely what is needed here is reform in belief and not in language."

16. Devitt and Sterelny, *Language and Reality*, 10 (original emphasis).

17. Ibid., 285.

18. Ibid., 10.

19. Wittgenstein, *Zettel*, §223 (original emphasis).

20. Wittgenstein, *Philosophical Investigations*, §241 (original emphasis).

21. Cf. Hallett, *Language and Truth*, 117–18.

22. Randall, "Talking and Looking," 16.

CHAPTER 12. Malcolm and the "Ordinary-Language" Debate

1. Malcolm, "Moore and Ordinary Language," 345.
2. Ibid., 347.
3. Ibid., 349 (Malcolm's emphasis).
4. Ibid. (Malcolm's emphasis).
5. Ibid., 350 (original emphasis).
6. Ibid.
7. Ibid. See Passmore, *A Hundred Years of Philosophy*, 435–38, on the similar views of John Wisdom and Morris Lazerowitz ("he operates with Wisdom's main thesis—that philosophical paradoxes are verbal recommendations").
8. Cf. C. A. Campbell, "Common-Sense Propositions," 221–23; Chisholm, "Philosophers and Ordinary Language," 324–25; Morris Lazerowitz, *The Language of Philosophy*, 112–16.
9. Chisholm, "Philosophers and Ordinary Language," 324.
10. Malcolm, "Moore and Ordinary Language," 368 (emphasis added).
11. Ibid., 358–59 (original emphasis).
12. Malcolm, Critical Notice, 97.
13. Chisholm, "Philosophers and Ordinary Language," 320 (Chisholm's italics).
14. In full illustration of this possible split between what people mean and what their words say, recall, for example, Russell's denial that we see physical objects other than our brains.
15. Chisholm, "Philosophers and Ordinary Language," 320n11 (original emphasis).
16. Tennessen, "Permissible and Impermissible Locutions," 503, and "Vindication of the Humpty Dumpty Attitude," 192–93.
17. Tennessen, "Permissible and Impermissible Locutions," 504 (original emphasis).
18. Ibid., 503 (original emphasis).
19. Ibid., 504 (original emphasis).
20. Mundle, *A Critique of Linguistic Philosophy*, 20.
21. Ibid., 16 (original in italics).

Chapter 13. Austin, Statements, and Their Truth

1. Austin, "Truth," 111.
2. Ibid., 113–14.
3. Ibid., 116. These conventions are, of course, ones existing at the time of the utterance, not past or future ones.

4. Ibid., footnote 9.

5. Künne, *Conceptions of Truth*, 250 (original emphasis).

6. On such argumentation, the kind I term "calculus-reasoning," see Hallett, *Essentialism*, 45–68.

7. Arguments that rule out utterances as truth bearers tend to overlook this fact and its relevance. Cf., for example, Künne, *Conceptions of Truth*, 264–68.

8. Davidson, "Truth Rehabilitated," 66. For similar assertions, which are plentiful, see for instance Quine, "Identity, Ostension, and Hypostasis," 79, and *Philosophy of Logic*, 11, quoted at the end of chapter 16.

9. Skorupski, "Meaning, Use, Verification," 47.

10. Austin, "Truth," 116, footnote 10.

11. Cf. Hallett, *Language and Truth*, 33.

12. Ibid., chap. 4.

13. Ibid., 45–46.

14. Ibid., 42.

15. Ibid., 110–12.

16. Strawson, "Truth," 144–45 (original emphasis).

17. Ibid., 144.

18. Ibid. (original emphasis).

19. Richard Kirkham (*Theories of Truth*, 128) draws a related distinction. Austin's account, he suggests, "tells us what it is for a statement to *be* true. It has nothing to say about the locutionary or illocutionary purposes of truth ascriptions."

20. Strawson, "Truth," 131.

21. Austin, "Truth," 113.

22. For fuller development of the case for statements as bearers of truth, see Knox, "Truth, Correspondence, and Ordinary Language," 520–21.

23. See Hallett, *Language and Truth*, chap. 5.

24. Strawson, "Truth," 153–54.

25. Ibid., 154.

26. Ibid.

27. Warnock, "Truth and Correspondence," 18.

28. See also Cousin, "Truth," 166; Knox, "Truth, Correspondence, and Ordinary Language," 526.

CHAPTER 14. A Lead Overlooked: From Meaning to Truth

1. Wittgenstein, *Philosophical Investigations*, §23 (original emphasis).

2. Wittgenstein, *Zettel*, §173.

3. Wittgenstein, *Philosophical Investigations*, §69 (original emphasis).

4. Ibid., §68 (original emphasis).

5. Ibid., §67.

6. Hallett, *A Middle Way to God*, 14 (revised from Hallett, *Language and Truth*, 91). For a fuller exposition and defense of such a formula than this chapter will or can present, consult the latter work.

7. Austin, "Truth," 116, footnote 9.

8. In this regard, see Smith, "Concepts and Categorization," for numerous complications the formula ignores.

9. Cf., for example, Waismann, "Language Strata," 23–24, on proverbs; Swinburne, "Analogy and Metaphor," 80–81, on metaphorical utterances; McMichael, "The Epistemology of Essentialist Claims," 41, on names: "Exactly parallel uncertainties arise concerning *the reference of proper names*. For example, suppose it should turn out that the writer of all those fabulous plays is not the man who actually bore the name 'Shakespeare.' What then should we say about our present utterances containing the name 'Shakespeare'? Are they true statements about the writer or false statements about the real bearer of the name? The answer, in any case, is not cut-and-dried" (original emphasis). Paul Grice ("Logic and Conversation," 25–26) reveals another sort of problem: If I say, smugly, "He is an Englishman, so he is brave," and am right about his nationality and his courage but not about the "so," is my statement true or false? Saul Kripke ("Naming and Necessity," 281) discusses a further complication, the weighting of similarities.

10. Cf. Baker and Hacker, *Wittgenstein: Understanding and Meaning*, 680 ("One common idea is that an explanation is correct only if it is 'complete,' i.e. only if it expressly states how to use the explained expression in every possible circumstance"); Popper, "Some Philosophical Comments," 398–99 ("there are still many philosophers who believe that any notion, for example the notion of truth, is logically legitimate only if a criterion exists which enables us to decide whether or not an object falls under that notion").

11. Baker and Hacker, *Wittgenstein: Meaning and Understanding*, 664.

12. Scriven, "The Argument from Ordinary Language," 269.

13. This take on truth fits well with Nicholas Rescher's idea of "standardism"—"namely, the policy of interpreting the generalizations of the field not as making their claims *universalistically* (i.e., exceptionlessly), but rather as making them *standardistically*, that is, as stating how matters stand 'normally' or 'as a rule'" (Rescher's italics). This approach "abandons the necessitarian pretensions of traditional philosophizing in favor of a more modest and cautious perspective that looks to what our experience of the world indicates to be its normal course of things" (*Philosophical Standardism*, 3). Specifically on truth, cf. David Wiggins's "An Indefinibilist cum Normative View of Truth and the Marks of Truth." In his critique of

Rescher's stance ("Rescher's Metaphilosophy"), Timm Triplett takes little note of the linguistic difficulties for valid generalization, or of the fact that, with no assurance of completeness, even the most refined version of a rule such as the Norm of Linguistic Correspondence would still have to be regarded as a rule of thumb, open to possible exceptions.

14. Wittgenstein, *Philosophical Investigations*, §88.

15. Wittgenstein's *Nachlass*, manuscript 108, page 134.

16. Cf., e.g., Hallett, *Language and Truth*, and *A Middle Way to God*, 13–17.

CHAPTER 15. Kripke, Putnam, and Rigid Designation

1. Putnam, "The Meaning of 'Meaning,'" 223–24.

2. Ibid., 233.

3. For Kripke's agreement, see "Naming and Necessity," 323.

4. For disagreement with Putnam's verdict, see, for example, John Campbell, "Extension and Psychic State," 69 ("The view opposed to Putnam's is that if there are quantities of such substances as XYZ anywhere in the known or unknown universe, then the extension of 'water,' for example, is not H_2O but [XYZ v H_2O]") and 79; Canfield, "Discovering Essence," 126–27; Donnellan, "Kripke and Putnam," 104; Double, "Twin Earths," 301–3; Dupré, "Natural Kinds and Biological Taxa," 72–73; Zemach, "Putnam's Theory," 119.

5. Putnam, "Is Semantics Possible?" 140–41.

6. Ibid., 139.

7. Putnam, "The Meaning of 'Meaning,'" 242.

8. Ibid., 232. Cf. ibid., 241.

9. Ibid., 235, 239, 240–41.

10. Kripke, "Naming and Necessity," 327.

11. Carney, "A Kripkean Approach," 150.

12. Putnam, "The Meaning of 'Meaning,'" 265 (emphasis omitted).

13. Cf. Double, "Twin Earths," 304n1.

14. Putnam, "The Meaning of 'Meaning,'" 238 (Putnam's emphasis).

15. Dupré, "Natural Kinds and Biological Taxa," 70.

16. Kripke, "Naming and Necessity," 254.

17. Ibid., 277. "My view is that proper names (except perhaps, for some quirky and derivative uses, that are not uses as *names*) *are* always rigid" (Kripke, "Speaker's Reference and Semantic Reference," 272).

18. Kripke, "Naming and Necessity," 269.

19. Ibid., 270.

20. Ibid. (Kripke's emphasis). "We are speaking of *Nixon* and asking what, in certain counterfactual situations, would have been true of *him*" (Kripke, "Identity and Necessity," 81; again, Kripke's emphasis).

21. Kripke, "Naming and Necessity," 270.
22. Kripke, "Identity and Necessity," 83.
23. Kripke, "Naming and Necessity," 279.
24. Ibid., 317.
25. Ibid., 318.
26. Ibid.
27. Zemach, "Putnam's Theory," 120.
28. Kripke, "Naming and Necessity," 281.
29. Ibid., 316.
30. Putnam, "The Meaning of 'Meaning,'" 244 (original emphasis).
31. Kripke, "Naming and Necessity," 330.
32. Ibid., 320 (original emphasis).
33. Ibid., 331.
34. Cassam, "Science and Essence," 97–98 (Cassam's emphasis).
35. Kripke, "Naming and Necessity," 313 (again, Kripke's characteristic emphasis).
36. Ibid., 265–66.
37. Cf. Wilkerson, *Natural Kinds*, 157.
38. Putnam, *Realism and Reason*, 73, 74.
39. Cf. John Campbell, "Extension and Psychic State," 74 ("What, however, is 'structural importance,' and how in general do we find out which of two properties say, being in a gaseous state and being a lead salt is the more structurally important?"); Donnellan, "Kripke and Putnam," 100–101 ("it seems to me not psychologically implausible for my Twin-Earthlings to be more taken with, so to speak, the isotope number of a bit of substance rather than with its atomic number"); Dupré, "Natural Kinds and Biological Taxa," 80–83 (on the varied reasons that motivate biological classifications, both scientific and nonscientific).
40. Kripke, "Naming and Necessity," 314.
41. Russell, "On Scientific Method in Philosophy," 84.
42. Cf., for example, Kripke, "Naming and Necessity," 330: "it is (metaphysically) *possible* that there should have been animals that resembled tigers but were not tigers" (Kripke's emphasis).
43. Ibid., 289 (Kripke's italics).
44. Wittgenstein, *Philosophical Investigations*, §89.

CHAPTER 16. Quine, Linguistic Truths, and Holistic Theory

1. Tarski, "The Concept of Truth," 263.
2. Quine, "Reply to Robert Nozick," 367. Cf. Quine, *Word and Object*, 24 ("Where it makes sense to apply 'true' is to a sentence couched in the terms of a given theory and seen from within the theory, complete with its posited reality").

3. Quine, "Two Dogmas of Empiricism," 42.

4. A lengthy footnote in Quine, *Word and Object*, 67–68, traces the history of this dichotomy, before and after "Two Dogmas." For a fuller sketch of its history and significance, see Orenstein, *Willard van Orman Quine*, 75–79.

5. Quine, "Two Dogmas of Empiricism," 21.

6. Elsewhere, Quine did cite Wittgenstein's identification of meaning with use, and made similar-sounding statements himself—statements that cause problems for his argument in "Two Dogmas." Cf. Canfield, "The Passage into Language," 120–21.

7. Quine, "Two Dogmas of Empiricism," 22.

8. Ibid., 27.

9. Ibid., 38.

10. Ibid., 40–41.

11. Ibid., 41.

12. Ibid., 42.

13. Ibid., 43. On Quine's shift to a more moderate form of holism, a shift that need not detain us here, see Gibson, "Quine's Philosophy: A Brief Sketch," 675–77.

14. Quine, "Two Dogmas of Empiricism," 41.

15. Grice and Strawson, "In Defense of a Dogma," 212.

16. Ibid., 203.

17. Ibid., 204.

18. See Nielsen, *On Transforming Philosophy*, 59–61.

19. Perhaps the later Quine would, too. The difference between "No unmarried man is married" and "No bachelor is married" ("Two Dogmas," 22–23) may account for Quine's mitigated claim later on (see below) that *many* sentences that are analytic by "popular philosophical acclaim" can be declared false when theoretical adjustments are made ("Reply to Jules Vuillemin," 619). Only the explicit tautology, "No unmarried man is married," rests on a logical law.

20. Grice and Strawson, "In Defense of a Dogma," 210–11. Cf. O'Grady, "Carnap and Two Dogmas of Empiricism," 1026.

21. Cf. Putnam, "The Analytic and the Synthetic," 34–35. Dummett writes: "I am therefore in entire agreement with the observation made by Donald Davidson, that it is at best very misleading to describe Quine's view as involving the rejection of the notion of meaning" ("Significance," 378).

22. Quine, "Reply to Robert Nozick," 364.

23. Burge, "Philosophy of Language and Mind," 27. Cf. Hacker, *Wittgenstein's Place*, 211–12.

24. Quine, *Philosophy of Logic*, 2.

25. Quine, *Word and Object*, 191.

26. Quine, *Philosophy of Logic*, 13.

27. Ibid.

28. Putnam, "Meaning Holism," 290.

29. Cf. ibid., 292.

30. According to Harman (*Reasoning, Meaning and Mind*, 140), "Society pages in newspapers will identify as eligible 'bachelors' men who are in the process of being divorced but are still married." I have not encountered such identifications; but suppose this usage has crept in without my noticing it, and has become widespread, and has therefore become "established use" by which truth and falsehood may be judged (cf. chapter 14's Principle of Relative Similarity): then "Bachelors are not married" is not analytic. However, in the contrary supposition it is. And the like may hold in other instances if not in this one, and doubtless does.

31. Quine, "Carnap and Logical Truth," 386.

32. Ibid. Cf. Quine, *Philosophy of Logic*, 14 ("When we call a sentence eternal, therefore, we are calling it eternal relative only to a particular language at a particular time"), *Mathematical Logic*, 1 ("A logically true statement has this peculiarity: basic particles such as 'is,' 'not,' 'and,' 'or,' 'unless,' 'if,' 'then,' 'neither,' 'nor,' 'some,' 'all,' etc. occur in the statement in such a way that the statement is true independently of its other ingredients"), *The Roots of Reference*, 79–80 ("a sentence is analytic if *everybody* learns that it is true by learning its words"), "Three Indeterminacies," 10, "Two Dogmas in Retrospect," 270: "Analyticity undeniably has a place at a common-sense level, and this has made readers regard my reservations as unreasonable. My threadbare bachelor example is one of many undebatable cases. It is intelligible and often useful in discussion to point out that some disagreement is purely a matter of words rather than of fact."

33. Cf., for example, Quine, "Carnap and Logical Truth," 402, and "Necessary Truth," 74–75.

34. Kneale, "Are Necessary Truths True by Convention?" 135–36. In a Wittgensteinian perspective, this becomes: "Analytic truths are rules in the guise of descriptions: 'Bachelors are unmarried' is a grammatical proposition, an explanation of the meaning of the word 'bachelor,' given in the material mode. It is a rule that licenses the inference from 'A is a bachelor' to 'A is unmarried'" (Hacker, "Wittgenstein and Quine," 21).

35. Giving prominence to this normative aspect, some have suggested that an utterance such as "No bachelors are married" be read as a prescriptive not a descriptive utterance—that is, as stating a rule against calling married people bachelors and not as denying the existence of married bachelors. In either alternative, language retains its authority, backing the assertion of the rule in one reading and backing the denial of exceptions in the other.

36. Putnam, "The Analytic and the Synthetic," 38.

37. Nielsen, *On Transforming Philosophy*, 56. Cf. Boyd, "Metaphor and Theory Change," 366.

38. Nielsen, *On Transforming Philosophy*, 56.

39. Ibid., 67.

40. Note here the crucial difference between married bachelors (quadrilateral triangles, liquid ice, etc.), on the one hand, and split atoms or black swans, on the other: both the atoms and the swans were *discovered*; they were not well-known candidates to whom the word was clearly, consistently refused, as "bachelor" is refused to countless married men. Hence, in the one case ("married bachelor") there clearly is conflict with established linguistic usage, in the others ("black swan," "split atom") there is not.

41. Quine, "Identity, Ostension, and Hypostasis," 79.

42. Quine, "On Empirically Equivalent Systems," 327. Cf. Quine, *Philosophy of Logic*, 11: "In speaking of the truth of a given sentence there is only indirection; we do better simply to say the sentence and so speak not about language but about the world. So long as we are speaking only of the truth of singly given sentences, the perfect theory of truth is what Wilfrid Sellars has called the disappearance theory of truth."

CHAPTER 17. Quine, Indeterminacy, and the Opacity of Language

1. Alston, "Quine on Meaning," 58.

2. Gibson, "Translation," 139.

3. Quine, *Word and Object*, 64.

4. Ibid., 29.

5. Ibid., 51–52; Quine, "Speaking of Objects," 1–3.

6. Quine, "Ontological Relativity," 35.

7. Ibid., 47.

8. Quine, *Word and Object*, 79.

9. Quine, "Ontological Relativity," 49.

10. Wittgenstein, *Philosophical Investigations*, §293.

11. Quine, *Word and Object*, 79.

12. Ibid., 78. Cf. ibid., 70 ("the most notable thing about the analytical hypotheses is that they exceed anything implicit in any native's dispositions to speech behavior"); Quine, *Theories and Things*, 23 ("I have argued that two conflicting manuals of translation can both do justice to all dispositions to behavior, and that, in such a case, there is no fact of the matter of which manual is right").

13. Wittgenstein, *Tractatus Logico-Philosophicus*, 4.002.

14. Mates, "Verification," 165.

15. Ibid. Cf. Scriven, "The Argument from Ordinary Language," 267: "Even John Austin's ear was sometimes at less than absolute pitch; he once spent half-an-hour arguing that the term 'prediction' *only* properly applies to statements about the future based on intuitive or extrasensory or magical perception, not to the conclusions of rational inference [as in weather predictions], a view that few would share."

16. Cavell, "Must We Mean," 174–75. In a similar vein, see Baier, "The Ordinary Use of Words," 52.

17. Cf. Fodor and Katz, "Availability," 60.

18. Vendler, *Linguistics in Philosophy*, 7.

19. Wittgenstein, *Zettel*, §455.

CHAPTER 18. Rorty, Stich, and Pragmatic Assertability

1. Ryle, "Use, Usage, and Meaning," 227.

2. Barnes, *The Philosophical Predicament*, 126.

3. Grice, "Logic and Conversation," 27.

4. Rorty, "Pragmatism, Relativism, and Irrationalism," 722–23.

5. Ibid., 724. Cf. Rorty, "Pragmatism, Davidson, and Truth," 131: "The Peircian pragmatist is right in thinking that the idealist and the physicalist share a common fallacy—namely that 'correspondence' is the name of a relation between pieces of thought (or language) and pieces of the world, a relation such that the relata must be ontologically homogeneous."

6. Rorty, *Consequences of Pragmatism*, xxv. See Rorty, *Objectivity, Relativism, and Truth*, 126–27.

7. Rorty, *Consequences of Pragmatism*, xiii. Cf. Rorty, "Science as Solidarity," 11.

8. Rorty, "Pragmatism, Relativism, and Irrationalism," 723. Cf. Rorty, *Contingency, Irony, and Solidarity*, 9 ("The method is to redescribe lots and lots of things in new ways, until you have created a pattern of linguistic behavior which will tempt the rising generation to adopt it, thereby causing them to look for appropriate new forms of non-linguistic behavior").

9. Wittgenstein, *Philosophical Investigations*, §129.

10. Rorty, *Contingency, Irony, and Solidarity*, 5.

11. Ibid.

12. "In this attitude," Rorty writes admiringly of Hans-Georg Gadamer, "getting the facts right (about atoms and the void, or about the history of Europe) is merely propaedeutic to finding a new and more interesting way of expressing ourselves, and thus of coping with the world" (*Philosophy and the Mirror of Nature*, 359).

13. Ramberg, "Post-Ontological Philosophy of Mind," 351.

14. Rorty, "Response to Bjørn Ramberg," 375.

15. Stich, *The Fragmentation of Reason*, 106.

16. Ibid., 124–25. Hugh Tomlinson carries the proliferation of truths even further and draws a similar conclusion: "There are as many truths as there are languages and the notion of truth can no longer provide a final and objective justification for science" ("After Truth," 47).

17. Stich, *The Fragmentation of Reason*, 124.

18. Ibid., 134–35.

19. Cf. Finnis, *Natural Law*, 74–75 ("The sceptical assertion that knowledge is not a good is operationally self-refuting"); Anthony Gottlieb's critique of Rorty (Review, 30): "The main problem with this idea is that not even Mr. Rorty himself can stay faithful to it. By his own lights, he ought to argue not that pragmatism is right but that it is useful. In fact, for the most part he uses good old-fashioned philosophical arguments to support it."

20. Stich, *The Fragmentation of Reason*, 121.

21. Hallett, *Language and Truth*, 110.

22. Lynch, *True to Life*, 4.

23. Ibid., 16 (original emphasis).

24. Ibid., 15–16.

CHAPTER 19. Habermas, Communicative Speech, and Validity

1. Kloppenberg, "Pragmatism," 46.

2. Habermas, *The Theory of Communicative Action*, vol. 1, 277–78. Cf. Habermas, "Questions and Counterquestions," 408.

3. Habermas, *The Theory of Communicative Action*, vol. 1, 86.

4. Ibid., 290 (Habermas's emphasis).

5. Habermas, "Some Further Clarifications," 340.

6. Habermas, *The Theory of Communicative Action*, vol. 1, 99, 278, 307–8; "Discourse Ethics," 58. Cf. Habermas, "Questions and Counterquestions," 408: "Here the validity dimensions of propositional truth, normative rightness, and subjective truthfulness (*Wahrhaftigkeit*) or authenticity are entwined with each other." In *The Theory of Communicative Action*, vol. 1, 99, truth is extended to include satisfaction of the "existential presuppositions of the propositional content." In his 1971 Gauss Lectures ("Reflections on the Linguistic Foundation of Sociology," 63–64, 85, 90), Habermas has a fourfold classification, adding "intelligibility."

7. Habermas, *The Theory of Communicative Action*, vol. 1, 308–9.

8. Habermas, "Communicative Rationality," 203.

9. Habermas, *The Theory of Communicative Action*, vol. 1, 311.

10. Bringing in the hearer as well as the speaker, Habermas enlarges this first-person perspective and indicates a further dimension of language's "authority": "As soon as the hearer accepts the guarantee offered by the speaker, obligations are assumed that have consequences for the interaction, obligations that are contained in the meaning of what was said. In the case of orders and directives, for instance, the obligations to act hold primarily for the hearer, in the case of promises and announcements, they hold for the speaker, in the case of agreements and contracts, they are symmetrical, holding for both parties, and in the case of substantive normative recommendations and warnings, they hold asymmetrically for both parties" ("Discourse Ethics," 59). Such are the implications contained in the meaning of what was said, and the meaning was determined by the language spoken. If these obligations arise, they arise, in part, from language.

CHAPTER 20. Past, Present, and Future: An Overview

1. Hoy and McCarthy, *Critical Theory*, 63. Cf. Føllesdal, "Triangulation," 719: "Philosophers and linguists have always said that language is a social institution. They have, however, immediately forgotten this and have adopted notions of meaning that are not publicly accessible and where it remains unclear how such entities are grasped by us."
2. Russell, *Inquiry*, 186.
3. Akiba, "Identity Is Simple," 393 (original emphasis).
4. Ibid. (original emphasis).
5. Gibbard, "Contingent Identity," 187.
6. Ibid., 202.
7. Ibid., 202–3.
8. Zagzebski, *Virtues of the Mind*, 266.
9. Von Wright, *The Tree of Knowledge*, 85. Hacker concurs, still more recently: "Analytic philosophy has been the predominant philosophical movement of the twentieth century" ("Analytic Philosophy," 3).
10. Quoted, without reference, in Kloppenberg, "Pragmatism," 31.
11. Rundle, *Grammar in Philosophy*, vii.
12. Hoy and McCarthy, *Critical Theory*, 66–67 (McCarthy's italics), expounding the thought of Harold Garfinkel.
13. Citing John McDowell, Donald Davidson, Stephen Schiffer, Richard Rorty, and Hilary Putnam, Robert Hanna surmises that "the analytic consensus in contemporary philosophy—as intellectually vigorous, institutionally secure, and one might even say bull-marketish, as it undoubtedly is—is speeding towards a crash" (*Kant and the Foundations*, 11). Cf. Baynes, Bohman, and McCarthy, *After Philosophy*, 5–6, 15–16.
14. James, *The Meaning of Truth*, 41.

BIBLIOGRAPHY

Achinstein, Peter. "Rudolf Carnap." *Review of Metaphysics* 19 (1965–66): 517–49, 758–79.

Akiba, Ken. "Identity Is Simple." *American Philosophical Quarterly* 37 (2000): 389–404.

Alston, William P. "Quine on Meaning." In Hahn and Schilpp, *The Philosophy of W. V. Quine*, 49–72.

Arrington, Robert L., and Hans-Johann Glock, eds. *Wittgenstein and Quine*. London: Routledge, 1996.

Austin, J. L. *How to Do Things with Words*. Oxford: Oxford University Press, 1962.

———. "A Plea for Excuses." *Proceedings of the Aristotelian Society* 57 (1956–57): 1–30. Rptd. in Austin, *Philosophical Papers*. Ed. J. O. Urmson and G. J. Warnock. Oxford: Clarendon, 1979. 175–204.

———. "Truth." *Proceedings of the Aristotelian Society*, suppl. no. 24 (1950): 111–28.

Ayer, A. J. "Comments on Professor Williams' 'Knowledge and Reasons.'" In von Wright, *Problems in the Theory of Knowledge*, 12–16.

———. *Language, Truth and Logic*. London: Victor Gollancz, 1950.

———, ed. *Logical Positivism*. Glencoe, Ill.: Free Press, 1959.

———. *Philosophy and Language*. Oxford: Clarendon, 1960.

Baier, Kurt. "The Ordinary Use of Words." *Proceedings of the Aristotelian Society* 52 (1951–52): 47–70.

Baker, G. P., and P. M. S. Hacker. *Wittgenstein: Understanding and Meaning*. Vol. 1 of *An Analytical Commentary on the Philosophical Investigations*. Chicago: University of Chicago Press, 1980.

Bar-Hillel, Yehoshua. "Do Natural Languages Contain Paradoxes?" *Studium Generale* 19 (1966): 391–97.

Barnes, Barry, David Bloor, and John Henry. *Scientific Knowledge: A Sociological Analysis*. Chicago: University of Chicago Press, 1996.

Barnes, Winston H. F. *The Philosophical Predicament*. London: Adam and Charles Black, 1950.

Barney, Rachel. *Names and Nature in Plato's* Cratylus. New York: Routledge, 2001.

Baynes, Kenneth, James Bohman, and Thomas McCarthy, eds. *After Philosophy: End or Transformation?* Cambridge, Mass.: MIT Press, 1987.

Beth, Evert W. *The Foundations of Mathematics: A Study in the Philosophy of Science*. Rev. ed. New York: Harper & Row, 1966.

Black, Max. *Language and Philosophy: Studies in Method*. Ithaca, N.Y.: Cornell University Press, 1949.

———. "Linguistic Relativity: The Views of Benjamin Lee Whorf." *Philosophical Review* 68 (1959): 228–38.

———. "Making Something Happen." In *Determinism and Freedom in the Age of Modern Science*. Ed. Sidney Hook. New York: New York University Press, 1958. 15–30.

Boyd, Richard. "Metaphor and Theory Change: What Is 'Metaphor' a Metaphor For?" In *Metaphor and Thought*. Ed. Andrew Ortony. Cambridge: Cambridge University Press, 1979. 356–408.

Brandom, Robert B., ed. *Rorty and His Critics*. Malden, Mass.: Blackwell, 2000.

Bunge, Mario. *Life Science, Social Science and Technology*. Vol. 7, pt. 2, of *Treatise on Basic Philosophy*. Dordrecht: Reidel, 1985.

Burge, Tyler. "Frege on Sense and Linguistic Meaning." In *The Analytic Tradition: Meaning, Thought, and Knowledge*. Ed. David Bell and Neil Cooper. Oxford: Blackwell, 1991. 30–60.

———. "Philosophy of Language and Mind: 1950–90." *Philosophical Review* 101 (1992): 3–51.

Campbell, C. A. "Common-Sense Propositions and Philosophical Paradoxes." *Proceedings of the Aristotelian Society* 45 (1944–45): 1–25. Rptd. in H. D. Lewis, *Clarity Is Not Enough*, 217–38.

Campbell, John. "Extension and Psychic State: Twin Earth Revisited." *Philosophical Studies* 42 (1982): 67–89.

Canfield, John V. "Discovering Essence." In Ginet and Shoemaker, *Knowledge and Mind*, 105–29.

[handwritten marginal note: "but not Reddy?"]

———. "The Passage into Language: Wittgenstein versus Quine." In Arrington and Glock, *Wittgenstein and Quine*, 118–43.

Cappelen, Herman, and Douglas G. Winblad. "'Reference' Externalized and the Role of Intuitions in Semantic Theory." *American Philosophical Quarterly* 36 (1999): 337–50.

Carnap, Rudolf. "The Elimination of Metaphysics through Logical Analysis of Language." Trans. Arthur Pap. In Ayer, *Logical Positivism*, 60–81.

———. "Intellectual Autobiography." In Schilpp, *The Philosophy of Rudolf Carnap*, 3–84.

———. *Logical Foundations of Probability*. 2nd ed. Chicago: University of Chicago Press, 1962.

———. *Meaning and Necessity: A Study in Semantics and Modal Logic*. 2nd ed. Chicago: University of Chicago Press, 1956.

———. "The Old and the New Logic." In Ayer, *Logical Positivism*, 133–46.

———. *Philosophy and Logical Syntax*. London: Kegan Paul, Trench, Trubner, 1935.

———. "Remarks on Induction and Truth." *Philosophy and Phenomenological Research* 6 (1945–46): 590–602.

———. "Replies and Systematic Expositions." In Schilpp, *The Philosophy of Rudolf Carnap*, 859–1013.

———. "Truth and Confirmation." In Feigl and Sellars, *Readings in Philosophical Analysis*, 119–27.

———. "The Two Concepts of Probability." *Philosophy and Phenomenological Research* 5 (1944–45): 513–32.

Carney, James D. "A Kripkean Approach to Aesthetic Theories." *British Journal of Aesthetics* 22 (1982): 150–57.

Cassam, Quassim. "Science and Essence." *Philosophy* 61 (1986): 95–107.

Cavell, Stanley. "Must We Mean What We Say?" *Inquiry* 1 (1958): 172–212.

Chisholm, Roderick M. "Philosophers and Ordinary Language." *Philosophical Review* 60 (1951): 317–28.

———. *Theory of Knowledge*. 2nd ed. Englewood Cliffs, N.J.: Prentice-Hall, 1977.

Cohen, L. Jonathan. *The Dialogue of Reason: An Analysis of Analytical Philosophy*. Oxford: Clarendon, 1986.

Cook, John W. "The Fate of Ordinary Language Philosophy." *Philosophical Investigations* 3 (1980): 1–72.

Copleston, F. C. *Aquinas*. Harmondsworth, UK: Penguin, 1955.

Cornforth, Maurice Campbell. *Marxism and the Linguistic Philosophy*. New York: International Publishers, 1966.

Cousin, D. R. "Truth." *Proceedings of the Aristotelian Society,* suppl. no. 24 (1950): 157–72.

Currie, Gregory. "Was Frege a Linguistic Philosopher?" *British Journal for the Philosophy of Science* 27 (1976): 79–92. Rptd. in *General Assessments and Historical Accounts of Frege's Philosophy*. Ed. Hans Sluga. New York: Garland, 1993. 171–84.

Danto, Arthur C. "The Paradigm Case Argument and the Free-Will Problem." *Ethics* 69 (1958–59): 120–24.

Davidson, Donald. "Truth Rehabilitated." In Brandom, *Rorty and His Critics*, 65–74.

Devitt, Michael. *Realism and Truth*. Princeton, N.J.: Princeton University Press, 1984.

Devitt, Michael, and Kim Sterelny. *Language and Reality: An Introduction to the Philosophy of Language*. 2nd ed. Cambridge, Mass.: MIT Press, 1999.

Donnellan, Keith S. "Kripke and Putnam on Natural Kind Terms." In Ginet and Shoemaker, *Knowledge and Mind*, 84–104.

———. "Paradigm-Case Argument." *The Encyclopedia of Philosophy*. Ed. Paul Edwards. Vol. 6. New York: Macmillan and Free Press, 1967. 39–44.

Double, Richard. "Twin Earths, Ersatz Pains, and Fool's Minds." *Metaphilosophy* 17 (1986): 300–10.

Dummett, Michael. "Can Analytical Philosophy Be Systematic, and Ought It to Be?" In Dummett, *Truth and Other Enigmas*, 437–58.

———. *Frege: Philosophy of Language*. 2nd ed. Cambridge, Mass.: Harvard University Press, 1981.

———. *The Interpretation of Frege's Philosophy*. Cambridge, Mass.: Harvard University Press, 1981.

———. *Origins of Analytical Philosophy*. Cambridge, Mass.: Harvard University Press, 1994.

———. "The Relative Priority of Thought and Language." In Dummett, *Frege and Other Philosophers*. Oxford: Clarendon, 1991. 315–26.

———. *The Seas of Language*. New York: Oxford University Press, 1993.

———. "The Significance of Quine's Indeterminacy Thesis." In Dummett, *Truth and Other Enigmas*, 375–419.

———. "Truth." *Proceedings of the Aristotelian Society* 59 (1958–59): 141–62. Rptd. in *Philosophical Logic*. Ed. P. F. Strawson. Oxford: Oxford University Press, 1967. 49–68.

———. *Truth and Other Enigmas*. Cambridge, Mass.: Harvard University Press, 1978.

Dupré, John. "Natural Kinds and Biological Taxa." *Philosophical Review* 90 (1981): 66–90.

Engelmann, Paul. *Letters from Ludwig Wittgenstein, with a Memoir*. Ed. B. McGuinness. Trans. L. Furtmüller. Oxford: Blackwell, 1967.

Eveling, H. S., and G. O. M. Leith. "When to Use the Paradigm-Case Argument." *Analysis* 18 (1957–58): 150–52.

Feigl, Herbert, and Wilfrid Sellars, eds. *Readings in Philosophical Analysis*. New York: Appleton-Century-Crofts, 1949.

Field, Hartry. "Tarski's Theory of Truth." *Journal of Philosophy* 69 (1972): 347–75.

Finnis, John. *Natural Law and Natural Rights*. Oxford: Clarendon, 1980.

Flew, Antony G. N. "Again the Paradigm." In *Mind, Matter and Method*. Ed. Paul K. Feyerabend and Grover Maxwell. Minneapolis: University of Minnesota Press, 1966. 261–72.

———. "*Apologia pro Philosophia Mea*." In Shanker, *Philosophy in Britain Today*, 72–97.

———. "Divine Omnipotence and Human Freedom." In *New Essays in Philosophical Theology*. Ed. Antony Flew and Alasdair MacIntyre. London: SCM, 1955. 144–69.

———, ed. *Logic and Language*. 2nd series. Oxford: Blackwell, 1973.

———. "The Paradigm Case Argument." *Journal of Philosophy of Education* 16 (1982): 115–21.

———. "Philosophy and Language." *Philosophical Quarterly* 5 (1955): 21–36.

Fodor, Jerry A., and Jerrold J. Katz. "The Availability of What We Say." *Philosophical Review* 72 (1963): 57–71.

Føllesdal, Dagfinn. "Triangulation." In *The Philosophy of Donald Davidson*. Ed. Lewis Edwin Hahn. Chicago: Open Court, 1999. 719–28.

Frege, Gottlob. *The Frege Reader*. Ed. Michael Beaney. Oxford: Blackwell, 1997.

———. *Funktion, Begriff, Bedeutung: Fünf logische Studien*. Ed. Günther Patzig. Göttingen: Vandenhoeck & Ruprecht, 1962.

———. *Translations from the Philosophical Writings of Gottlob Frege*. Ed. Peter Geach and Max Black. 3rd ed. Totowa, N.J.: Rowman & Littlefield, 1980.

Gellner, Ernest. *Words and Things: A Critical Account of Linguistic Philosophy and a Study in Ideology*. Boston: Beacon, 1960.

Gibbard, Allan. "Contingent Identity." *Journal of Philosophical Logic* 4 (1975): 187–221.

Gibson, Roger F., Jr. "Quine's Philosophy: A Brief Sketch." In Hahn and Schilpp, *The Philosophy of W. V. Quine*, 667–83.

———. "Translation, Physics, and Facts of the Matter." In Hahn and Schilpp, *The Philosophy of W. V. Quine*, 139–54.

Ginet, Carl, and Sydney Shoemaker, eds. *Knowledge and Mind: Philosophical Essays*. New York: Oxford University Press, 1983.

Gottlieb, Anthony. Review of *Philosophical Papers*, by Richard Rorty. *New York Times Book Review*, June 2, 1991, 30.

Grice, Paul. "Logic and Conversation." In Grice, *Studies in the Way of Words*, 22–40.

———. *Studies in the Way of Words*. Cambridge, Mass.: Harvard University Press, 1989.

Grice, Paul, and P. F. Strawson. "In Defense of a Dogma." *Philosophical Review* 65 (1956): 141–58. Rptd. in Grice, *Studies in the Way of Words*, 196–212.

Habermas, Jürgen. "Communicative Rationality and the Theories of Meaning and Action (1986)." In Habermas, *On the Pragmatics of Communication*, 183–213.

———. "Discourse Ethics: Notes on a Program of Philosophical Justification." In Habermas, *Moral Consciousness and Communicative Action*. Oxford: Blackwell, 1973. 43–115.

———. *On the Pragmatics of Communication*. Ed. Maeve Cooke. Cambridge, Mass.: MIT Press, 1998.

———. *On the Pragmatics of Social Interaction: Preliminary Studies in the Theory of Communicative Action*. Trans. Barbara Fultner. Cambridge, Mass.: MIT Press, 2001.

———. "Questions and Counterquestions (1985)." In Habermas, *On the Pragmatics of Communication*, 403–33.

———. "Reflections on Communicative Pathology." In Habermas, *On the Pragmatics of Social Interaction*, 131–70.

———. "Reflections on the Linguistic Foundation of Sociology: The Christian Gauss Lectures (Princeton University, February–March 1971)." In Habermas, *On the Pragmatics of Social Interaction*, 3–103.

———. "Some Further Clarifications of the Concept of Communicative Rationality (1996)." In Habermas, *On the Pragmatics of Communication*, 307–42.

———. *The Theory of Communicative Action*. Vol. 1, *Reason and the Rationalization of Society*. Trans. Thomas McCarthy. Boston: Beacon, 1984.

Hacker, P. M. S. "Analytic Philosophy: What, Whence, and Whither?" In *The Story of Analytic Philosophy: Plot and Heroes*. Ed. Anat Biletzki and Anat Matar. London: Routledge, 1998. 3–34.

———. "Frege and the Later Wittgenstein." In *German Philosophy since Kant*. Ed. Anthony O'Hear. Cambridge: Cambridge University Press, 1999. 223–47.

———. "Wittgenstein and Quine: Proximity at Great Distance." In Arrington and Glock, *Wittgenstein and Quine*, 1–38.

———. *Wittgenstein's Place in Twentieth-Century Analytic Philosophy*. Oxford: Blackwell, 1996.

Hacking, Ian. *Why Does Language Matter to Philosophy?* Cambridge: Cambridge University Press, 1975.

Hahn, Lewis Edwin, and Paul Arthur Schilpp, eds. *The Philosophy of W. V. Quine*. 2nd ed. Chicago: Open Court, 1998.

Hallett, Garth L. *A Companion to Wittgenstein's "Philosophical Investigations."* Ithaca, N.Y.: Cornell University Press, 1977.

———. *Essentialism: A Wittgensteinian Critique*. Albany: State University of New York Press, 1991.

———. *Language and Truth*. New Haven, Conn.: Yale University Press, 1988.

———. *A Middle Way to God*. New York: Oxford University Press, 2000.

———. "The Theoretical Content of Language." *Gregorianum* 54 (1973): 307–36.

Hancock, Roger. "Ideas of Freedom." *Ethics* 69 (1958-1959): 285–90.

Hanfling, Oswald. *Logical Positivism.* New York: Columbia University Press, 1981.

———. *Philosophy and Ordinary Language: The Bent and Genius of Our Tongue.* London: Routledge, 2000.

Hanna, Robert. *Kant and the Foundations of Analytic Philosophy.* Oxford: Oxford University Press, 2001.

Harman, Gilbert. "Knowledge, Inference, and 'Explanation.'" *American Philosophical Quarterly* 5 (1968): 164–73.

———. *Reasoning, Meaning and Mind.* Oxford: Clarendon, 1999.

Harris, Roy. *The Language Myth.* New York: St. Martin's, 1981.

Herder, Johann Gottfried. *Fragmente über die neuere deutsche Literatur.* In *Herders Werke,* vol. 19. Ed. Heinrich Dünker. Berlin: Gustav Hempel. 1877.

Hintikka, Jaakko. "The Emperor's New Intuitions." *Journal of Philosophy* 96 (1999): 127–47.

Hoenen, Peter. *Reality and Judgment according to St. Thomas.* Trans. Henry F. Tiblier. Chicago: Henry Regnery, 1952.

Hoy, David Couzens, and Thomas McCarthy. *Critical Theory.* Oxford: Blackwell, 1994.

James, William. *The Meaning of Truth.* 1909. Cambridge, Mass.: Harvard University Press, 1975.

Katz, Jerrold J. *The Philosophy of Language.* New York: Harper & Row, 1966.

Kirkham, Richard L. *Theories of Truth: A Critical Introduction.* Cambridge, Mass.: MIT Press, 1992.

Klein, Peter D. "Knowledge, Concept of." *Routledge Encyclopedia of Philosophy.* Ed. Edward Craig. Vol. 5. London: Routledge, 1998. 266–76.

Kloppenberg, James T. "Pragmatism: An Old Name for Some New Ways of Thinking?" In *A Pragmatist's Progress? Richard Rorty and American Intellectual History.* Ed. John Pettegrew. Lanham, Md.: Rowman & Littlefield, 2000, 19–60.

Kneale, William. "Are Necessary Truths True by Convention?" *Proceedings of the Aristotelian Society,* suppl. no. 21 (1947): 118–33. Rptd. in Lewis, *Clarity Is Not Enough,* 133–46.

Knox, John, Jr. "Truth, Correspondence, and Ordinary Language." *Personalist* 52 (1971): 515–34.

Kripke, Saul. "Identity and Necessity." In Kripke, *Naming, Necessity, and Natural Kinds*. Ed. Stephen P. Schwartz. Ithaca, N.Y.: Cornell University Press, 1977. 66–101.

———. "Naming and Necessity." In *Semantics of Natural Language*. Ed. Donald Davidson and Gilbert Harman. Dordrecht: Reidel, 1972. 253–355, 763–69.

———. "Speaker's Reference and Semantic Reference." In *Studies in the Philosophy of Language*. Ed. Peter A. French, Theodore E. Uehling Jr., and Howard K. Wettstein. Midwest Studies in Philosophy 2. Morris: University of Minnesota, 1977. 255–76.

Künne, Wolfgang. *Conceptions of Truth*. Oxford: Clarendon, 2003.

Lafont, Christina. *The Linguistic Turn in Hermeneutic Philosophy*. Trans. José Medina. Cambridge, Mass.: MIT Press, 1999.

Lawson, Hilary, and Lisa Appignanesi, eds. *Dismantling Truth: Reality in the Post-Modern World*. New York: St. Martin's, 1989.

Lazerowitz, Alice Ambrose. "Linguistic Approaches to Philosophical Problems." *Journal of Philosophy* 49 (1952): 289–301. Rptd. in *The Linguistic Turn: Recent Essays in Philosophical Method*. Ed. Richard Rorty. Chicago: University of Chicago Press, 1967. 147–55.

Lazerowitz, Morris. *The Language of Philosophy: Freud and Wittgenstein*. Dordrecht: Reidel, 1977.

Lee, Patrick. "Aquinas on Knowledge of Truth and Existence." *New Scholasticism* 60 (1986): 46–71.

Levin, Susan B. "What's in a Name?: A Reconsideration of the *Cratylus'* Historical Sources and Topics." *Ancient Philosophy* 15 (1995): 91–115.

Levison, A. B. "Logic, Language, and Consistency in Tarski's Theory of Truth." *Philosophy and Phenomenological Research* 25 (1964–65): 384–92.

Lewis, David K. *Convention: A Philosophical Study*. Cambridge, Mass.: Harvard University Press, 1969.

Lewis, H. D., ed. *Clarity Is Not Enough*. New York: Humanities, 1963.

Lynch, Michael P. *True to Life: Why Truth Matters*. Cambridge, Mass.: MIT Press, 2004.

Mackenzie, I. E. *Introduction to Linguistic Philosophy*. Thousand Oaks, Calif.: Sage, 1997.

Mackie, J. L. *Contemporary Linguistic Philosophy—Its Strength and Its Weakness*. Dunedin, New Zealand: University of Otago, 1956.

Magee, Bryan. *Men of Ideas*. New York: Viking, 1979.

———, ed. *Modern British Philosophy*. London: Secker and Warburg, 1971.

Malcolm, Norman. Critical Notice of Alan R. White, *G. E. Moore: A Critical Exposition*. *Mind* 69 (1960): 92–98.

———. "Moore and Ordinary Language." In Schilpp, *The Philosophy of G. E. Moore*, 345–68.

Martinich, A. P. "Ordinary Language Philosophy." *Routledge Encyclopedia of Philosophy*. Ed. Edward Craig. Vol. 7. London: Routledge, 1998. 143–47.

Mates, Benson. "On the Verification of Statements about Ordinary Language." *Inquiry* 1 (1958): 161–71.

McMichael, Alan. "The Epistemology of Essentialist Claims." In *Midwest Studies in Philosophy*. Vol. 11, *Studies in Essentialism*. Ed. Peter A. French, Theodore E. Uehling Jr., and Howard K. Wettstein. Minneapolis: University of Minnesota Press, 1986. 33–52.

Modrak, Deborah K. W. *Aristotle's Theory of Language and Meaning*. New York: Cambridge University Press, 2001.

Moore, George Edward. *Commonplace Book 1919–1953*. Ed. Casimir Lewy. London: Allen & Unwin, 1962.

———. *Philosophical Papers*. London: Allen & Unwin, 1959.

———. *Principia Ethica*. 1903. Rev. ed. Ed. Thomas Baldwin. Cambridge: Cambridge University Press, 1993.

———. "A Reply to My Critics." In Schilpp, *The Philosophy of G. E. Moore*, 535–677.

———. *Some Main Problems of Philosophy*. London: Allen & Unwin, 1953.

Mundle, C. W. K. *A Critique of Linguistic Philosophy*. Oxford: Clarendon, 1970.

Nagel, Ernest. "Russell's Philosophy of Science." In Schilpp, *The Philosophy of Bertrand Russell*, 319–49.

Nielsen, Kai. *On Transforming Philosophy: A Metaphilosophical Inquiry*. Boulder, Colo.: Westview, 1995.

Noonan, John T., Jr. "Responding to Persons: Methods of Moral Argument in Debate over Abortion." *Theology Digest* 21 (1973): 291–307.

O'Callaghan, John P. *Thomistic Realism and the Linguistic Turn: Toward a More Perfect Form of Existence*. Notre Dame, Ind.: University of Notre Dame Press, 2003.

O'Grady, Paul. "Carnap and Two Dogmas of Empiricism." *Philosophy and Phenomenological Research* 59 (1999): 1015–27.

Orenstein, Alex. *Willard van Orman Quine*. Boston: Twayne, 1977.

Panaccio, Claude. "Aquinas on Intellectual Representation." In *Ancient and Medieval Theories of Intentionality*. Ed. Dominik Perler. Leiden: Brill, 2001. 185–201.

Passmore, John. *A Hundred Years of Philosophy*. London: Duckworth, 1957.

———. *Philosophical Reasoning*. London: Duckworth, 1961.

———. "Reflections on 'Logic and Language.'" *Australasian Journal of Philosophy* 30 (1952): 153–76.

Pinker, Steven. *The Language Instinct*. New York: Morrow, 1994.

Popper, Karl R. "Some Philosophical Comments on Tarski's Theory of Truth." In *Proceedings of the Tarski Symposium*. Ed. Leon Henkin et al. Providence, R.I.: American Mathematical Society, 1974. 397–409.

Purtill, Richard L. "Flew and the Free Will Defence." *Religious Studies* 13 (1977): 477–83.

Putnam, Hilary. "The Analytic and the Synthetic." In Putnam, *Mind, Language and Reality*, 33–69.

———. "Is Semantics Possible?" In Putnam, *Mind, Language and Reality*, 139–52.

———. "Language and Philosophy." In Putnam, *Mind, Language and Reality*, 1–32.

———. "Meaning Holism." In Putnam, *Realism with a Human Face*. Ed. James Conant. Cambridge, Mass.: Harvard University Press, 1990. 278–302.

———. "The Meaning of 'Meaning.'" In Putnam, *Mind, Language and Reality*, 215–71.

———. *Mind, Language and Reality*. Philosophical Papers 2. Cambridge: Cambridge University Press, 1975.

———. *Pragmatism: An Open Question*. Oxford: Blackwell, 1995.

———. *Realism and Reason*. Philosophical Papers 3. Cambridge: Cambridge University Press, 1983.

Quine, Willard Van Orman. "Carnap and Logical Truth." In Schilpp, *The Philosophy of Rudolf Carnap*, 385–406.

———. *From a Logical Point of View: Logico-Philosophical Essays*. 2nd ed. Cambridge, Mass.: Harvard University Press, 1964.

———. "Identity, Ostension, and Hypostasis." In Quine, *From a Logical Point of View*, 65–79.

———. *Mathematical Logic*. Rev. ed. New York: Harper, 1962.

———. "Necessary Truth." In Quine, *Ways of Paradox and Other Essays*. Rev. ed. Cambridge, Mass.: Harvard University Press, 1976. 68–76.

———. "On Empirically Equivalent Systems of the World." *Erkenntnis* 9 (1975): 313–28.

———. "Ontological Relativity." In Quine, *Ontological Relativity and Other Essays*, 26–68.

———. *Ontological Relativity and Other Essays*. New York: Columbia University Press, 1969.

———. *Philosophy of Logic*. Englewood Cliffs, N.J.: Prentice-Hall, 1970.

———. "Reply to Jules Vuillemin." In Hahn and Schilpp, *The Philosophy of W. V. Quine*, 619–22.

———. "Reply to Robert Nozick." In Hahn and Schilpp, *The Philosophy of W. V. Quine*, 364–67.

———. *The Roots of Reference*. LaSalle, Ill.: Open Court, 1974.

———. "Speaking of Objects." In Quine, *Ontological Relativity and Other Essays*, 1–25.

———. *Theories and Things*. Cambridge, Mass.: Harvard University Press, 1981.

———. "Three Indeterminacies." In *Perspectives on Quine*. Ed. Robert B. Barrett and Roger F. Gibson. Oxford: Blackwell, 1990. 1–16.

———. "Two Dogmas of Empiricism." *Philosophical Review* 60 (1951): 20–43. Rptd. in Quine, *From a Logical Point of View*, 20–46.

———. "Two Dogmas in Retrospect." *Canadian Journal of Philosophy* 21 (1991): 265–74.

———. *Word and Object*. Cambridge, Mass.: MIT Press, 1960.

Ramberg, Bjørn. "Post-Ontological Philosophy of Mind: Rorty versus Davidson." In Brandom, *Rorty and His Critics*, 351–70.

Randall, John Herman, Jr. "Talking and Looking." *Proceedings and Addresses of the American Philosophical Association* 30 (1956–57): 5–24.

Rescher, Nicholas. *Philosophical Standardism: An Empiricist Approach to Philosophical Methodology*. Pittsburgh: University of Pittsburgh Press, 1994.

Ricoeur, Paul. "Philosophie et langage." In *Contemporary Philosophy: A Survey.* Vol. 3: *Metaphysics, Phenomenology, Language and Structure.* Ed. Raymond Klibansky. Florence: La Nuova Italia, 1969. 272–95.

Rorty, Richard. *Consequences of Pragmatism (Essays: 1972–1980).* Minneapolis: University of Minnesota Press, 1982.

———. *Contingency, Irony, and Solidarity.* Cambridge: Cambridge University Press, 1989.

———. *Objectivity, Relativism, and Truth.* Cambridge: Cambridge University Press, 1991.

———. *Philosophy and the Mirror of Nature.* Princeton, N.J.: Princeton University Press, 1980.

———. "Pragmatism, Davidson and Truth." In Rorty, *Objectivity, Relativism, and Truth*, 126–50.

———. "Pragmatism, Relativism, and Irrationalism." *Proceedings and Addresses of the American Philosophical Association* 53 (1979–80): 719–38.

———. "Response to Bjørn Ramberg." In Brandom, *Rorty and His Critics*, 370–77.

———. "Science as Solidarity." In Lawson and Appignanesi, *Dismantling Truth*, 6–22.

Routley, Richard. "The Semantical Metamorphosis of Metaphysics." *Australasian Journal of Philosophy* 54 (1976): 187–205.

Rundle, Bede. *Grammar in Philosophy.* New York: Oxford University Press; Oxford: Clarendon, 1979.

Russell, Bertrand. *The Analysis of Matter.* London: Allen & Unwin, 1954.

———. *The Analysis of Mind.* London: Allen & Unwin, 1921.

———. "The Cult of 'Common Usage.'" *British Journal for the Philosophy of Science* 3 (1952–53): 303–7.

———. *An Inquiry into Meaning and Truth.* London: Allen & Unwin, 1940.

———. *Logic and Knowledge: Essays 1901–1950.* Ed. Robert Charles Marsh. New York: Macmillan, 1956.

———. "On Scientific Method in Philosophy." In Russell, *Mysticism and Logic.* London: Allen & Unwin, 1963. 75–93.

———. "Reply to Criticisms." In Schilpp, *The Philosophy of Bertrand Russell*, 681–741.

———. *The Scientific Outlook*. Glencoe, Ill.: Free Press, 1931.

Ryle, Gilbert. "Use, Usage and Meaning." *Proceedings of the Aristotelian Society*. Suppl. no. 35 (1961): 223–30.

Sapir, Edward. *Selected Writings in Language, Culture and Personality*. Ed. David G. Mandelbaum. Berkeley: University of California Press, 1985.

Schaff, Adam. *Language and Cognition*. Ed. Robert S. Cohen. Trans. Olgierd Wojtasiewicz. New York: McGraw-Hill, 1973.

Schilpp, Paul Arthur, ed. *The Philosophy of Bertrand Russell*. Evanston, Ill.: Northwestern University Press, 1944.

———, ed. *The Philosophy of G. E. Moore*. 3rd ed. LaSalle, Ill.: Open Court, 1968.

———, ed. *The Philosophy of Rudolf Carnap*. LaSalle, Ill.: Open Court, 1963.

Scriven, Michael. "The Argument from Ordinary Language." In *Principles of Philosophical Reasoning*. Ed. James H. Fetzer. Totowa, N.J.: Rowman & Allanheld, 1984. 261–77.

Shanker, S. G., ed. *Philosophy in Britain Today*. Albany: State University of New York Press, 1986.

Skorupski, John. "Meaning, Use, Verification." In *A Companion to the Philosophy of Language*. Ed. Bob Hale and Crispin Wright. Oxford: Blackwell, 1997. 29–59.

Smith, Edward E. "Concepts and Categorization." In *Thinking*. Ed. Edward E. Smith and Daniel N. Osherson. 2nd ed. Cambridge, Mass.: MIT Press, 1995. 3–33.

Soames, Scott. *Philosophical Analysis in the Twentieth Century*. Vol. 2, *The Age of Meaning*. Princeton, N.J.: Princeton University Press, 2003.

Sorensen, Roy. "Vagueness and the Desiderata for Definition." In *Definitions and Definability: Philosophical Perspectives*. Ed. James H. Fetzer, David Shatz, and George N. Schlesinger. Synthese Library 216. Dordrecht: Kluwer, 1991. 71–109.

Speake, Jennifer, ed. *A Dictionary of Philosophy*. New York: St. Martin's, 1979.

Stern, David G. *Wittgenstein on Mind and Language*. New York: Oxford University Press, 1995.

Stich, Stephen P. *The Fragmentation of Reason: Preface to a Pragmatic Theory of Cognitive Evaluation*. Cambridge, Mass.: MIT Press, 1990.

———. "What Is a Theory of Mental Representation?" In *Mental Representation: A Reader*. Ed. Stephen P. Stich and Ted A. Warfield. Oxford: Blackwell, 1994. 347–64.

Strawson, P. F. "Carnap's Views on Constructed Systems versus Natural Languages in Analytic Philosophy." In Schilpp, *The Philosophy of Rudolf Carnap*, 503–18.

———. "Truth." *Proceedings of the Aristotelian Society*, suppl. no. 24 (1950): 129–56.

Stroll, Avrum. "Is Everyday Language Inconsistent?" *Mind* 63 (1954): 219–25.

Stump, Eleonore. *Aquinas*. London: Routledge, 2003.

Swinburne, Richard. "Analogy and Metaphor." In *The Philosophical Assessment of Theology: Essays in Honour of Frederick C. Copleston*. Ed. Gerard Hughes. Washington, D.C.: Georgetown University Press, 1987. 65–84.

Tarski, Alfred. "The Concept of Truth in Formalized Languages." In Tarski, *Logic, Semantics, Metamathematics*, 152–278.

———. "The Establishment of Scientific Semantics." In Tarski, *Logic, Semantics, Metamathematics*, 401–8.

———. *Logic, Semantics, Metamathematics: Papers from 1923 to 1938*. Trans. J. H. Woodger. Oxford: Clarendon, 1956.

———. "The Semantic Conception of Truth." *Philosophy and Phenomenological Research* 4 (1943–44): 341–75. Rptd. in Feigl and Sellars, *Readings in Philosophical Analysis*, 52–84.

Taylor, C. "Phenomenology and Linguistic Analysis: I." In *Analytic Philosophy and Phenomenology*. Ed. Harold A. Durfee. The Hague: Nijhoff, 1976. 217–31.

Tennessen, Herman. "Permissible and Impermissible Locutions." *Synthese* 12 (1960): 495–508.

———. "Vindication of the Humpty Dumpty Attitude towards Language." *Inquiry* 3 (1960): 185–98.

Thomas Aquinas. *Commentary on the Metaphysics of Aristotle*. 2 vols. Trans. John P. Rowan. Chicago: Henry Regnery, 1961.

Thompson, Manley. "When Is Ordinary Language Reformed?" *Journal of Philosophy* 58 (1961): 498–504.

Tomlinson, Hugh. "After Truth: Post-Modernism and the Rhetoric of Science." In Lawson and Appignanesi, *Dismantling Truth*, 43–57.

Triplett, Timm. "Rescher's Metaphilosophy." *Metaphilosophy* 30 (1999): 209–30.

Tugendhat, Ernst. *Traditional and Analytical Philosophy: Lectures on the Philosophy of Language*. Trans. P. A. Gorner. Cambridge: Cambridge University Press, 1982.

Urban, Wilbur Marshall. *Language and Reality: The Philosophy of Language and the Principles of Symbolism*. New York: Books for Libraries Press, 1939.

Urmson, J. O.. "Some Questions concerning Validity." In *Essays in Conceptual Analysis*. Ed. Antony Flew. New York: St. Martin's, 1966. 120–33.

Vendler, Zeno. *Linguistics in Philosophy*. Ithaca, N.Y.: Cornell University Press, 1967.

Von Wright, Georg Henrik, ed. *Problems in the Theory of Knowledge*. The Hague: Martinus Nijhoff, 1972.

———. *The Tree of Knowledge and Other Essays*. Leiden: Brill, 1993.

Waismann, F. "Language Strata." In Flew, *Logic and Language*, 11–31.

———. *The Principles of Linguistic Philosophy*. Ed. R. Harré. New York: St. Martin's, 1965.

Warnock, Geoffrey. "Ordinary Language Philosophy, School of." *Routledge Encyclopedia of Philosophy*. Ed. Edward Craig. Vol. 7. London: Routledge, 1998. 147–53.

———. "Truth and Correspondence." In *Knowledge and Experience*. Ed. C. D. Rollins. Pittsburgh: University of Pittsburgh Press, 1962. 11–20.

Watkins, J. W. N. "Farewell to the Paradigm-Case Argument." *Analysis* 18 (1957–58): 25–33.

Weingartner, Rudolph H. *The Unity of the Platonic Dialogue: The Cratylus, the Protagoras, the Parmenides*. Indianapolis, Ind.: Bobbs-Merrill, 1973.

White, Nicholas P. *Plato on Knowledge and Reality*. Indianapolis, Ind.: Hackett, 1976.

Whitehead, Alfred North, and Bertrand Russell. *Principia Mathematica*. 2nd ed. Cambridge: Cambridge University Press, 1950.

Whiteley, C. H. "Let Epimenides Lie!" *Analysis* 19 (1958–59): 23–24.

Whorf, Benjamin Lee. *Language, Thought, and Reality*. Ed. John B. Carroll. Cambridge, Mass.: MIT Press, 1967.

Wiggins, David. "An Indefinibilist cum Normative View of Truth and Marks of Truth." In *What Is Truth?* Ed. Richard Schanta. Berlin: de Gruyter, 2002. 316–32.

Wilkerson, T. E. *Natural Kinds*. Aldershot, UK: Avebury, 1995.

Williams, Bernard. "Knowledge and Reasons." In von Wright, *Problems in the Theory of Knowledge*, 1–11.

Wisdom, John. "Ludwig Wittgenstein, 1934–1937." In *Ludwig Wittgenstein: The Man and His Philosophy*. Ed. K. T. Fann. New York: Dell, 1967. 46–48.

Wittgenstein, Ludwig. *The Blue and Brown Books*. Oxford: Blackwell, 1960.

———. *Last Writings on the Philosophy of Psychology*. Vol. 1, *Preliminary Studies for Part II of the* Philosophical Investigations. Ed. G. H. von Wright and Heikki Nyman. Trans. C. G. Luckhardt and Maximilian A. E. Aue. Chicago: University of Chicago Press, 1982.

———. *Lectures and Conversations on Aesthetics, Psychology and Religious Belief*. Ed. Cyril Barrett. Oxford: Blackwell, 1966.

———. *Notebooks 1914–1916*. Ed. G. H. von Wright and G. E. M. Anscombe. Trans. G. E. M. Anscombe. Oxford: Blackwell, 1961.

———. *Philosophical Grammar*. Ed. Rush Rhees. Trans. Anthony Kenny. Berkeley: University of California Press, 1974.

———. *Philosophical Investigations*. Trans. G. E. M. Anscombe. 2nd ed. Oxford: Blackwell, 1958.

———. *Philosophical Remarks*. Ed. Rush Rhees. Trans. Raymond Hargreaves and Roger White. Chicago: University of Chicago Press, 1980.

———. *Schriften*, vol. 5. Frankfurt am Main: Suhrkamp, 1970.

———. "Some Remarks on Logical Form." *Proceedings of the Aristotelian Society*, suppl. no. 9 (1929): 162–71. Rptd. in *Essays on Wittgenstein's 'Tractatus.'* Ed. Irving M. Copi and Robert W. Beard. New York: Hafner, 1973. 31–37.

———. *Tractatus Logico-Philosophicus*. Trans. D. F. Pears and B. F. McGuinness. New York: Humanities, 1961.

———. *Zettel*. Ed. G. E. M. Anscombe and G. H. von Wright. Trans. G. E. M. Anscombe. Oxford: Blackwell, 1967.

Wright, Crispin. "Theories of Meaning and Speakers' Knowledge." In Shanker, *Philosophy in Britain Today*, 267–307.

Zagzebski, Linda Trinkaus. *Virtues of the Mind*. Cambridge: Cambridge University Press, 1996.

Zemach, Eddy M. "Putnam's Theory on the Reference of Substance Terms." *Journal of Philosophy* 73 (1976): 116–27.

INDEX

<u>Letter to Hallett</u>

    ments Reddy (H cites another art. in <u>Metaphor</u>
        <u>& Thought</u>)

At 176 N.8., GH's "Issue of Language's Authority"
seems to fit re controversy over "contingent identity